Rethinking US Election Law

RETHINKING LAW

The Rethinking Law series is a forum for innovative scholarly legal writing from across all substantive fields of law. The series aims to enrich the study of law by promoting a cutting-edge approach to legal analysis.

Despite the old maxim that nothing is new under the sun, it is nevertheless true that laws evolve and contexts in which laws operate change. Law faces new and previously unforeseen challenges, responds to shifting motivations and is shaped by competing interests and experiences. Academic scrutiny and challenge is an essential component in the development of law, and the act of re-thinking and re-examining principles and precepts that may have been long-held is imperative.

Rethinking Law showcases authored books that address their field from a new angle, expose the weaknesses of existing frameworks, or 're-frame' the topic in some way. This might be through the introduction of a new legal framework, through the integration of perspectives from other fields or even other disciplines, through challenging existing paradigms, or simply through a level of analysis that elevates or sharpens our understanding of a subject. While each book takes its own approach, all the titles in the series use an analytical lens to open up new thinking.

Titles in the series include:

Rethinking Contract Law and Contract Design
Victor P. Goldberg

Rethinking Cyberlaw
A New Vision for Internet Law
Jacqueline Lipton

Rethinking International Commercial Arbitration
Towards Default Arbitration
Gilles Cuniberti

Rethinking Intellectual Property
Balancing Conflicts of Interest in the Constitutional Paradigm
Gustavo Ghidini

Rethinking Legal Reasoning
Geoffrey Samuel

Rethinking the Jurisprudence of Cyberspace
Chris Reed and Andrew Murray

Rethinking US Election Law
Unskewing the System
Steven Mulroy

Rethinking US Election Law

Unskewing the System

Steven Mulroy

Bredesen Professor of Law, University of Memphis, School of Law, USA

RETHINKING LAW

Cheltenham, UK • Northampton, MA, USA

Published by
Edward Elgar Publishing Limited
The Lypiatts
15 Lansdown Road
Cheltenham
Glos GL50 2JA
UK

Edward Elgar Publishing, Inc.
William Pratt House
9 Dewey Court
Northampton
Massachusetts 01060
USA

Paperback edition 2020

A catalogue record for this book
is available from the British Library

Library of Congress Control Number: 2018958446

This book is available electronically in the **Elgar**online
Law subject collection
DOI 10.4337/9781788117517

ISBN 978 1 78811 750 0 (cased)
ISBN 978 1 78811 751 7 (eBook)
ISBN 978 1 83910 669 9 (paperback)

Typeset by Servis Filmsetting Ltd, Stockport, Cheshire
Printed and bound by CPI Group (UK) Ltd, Croydon CR0 4YY

Contents

About the author

Steven Mulroy is the Bredesen Professor of Law at the University of Memphis, where he teaches, among other things, Constitutional Law, Civil Rights, and Election Law. He has litigated voting rights and election law cases, including cases involving the use of non-district voting systems, for both the U.S. Justice Department's Voting Section and as a law professor. As a former elected County Commissioner in Memphis, he oversaw that body's redistricting process, and led the effort to have instant runoff voting adopted by referendum in Memphis, Tennessee, where he lives with his long-suffering wife Amy. His hobbies include procrastinating and high-impact skydiving.

Acknowledgments

I gratefully acknowledge the assistance provided by Rob Richie, Drew Spencer Penrose, Chris Hughes, and the staff of Fairvote as I researched and wrote this book, as well as the assistance provided by Gary Bartlett, Karen Brinson Bell, and George Gilbert of the Ranked Choice Voting Resource Center. Former University of Memphis law professor Gene Shapiro provided comments on a draft chapter, for which I thank him. For a useful international perspective, I thank Damon Muller of the Australian Parliamentary Library and Paul Pirani of the Australian Election Commission, as well as Profs. Ron Levy, Ryan Goss, and other faculty at the wonderful Australian National University College of Law.

For excellent research assistance, I thank University of Memphis law students Hayden Phillips, Liz Stagich, and Patrick Treadwell. I am also grateful for graphic design help from Ryan Jones, Jacques Lerner, and Rick Maynard, and editing help from my assistant Karol Landers. Anything you like about this book is due to me, and any errors are the fault of those listed above. Finally, a heartfelt thanks to my wife Amy for her consistent support.

1. Introduction

Observers of recent U.S. elections could note the following somewhat surprising facts:

1. *In 2016, 3 million more Americans voted for Hillary Clinton than for Donald Trump for President. Yet Donald Trump became President.*
2. *In 2012, more Americans voted for Democratic candidates for U.S. House seats than for Republican House candidates. Yet the GOP[1] maintained majority control of the House (by 30 seats).*
3. A similar comparison for the U.S. Senate is slightly more complicated because Senate terms are staggered and it takes 3 consecutive elections for all 100 Senate seats to be up for election. *But in the first 3 elections in this decade (2010, 2012, and 2014), more Americans voted for Democratic Senate candidates than Republican Senate candidates (52%), and yet Democrats won only 46% of the Senate seats.*

This seems to go against basic assumptions about democracy and majority rule. Our middle-school civics class understanding of American government has always been that the candidate or party who gets the most votes wins. If they get more votes than the other party, they control. They certainly shouldn't take a back seat to a candidate or party that gets *fewer* votes. We can call this the "majority criterion."

Unfortunately, the above scenarios are not freakish, once-in-a-lifetime occurrences. They happen periodically throughout our nation's history. They have affected both parties, both nationally and at the state level. In New Jersey, for example, Republican candidates garnered 51% of the statewide vote for State Assembly in 2013 but Democrats controlled 60% of the seats.

How to explain these anomalous results? Although the scenarios above are superficially different, the same dynamic underlies all three. They all divide the electorate into lots of smaller subunits and hold a "winner-take-all" election within each—a situation sometimes called "the unit

---

[1] 'Grand Old Party'—a nickname for the Republican Party.

rule."[2] Whenever you do that, you create the possibility that there will be a significant deviation between (i) the percentage of votes a party receives, and (ii) the percentage of seats the party receives (or, in the case of presidential elections, the number of states the party carries). In close elections, that "skew" between votes and seats can mean that the majority party becomes the loser and the minority party becomes the winner. But even when this "winner loses" situation doesn't occur, there is almost always a gap between votes and seats, with the majority party either getting robbed of some seats it otherwise earned, or getting a windfall of extra seats it doesn't deserve.

In the parlance of political scientists, the culprits are *winner-take-all systems*. They allow for a majority-supported candidate or party to "waste" its votes—to distribute them in a less than ideally efficient manner. This can be done in two ways: by "packing" and by "cracking."

Presidential elections create a good example of packing, thanks to the Electoral College. Under our Constitution, we do not vote directly for our President. Instead, we vote to determine whether our state's Electoral College votes go to one candidate or another, with the winner being the candidate who receives a nationwide majority of Electoral votes. Each state has a number of Electoral votes equal to its number of House and Senate members. Almost all states allocate these Electoral votes on a winner-take-all basis: the party that gets 50.1% or more of the votes in the state gets all its Electoral votes. Because of this, it is easy for a candidate to waste votes by running up an unnecessary and useless supermajority in some states, and coming up just short in others.

See Figure 1.1 as an example. It shows a hypothetical, simple 5-state presidential election, where each state gets 1 Electoral vote. In New York and California, the Democratic candidate gets over 80% of the vote. In Wisconsin, Texas, and Tennessee, she gets just barely under 50%. If you add up all the votes in the 5 states combined, she clearly has a majority overall (even if all states had the same population)—indeed, a 60% total, normally considered a landslide victory. But under the Electoral College system, she loses 3 States to 2.

She wasted her votes because her votes were "packed" into New York and California. In those states, every vote above a simple majority counts

---

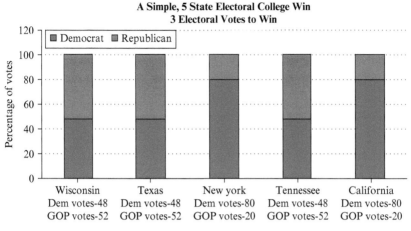

A Simple, 5 State Electoral College Win
3 Electoral Votes to Win

	Wisconsin	Texas	New york	Tennessee	California
Dem votes	48	48	80	48	80
GOP votes	52	52	20	52	20

TOTAL VOTES: DEMOCRATS - 304; GOP - 196
GOP WINS 3 STATES TO 2

Figure 1.1   A simple illustration of packing

for nothing; it does her no good. The votes for the Republican candidate, by contrast, were distributed *efficiently*: just enough to make a majority in each state, and no more, in just enough red states to make the state-by-state count favor the GOP. On a larger scale, this is essentially what happened in 2016 with Trump and Clinton, and in 2000 with Bush and Gore.

Packing is also at work in the U.S. Senate. Democrats rack up huge supermajorities in populous states like New York and California, with lots of wasted votes. Republicans do likewise in some states like Texas, but Democrats waste more votes like this. At the same time, smaller, less populated states get overrepresented because they get the same number of Senators as larger states. Controlling elections in those smaller and mid-size states thus takes fewer votes for the same number of seats. The party that controls more of those states is more efficiently distributing its votes nationwide. That party currently happens to be the GOP.

House of Representatives elections can illustrate both packing and cracking, the two tools of gerrymandering. A gerrymandered redistricting plan uses both tools to force the "victim" party to waste its votes. It can pack supermajorities of one party in a few districts, draining surrounding districts of the voters needed to get majorities in those neighboring districts. Or it can take a geographic concentration of voters of that party and slice it in half by drawing the district line right through it, with the result that neither remaining concentration on either side of the line is big enough to be a majority in any district.

We have had gerrymandering as long as we have had House districts. But the gerrymandering has been getting worse as computer map-drawing programs have been getting better. Since World War II, there has been an average of 6% deviation between the percentage of the countrywide vote a major party yields, and the percentage of House seats that party receives. For much of that time, the skew favored Democrats. In more recent elections, it has favored Republicans. Much of the skew (though not all) is due to gerrymandering, with almost all districts drawn in such a way that the general election result is a foregone conclusion. In a very real sense, in the House, the voters do not choose their representatives; the representatives choose their voters.

The dysfunction goes beyond the votes–seats skew of the major parties. The Electoral College encourages candidates to focus only on 10 "swing" states and to ignore the rest, a pattern that continues into governance once the candidate is elected.

In both presidential and congressional elections, winner-take-all systems lock us into the tyranny of the two-party system, freezing out any realistic chance for third parties to offer alternatives. Voting for a third party, or indeed any up-and-comer candidate who is not perceived as sufficiently well known, well funded, and mainstream to be electable, is "throwing away your vote." Because it is winner-take-all, candidates are also encouraged to attack their opponents in a zero-sum environment.

Winner-take-all elections also tend to dilute the voting strength of racial and ethnic minorities. We partially alleviate this by drawing a few single-member districts with racial and ethnic minorities in mind. But they are too few to fairly represent such minorities, and enough could never be drawn because of the way minority voters are dispersed. The overwhelming majority of such minority voters will always live outside such districts, and that problem will only get worse as minority voters move out of the ghettos and barrios. As a civil rights strategy, minority districting perversely depends on racial segregation to be effective.

Single-member districts (SMDs) add their own special dysfunctions. Because gerrymandered districts lead to "safe" seats for Republicans and Democrats alike, general election outcomes are usually preordained, reducing competition, making voting seem futile, and depressing voter participation. The only true competition is in the primaries. This incentivizes candidates to take extreme positions on the left and the right, discouraging bipartisan compromise, increasing polarization, and baking in gridlock.

Every one of these dysfunctions occurring with the House simultaneously occurs at the state and local level in the U.S. (and indeed around the world). It is not dependent on the demographics or political culture of the city or state (or country) involved. It is a universal dynamic, an inherent problem with winner-take-all and single-member district systems.

Can anything be done about all this? The answer is yes, but in perhaps surprising ways. No federal constitutional amendment is needed. The chief hope lies in reforms to be undertaken on a state-by-state basis by each state's legislature. The usual suspects of reform in these areas are partial solutions at best, or flat-out nonstarters at worst.

Take the Electoral College. In decades past, reformers called for a constitutional amendment to abolish it. But even with the best of causes, amending the U.S. Constitution is a Herculean task, requiring supermajority votes of both Houses of Congress and the state legislatures. With an issue like the Electoral College, which favors some states over others, such that some states would stand to lose out with reform, it is politically impossible.

Fortunately, though, there is a workaround: the National Popular Vote (NPV) Compact. This is an agreement among certain states that they will all allocate all their Electoral College votes to whoever wins the NPV. It takes effect once enough states have signed on to control the outcome of a presidential election. Currently, NPV is almost two-thirds of the way there, after only a decade or so of trying. It is very likely that in our lifetime, we will see the Electoral College not abolished, but rendered harmless.

The Senate is a tougher nut to crack. The fundamental anti-democratic feature (or bug, really) of the Senate is that low-population states get the same representation as high-population states. Wyoming has the same say in ratifying treaties, confirming Supreme Court Justices, and passing laws as California, making a Wyomingan's vote worth over 60 times more than a Californian's. Unfortunately, there is nothing that can be done about that. Not only is this bug hard-wired into the CPU, the program cannot be altered by the user. The Constitution itself says that this part of the Constitution cannot be amended. Though there is a partial fix which could help slightly through coordinated action by Congress and state legislatures, it would be a long walk for a short beer. This small- and mid-state bias unfairly advantages states which tend to skew Republican.[3]

Instead, reformers should be content to change another anti-democratic feature of the Senate: the filibuster. Like gerrymandering, it has only gotten worse in recent decades, with the current practical reality that

---

[3]   Earlier in our history, the pro-rural bias helped Democrats, and was equally problematic.

nothing can get done legislatively without 60 votes in the Senate. Worse, a Senator can single-handedly and *anonymously* halt all Senate action on a nomination or legislation without ever revealing herself, unless 60 Senators from both parties can come together to break the logjam. Again, no constitutional amendment is needed to change this.

The above solutions—the NPV, filibuster reform—are fairly straight-forward. The solution needed to address House gerrymandering is some-what more involved and requires a basic reexamination of the way we do elections.

Some reformers urge that courts should rule gerrymanders illegal and force states to draw fair district lines for U.S. House (and state legisla-tive) elections. While courts have long been aggressive in policing *racial* gerrymanders, they have been unwilling to do so with regard to *partisan* gerrymanders, out of a sense that this is a "political question" unsuitable for intervention by unelected judges. This should change, but so far it hasn't. The Supreme Court recently passed on some great opportunities to fix this problem.

But even if courts did get more aggressive in policing gerrymander-ing, we would only be working at the edges of the problem. Courts will continue to be hesitant to get too involved in political fights and micromanage the elected representatives drawing the maps. Perhaps more important, the legal doctrine focuses only on *intentional* gerrymanders, instances where the proof is clear that the party temporarily in power was deliberately trying to disadvantage the party temporarily out of power. Because of these interrelated factors, under the best scenarios, courts will only address the most extreme of the gerrymanders, leaving a lot of other cartographical skewing intact.

More promising is a solution that is more proactive: nonpartisan redistricting commissions. Such commissions have worked well around the world. Indeed, we are the only Western democracy left which allows elected legislators to draw their own district lines. All others leave it to the technocrats: appointed nonpartisan experts working with set criteria, sometimes with the help of equal number of politicos from both major parties. In recent years, a few U.S. states have been attempting similar approaches.

The results have been mixed. Some states have created plans with a minimum of partisan skew—i.e., a pretty close relationship between votes received and seats obtained. Other states have repeated significant partisan skews anyway. A 2002 study of such redistricting plans showed a median partisan bias in redistricting commissions states of 4.7%, compared to 8.6% in states with traditional politician-drawn maps. Better, to be sure, but there's still a median skew of almost 5%; since that's *median*, there are states with partisan biases higher than that, even using nonpartisan commissions. In a closely divided polity like ours, a 5% deviation can mean the difference between majority control and minority control. Even where the skew doesn't have such a dramatic effect, it seems intuitively problematic that there is any such skew *at all*, unless it is necessary for other, sound, democratic reasons.

In some cases, the less-than-stellar results of nonpartisan redistricting commissions can be attributed to bad design of the makeup of the commission or bad execution by the particular individuals involved. But in other cases, deviations occur despite the best structure and best intentions of the participants. This is because of the phenomenon of *demographic clustering*, known more colloquially as "The Big Sort."

Since World War II, America has seen a slow-motion interior migration. People have been concentrating in areas where people vote like themselves—not deliberately, to be sure, but as a natural by-product of other demographic and residential trends. Most notably, Democrats tend to over-cluster in urban areas, especially those on the coasts. As a result, they are naturally "packing" themselves. When redistricters draw SMDs, which must have equal populations and which normally are expected to be somewhat compact in shape, the inevitable result is that Democrats are packed, and the resulting plans underrepresent them. Just like the Senate, with its pro-small, pro-rural, and thus pro-GOP bias, the modern House has a natural, structural, anti-Democratic bias.

Even though this demographic clustering is particularly acute in 21st-century America because of the post-World War II Big Sort, it is not limited to 21st-century America. It happens naturally in any advanced, pluralistic society, such that single-member districting inevitably imposes a representational skew. Even Australia's technocratic Election Commission, the gold standard for nonpartisan commission map-drawing, occasionally gets it wrong due to demographic clustering. In 1990, the Liberal Party won a majority of the nationwide vote, but the Labor Party won a majority of the seats. In 1998, it was the Labor Party's turn to get robbed.

These "naturally occurring gerrymanders" should not surprise us once we consider how many conflicting demands redistricting places on line-drawers. Under U.S. federal law, they have to draw districts that are very nearly perfectly equal in population, while also fairly reflecting racial and ethnic minority voting strength. Under state law and custom, they additionally must draw maps which keep cities and counties intact as much as possible, and are reasonably regular in shape. All these criteria can conflict with each other.

Beyond that, reformers like to have as many "competitive" or "swing" districts as possible so that general election outcomes are not always a foregone conclusion. Drawing competitive districts often conflicts with the goal of having a number of majority-Democratic and majority-Republican districts that fairly reflects the statewide partisan makeup of voters—i.e., of minimizing the skew. Put cartographic pen to paper, and something's gotta give—usually a lot of somethings, including important things like partisan and racial fairness.

People simply do not naturally sort themselves into efficient, compact-district-shaped concentrations of voters. Their residential patterns are stubbornly complex, messy, and ever-changing. And the "ever-changing" part brings with it another headache. For, even if you were somehow to manage to balance perfectly all these many and varied criteria, at the end of the decade, you'll have to start from scratch. (Redistricting occurs every 10 years, after the U.S. Census.)

So, while nonpartisan redistricting commissions, like court decisions policing gerrymanders, are certainly worthwhile reforms, they alone will not fully resolve the problem of unrepresentative election outcomes. This problem is inherent in the idea of carving up the polity into states or SMDs and imposing a winner-take-all construct within each. This is why the courts' search for intentional gerrymanders addresses only part of the problem. As the failures of even the best nonpartisan redistricting commissions show, *unintentional* gerrymanders are commonplace. As long as you have SMDs, you will have gerrymandering.

So, what is the solution then? The solution is to avoid drawing districts in the first place. Or, at least, to draw as few as possible. Fewer districts, less gerrymandering, less fighting and litigating every 10 years. We can do that through American forms of *proportional representation* (PR).

PR can be used in any election where one is electing multiple legislators at the same time to fill multiple seats on a legislative assembly. Under PR, a majority of the votes yields a majority of the seats. And a minority party, or racial group, which makes up 37% of the vote will get roughly 37% of the representation. It's not "winner-take-all"; it's "majority take most, and minority take its fair share."

Why should 50.1% of the vote control 100% of the power? Why should a politically cohesive minority (racial, partisan, ideological, or whatever) that consistently gets 40% of the vote repeatedly get 0% of the power? When the latter happens, that minority gets alienated. It thinks of elections as futile endeavors, and starts participating at a lower rate. Under PR, almost everyone can point to at least one winning candidate and say, "I voted for that person. She is *my* representative." Elections are more competitive, and voter engagement improves.

PR is used around the world, at the national, state, and local level. Indeed, every industrialized democracy uses some form of PR for at least part of its nationwide elections—except for the U.S. and Canada, which inherited our outdated election system from the U.K. Traditionalists sometimes ask, "If PR is so good, how come our Founding Fathers didn't adopt it?" The simple answer: it hadn't been invented yet.

One can use a variety of electoral mechanisms to implement PR. Many countries using PR eschew primary elections; use parliamentary systems, where the chief executive is chosen by the legislature rather than being elected by the people; run elections where you vote for the party, not the candidate; and other things alien to our American experience. For a variety of reasons, those mechanisms aren't suitable for use in the U.S. The common objections to those methods (some of them legitimate) are irrelevant to this book. This book argues for the *single transferable vote* method of PR elections, which in turn requires the use of Ranked Choice Voting (RCV).

Under RCV, voters rank candidates in order of preference: 1st, 2nd, 3rd, etc. Under single transferable vote (STV), these rankings are used in successive rounds of vote-counting to fill multiple legislative seats in such a way that it produces proportional results. The vote-counting rules are designed to minimize wasted votes. This includes both votes for candidates who get too few votes, and are eliminated in early rounds; and "surplus" votes, where popular candidates get way more votes than they need to qualify for a seat on the legislature. These two types of wasted votes are roughly analogous to cracking and stacking, respectively, underscoring how STV helps with gerrymandering-type issues.

In addition to permanently solving the problem of gerrymandering, STV also leads to results more accurately reflective of the popular will. It opens opportunities for third parties, as well as racial, ethnic, and gender diversity.

Australia is a natural experiment to test this proposition. For the last 70 years, it has simultaneously had a single-member-district, winner-take-all system for the federal House, and a geographically overlapping STV system for its Senate, used at the same time and place. The Senate has consistently had more proportional representation of the major parties; has the majority party control; has substantially more proportional representation of third parties; and has a higher percentage of women. The same is true of Germany. Closer to home, STV is used in both Minneapolis, Minnesota, and Cambridge, Massachusetts, with similar results for minorities and women.

The RCV involved in STV has further advantages—not only in House elections, but in elections for the U.S. Senate and President, and at the state and local level as well. RCV creates more opportunities for third parties and lesser-known, lesser-funded candidates. Under a winner-take-all system, voters are legitimately reluctant to vote for such candidates, even if such candidates are their personal favorite, lest they "throw away their vote" on candidates that don't seem to have a good chance of winning. This of course triggers a vicious cycle: such voter reluctance perpetuates their perceived loser status, so they never get a chance.

Worse, under winner-take-all, a vote for a favored long-shot candidate can actually backfire and end up helping the major candidate you dislike the most: a vote for Green Party candidate Jill Stein is really a vote for Trump, and a vote for Libertarian Gary Johnson is really a vote for Clinton. RCV breaks this cycle. You can list Ralph Nader as your first choice and Al Gore as your second choice. If Nader doesn't get enough votes to advance, your vote will transfer to Gore. You won't be helping Bush.

And lest the above examples suggest a pro-Democratic bias, it should be made clear that PR helps all minority groups everywhere. It would help Republicans in Massachusetts and conservatives in San Francisco. Legislatures in all jurisdictions would be more diverse, by race, ethnicity, gender, party, and ideology.

STV is a natural for local elections, in cities small enough where you can run the election at-large. But how would one structure it for U.S. House elections? A bill currently pending in Congress has a decent answer. Under the Fair Representation Act, states with 5 or fewer House seats would run STV elections at-large: no districts at all. No gerrymandering, because no districting. For a state with 6 or more House seats, a nonpartisan redistricting commission would carve the state up into a few multimember districts, each electing between 3 and 5 House members. STV would be used within each multimember district. Districting would be kept to a minimum, as would gerrymandering. Mathematically and cartographically speaking, it is much harder to do real gerrymandering mischief in drawing 3 large multimember districts compared to 15 small SMDs. Even if that particular bill never passes, the general idea of moving to PR, STV, and RCV, on the federal as well as state/local level, is well worth considering.

This book examines the structural electoral issues implicated by the three anomalous results at the top of this chapter. It outlines in more detail the problems and solutions discussed in this chapter, including the legal issues and political practicalities involved. Chapter 2 discusses the Electoral College and the NPV Compact. Chapter 3 discusses the structural representational problems of the Senate as well as filibuster reform. Chapter 4 outlines the extent of House gerrymandering and why it's now worse than ever. Chapters 5 and 6 discuss two potential solutions to gerrymandering, judicial policing and redistricting commissions, respectively, and explain why they are, at best, partial solutions. Chapter 7 introduces the concept of RCV by discussing its simplest form, Instant Runoff Voting, which is used to fill one office at a time (as in a mayoral race, or in a single-member district). Chapter 8 builds on Chapter 7 to explain how STV uses Ranked Choice Voting to yield proportional results, and why reforms like the Fair Representation Act deserve serious consideration. Chapter 9 discusses how these ideas can apply at the state and local level, and Chapter 10 offers concluding thoughts.

Are these ideas far-fetched? Perhaps some, at least for now. But these reforms are part of a growing national movement. Ten years ago, the NPV movement was purely academic; today its advocates are almost two-thirds of the way toward making it effective. Twenty years ago, the idea of using RCV in the U.S. seemed quixotic. It is now used in over a dozen cities, including major cities, and is used statewide in Maine for major elections like governor and U.S. Senate. STV has gained a foothold in Minneapolis and Cambridge, and the Fair Representation Act itself has seen a growing list of co-sponsors.

Like all fundamental democratic reforms, these ideas will take years or decades of sustained consideration. But such sustained attention is as appropriate as our current democracy's structural flaws are fundamental.

2. The Electoral College

A. OUR UNDEMOCRATIC PRESIDENTIAL ELECTION SYSTEM

It's by now common knowledge that about 3 million more people voted for Hillary Clinton than for Donald Trump. Trump became President because of the anachronistic Electoral College, a system viewed as a genius compromise at the time it was created but which legitimately strikes many today as an anti-democratic Rube Goldberg contrivance. Under this system, each state has as many presidential Electors as it has representatives in Congress—that is, a certain number for House members based on state population, plus 2 for each state representing Senators. Each state selects a slate of Electors for one party or another on Election Day. Some weeks later, each state's slate of Electors meets in their respective states and casts official Electoral votes for a given candidate. It's the candidate with the most Electoral votes, not the most regular votes nationwide, who gets to take the oath of office.[1]

Less common knowledge is that Americans have no constitutional right to vote for President. State legislatures have full authority to choose which Electors they'll select in any manner they choose.[2] Although by 1876, all state legislatures had decided to do this through popular election,[3] there is nothing stopping Tennessee tomorrow from canceling presidential elections and announcing that henceforth, all 11 of its Electoral College votes would go to whomever the Republican nominee is.

Nor is there any constitutional requirement that the Electors obey the instructions given them by the state legislatures. While most states have laws requiring that Electors abide by the results of their state's presidential election, not all do. And even in those that do, there is usually no explicit provision for canceling the non-conforming vote or punishing the so-called "faithless elector."[4] Normally, this punishment is no more than

---

[1] U.S. Const. Art. II, § 1.

[2] *Id.*; McPherson v. Blacker, 146 U.S.1 (1892).

[3] John R. Koda et al., Every Vote Equal 5–6 (2013).

[4] Only 30 states and D.C. require Electors to abide by the state's election results. Of those, only 6 explicitly provide for cancellation of the stray vote; only 5 provide for a penalty against the faithless Elector; and 2 states do both. *See*

a light fine, hardly a deterrent for the determined zealot who has had a change of heart since originally getting selected by his party to serve as an Elector.

Such "faithless electors" pop up every now and then throughout our history, always in small numbers, and never enough to change the outcome of an election. But there's no legal reason why they couldn't play such an outcome-determinative role, including giving the presidency to someone who didn't earn the most support from the voters. Indeed, there were a record number of faithless Electoral votes counted—7—in the 2016 presidential election.[5]

But as a practical matter, the main fear of those concerned about the Electoral College is not the specter of faithless Electors, but a scenario like 2016, where the system worked as designed and awarded the Oval Office to a candidate who got fewer votes nationwide than a rival. Even when all the state legislatures and Electors play along with the democratic norm of respecting the will of the voters, the system itself can violate that norm.

This is because almost all states allocate Electors in a *winner-take-all* manner, meaning that a candidate with 51% of the state's vote gets 100% of the state's Electors.[6] Thus, it's possible for a presidential candidate to "waste" votes—e.g., by running up huge margins in certain population-rich states. If such a candidate's opponent is more efficient with his vote distribution, by getting slight majorities in a lot of states, he may end up with more Electoral votes even if he has fewer total votes. In fact, National Public Radio has calculated that with the right combination of states, and winning those states by just one vote, it is theoretically possible to win the presidency with just 23% of the popular vote, even if 77% of the voters chose that person's opponent.[7]

2016 was of course not the only time this happened. Only four presidential elections earlier, Al Gore lost to George W. Bush in 2000 despite receiving over half a million more votes nationwide. In fact, the

---

FairVote, *Faithless Elector State Laws*, available at http://www.fairvote.org/faithless_elector_state_laws.

[5] *See* Juila Boccagno, *Which Candidates Did the Seven 'Faithless' Electors Support?*, CBS NEWS (Dec. 21, 2016), available at https://www.cbsnews.com/news/which-candidates-did-the-seven-faithless-electors-support-election-2016/.

[6] The only exceptions are Maine and Nebraska, which allocate votes by congressional district, with the winner of the state overall receiving the extra 2 electoral votes corresponding to the state's 2 senators.

[7] *See* Danielle Kurtzleben, *How to Win the Presidency with 23 Percent of the Popular Vote* (Nov. 12, 2012), available at https://www.npr.org/2016/11/02/500 112248/how-to-win-the-presidency-with-27-percent-of-the-popular-vote.

Electoral College has caused this anomalous "winner becomes loser"
result five times in our history. In 1876, Democrat Samuel Tilden had
more votes than eventual President Republican Rutherford B. Hayes.[8]
In 1888, Democrat Grover Cleveland lost to Benjamin Harrison despite
having more of the popular vote.[9] In 1824, John Quincy Adams beat
Andrew Jackson despite having fewer nationwide votes.[10] All in all, this
has happened 5 times in 59 presidential elections, meaning the "winner
loses" about 8% of the time. It's been happening more frequently in
recent elections because of our highly polarized, roughly evenly split
electorate.[11]

---

[8]   Strictly speaking, the Electoral College was not the sole culprit here. The
1876 election results were contested, with the final tallies in four states uncertain.
A special bipartisan panel was convened to resolve the dispute. Eventually, key
members of the panel agreed to vote to support Hayes' claim if the Republicans
promised to remove federal troops from the South. Hayes became President
and removed the troops, thus ending Reconstruction and clearing the way for
Jim Crow. Eric Foner, RECONSTRUCTION: AMERICA'S UNFINISHED REVOLUTION,
1863–1877, 575–583 (1988).

[9]   James L. Baumgarden, *The 1888 Presidential Election: How Corrupt?* 14
PRESIDENTIAL STUDIES QUARTERLY 416–427 (1984). Cleveland later went on to win
the election four years later in 1892, the only President to serve two nonconsecutive
terms. *See* David Leip, "1892 Presidential Election Results". *Dave Leip's Atlas of
U.S. Presidential Elections.*

[10]   In fact, Jackson also had more *Electoral* votes too. But because neither
had a majority of all Electoral votes, the election went to the U.S. House of
Representatives according to provisions of the Constitution (see Article II, Section
1, and the Twelfth Amendment), and the House chose Adams.

  Some historians argue that we should add a sixth presidential election to the
list of instances where the popular vote winner nonetheless lost the Presidency
thanks to the Electoral College. Although most historians state that John F.
Kennedy won the national popular vote majority in 1960, that conclusion
depends on a particular way of counting the popular vote in Alabama, where
voters were allowed to choose between Nixon Electors, Kennedy Electors,
"undeclared" Electors, and pro-Southern "Dixiecrat" Electors who ultimately
voted for West Virginia Senator Robert Byrd. Reasonable minds could differ
about how to "score" these latter two classes of votes. If you award Alabama's
popular vote to Byrd rather than Kennedy, then ultimate loser Nixon would
have won the popular vote majority. *See* Gordon Tullock, *Nixon, Like Gore, also
Won Popular Vote, but Lost Election*, 37(1) PS: POLITICAL SCIENCE & POLITICS
1–2 (2004).

[11]   *See* Nate Cohn, *Polarization Is Dividing American Society, Not Just Politics*,
NEW YORK TIMES (June 12, 2014), available at https:// www.nytimes.com/2014/06/12/
upshot/polarization-is-dividing-american-society-not-just-politics.html.

B. WHY THE SYSTEM WAS CREATED

The Framers did consider a direct national popular vote during the Constitutional Convention but rejected it. As with any group decision, there were a number of different reasons for the rejection, motivating different decision-makers to different degrees. But from the evidence a few key reasons emerge.

Distrust of the Voters. A main reason was the Founders' belief that the people were too rash and ignorant to elect the President. Virginia's George Mason said to give the people a direct vote was as unnatural as "to give a trial of colours to a blind man."[12] Massachusetts' Elbridge Gerry, who the gerrymander was named after (see Chapter 4), feared that "the ignorance of the people" would make them too subject to manipulation by an organized group.[13] Alexander Hamilton, whose Federalist Papers were influential in the subsequent ratification debate, wrote that the selection should be made by "a small number of persons, selected . . . from the general mass," who would "possess the information and discernment requisite to such complicated investigations."[14] As an early and definitive scholar of the Constitution, the Supreme Court Justice and Harvard Law Professor Joseph Story, described it, the Framers preferred Electors over direct popular vote because it was thought the Electors would be "most capable of . . . deliberation" and most "judicious."[15] Popular election, by contrast, would lead to "excitements and interests," "heats and ferments," and "tumult and disorder."[16]

Concession to Small States. There were other objections. For one thing, some Framers feared that the people would simply favor candidates from their own states. This could advantage the large states.[17] The small states'

---

[12] James Madison, NOTES ON THE DEBATES IN THE FEDERAL CONVENTION, July 17, 1787, YALE L.S.: THE AVALON PROJECT, available at http://avalon.law.yale.edu/18th_century/debates_717.asp.

[13] James Madison, NOTES ON THE DEBATES IN THE FEDERAL CONVENTION, July 19, 1987, YALE L.S.: THE AVALON PROJECT, available at http://avalon.law.yale.edu/18th_century/debates_717.asp.

[14] THE FEDERALIST No. 68, at 347 (Alexander Hamilton) (Gary Wills ed., 1982).

[15] Joseph Story, COMMENTARIES ON THE CONSTITUTION 531 (1833) (reprinted, Ronald D. Rotunda & John E. Nowak, eds., 1980).

[16] *Id.* (citing Alexander Hamilton, FEDERALIST No. 68). The "tumult and disorder" and "heats and ferments" phrases came from Hamilton's FEDERALIST No. 68. They could plausibly be read as referring to popular election; selection of the President by Congress; a plenary meeting of the entire Electoral College rather than having them each meet separately in their own states; or all three.

[17] Shlomo Slonin, *The Electoral College at Philadelphia*, 73 JOURNAL OF AMERICAN HISTORY 35, 40 (1986).

fears of dominance of *Congress* by the large states were assuaged by the so-called Great Compromise, where each state got an equal number of Senators. By giving each state a number of Electors equal to the number of representatives in the House and Senate, the Electoral College recreated this small state/large state balancing act.

Concession to Southern States. This tendency of large-state voters to favor their native sons could also disadvantage the Southern states, which had limited suffrage. James Madison, known as the Father of the Constitution, stated this rationale quite explicitly as a major political impediment to the Constitutional Convention's acceptance of direct popular vote, which he personally favored.[18] In the South, many people counted for the purpose of allocating Electoral College votes were nonetheless ineligible to vote. Some of them were white males who lacked property or income.[19] Others were slaves, a significant fraction of the states' population,[20] who counted as three-fifths of a person for purposes of representation in the House and therefore for Electoral College votes as well.[21] This was quite a good deal for Southern white males with property, who got to use the many disenfranchised in their states (slave and free) to swell their representation in the House and Electoral College, while reserving for themselves (a relatively small subset of the population) the actual power to make decisions. A direct popular presidential vote, though, would not give the Southern states the advantage they enjoyed in the House from the three-fifths compromise. This motivated Southern opposition to a national popular presidential vote, pushing pro-Constitution advocates to look for a compromise.

In sum, while some Framers favored direct popular election, it was unpopular among most for several overlapping reasons: the Framers didn't trust the people; and as a political compromise to gain the support of both small states and Southern, largely disenfranchised, states.

---

[18]   *See* Max Farrand, THE RECORDS OF THE FEDERAL CONVENTION 1787, Vol. 2, 56–57.

[19]   Steffen W. Schmidt, AMERICAN GOVERNMENT AND POLITICS TODAY: 2007–2008 chapter 9 (2008).

[20]   *See, e.g.*, U.S. Census of 1790 [for Virginia, the Carolinas, and Georgia, the slave percentage of total population ranged from 27% (NC) to 43% (SC)]. In fact, there were more slaves than eligible voters in each state. *Id.* (showing that slave population in each such state exceeded white males over 16). "Heads of Families at the First Census of the United States Taken in the Year of 1790." *Department of Commerce and Labor Bureau of the Census* (1908), p. 8.

[21]   U.S. CONST. Art. I, § 2.

C. THE WEAKNESS OF THE ORIGINAL RATIONALES

All this may sound elitist and undemocratic to modern ears. That's because it is.

Today, it's not obvious why a candidate with fewer votes should prevail over one with more votes. Nor is it obvious that there's anything wrong with states containing more people having more of a say in who becomes President. And we're certainly not inclined to feel sympathy for a state because it chooses to deny the vote to large chunks of its population, enslaved or otherwise. Given modern universal suffrage among competent adult citizens of all races, that latter rationale is clearly moot anyway.

Protecting Small States? Beyond that, it's not even clear how well the College achieved its intended purposes. Take, for example, the idea that it protects smaller states, a supposed virtue cited by modern-day defenders of the College. To be sure, the modern Electoral College certainly does give a numerical advantage to smaller states. For example, Wyoming has only about 200,000 persons per Electoral College vote, while California, Texas, New York, Florida, Illinois, and Pennsylvania have more than three times as many per Electoral vote. A Wyoming voter's vote counts more than four times as much as a Californian's.

Certainly, a Wyoming voter is given more mathematical impact on the outcome than a California voter. For those who do not see the wisdom of giving smaller voters in small states disproportionate influence, and who see it instead as unfairly playing favorites, that is reason enough to decry the Electoral College.

But even for those who see value in protecting small states, the Electoral College should be cold comfort. In a very practical sense, large states still rule the day. Because most states use a winner-take-all rule, where the candidate who earns even a bare majority of the votes still receives all the Electoral College votes, the large states are seen as Elector-rich fields with outsize influence. Among the dozen or so "swing states" which could realistically go Democratic or Republican in a presidential election, the larger states receive the lion's share of the attention by the candidates during the campaign, which translates into disproportionate influence on policy outcomes once the campaign ends and governing begins. Indeed, the dozen biggest states by themselves (swing and non-swing alike) have enough Electoral votes to determine the outcome.

Even if the College actually did protect small-state sovereignty, and we were willing to overlook the manifest unfairness of giving more weight to a Rhode Island voter's preference than that of a New Yorker's preference, the sovereignty of individual states has far less salience in the 21st century than it did at the time the College was created. At the Founding, small states were considered sovereign entities. In many respects, this was true. They had their own currencies and often imposed tariffs on goods from other states. Commerce and transportation across state lines was by no means effortless, as it is today. In addition, psychologically, most people felt primary allegiance to their state over their country. If you asked the average citizen back then to identify himself or herself by location or citizenship, he or she would likely say, "I'm a Pennsylvanian," or "I'm a Georgian," rather than "I'm an American." During the Revolutionary War, New Jersey troops refused General Washington's request to swear allegiance to the United States, insisting, "New Jersey is our country!"[22]

Not so today. The Constitution curbed the powers of the states as it strengthened federal power.[23] The Civil War amendments altered the legal federal–state balance even more.[24] And our modern mobile, Internet-homogenized society has given us an ocean-to-ocean unified culture. Most people would identify themselves as "Americans" today. It is either already the case, or close to being the case, that state boundaries are arbitrary markers on the soil, rather than delineators of a distinct and sovereign polity. And, to the extent this "protect small states" rationale theoretically remains, it isn't even particularly served well by the modern Electoral College, as discussed above.[25]

---

[22]   Catherine Drinker Bowen, MIRACLE AT PHILADELPHIA 7 (2d ed. 1986).

[23]   For example, the Constitution gave Congress strong power to regulate and facilitate interstate commerce, see U.S. CONST. Art. I, § 8; forbade states from discriminating against out-of-staters, see Art IV, § 1; required each state to give "full faith and credit" to the judgments of other states, see Art. IV, § 1; and provided that treaties and laws agreed to by the federal government were binding on the States, even if State law had been to the contrary, see Art. VI, cl.2.

[24]   For example, the Fourteenth Amendment provided that anyone born or naturalized anywhere in the United States was a citizen of the state where she lived, *see* Amen. 14, § 1; and required each State to provide all its citizens due process and the equal protection of the laws, Amen. 14, § 1; and provided that Congress had the power to enforce all these requirements through appropriate legislation, Amen. 14, § 5.

[25]   Indeed, some defenders of the College argue as an *advantage* of the College that it, as currently constituted, gives power to large states because their winner-take-all allocation systems make them Electoral vote-rich prizes that receive much attention. *See, e.g.,* Richard Posner, *In Defense of the Electoral College,* SLATE (Nov. 12, 2012), available at http://www.slate.com/articles/news_and_politics/ view_from_chicago/2012/11/defending_the_electoral_college.html. This is a good thing, the argument goes, because it compensates for the improper, undemocratic advantage given the small states in the Senate as part of the Great Compromise. It is somewhat problematic to argue that the College, which replicates a feature of the Senate designed to protect small states, somehow redounds to the benefit

The Rise of Swing States. But of course, most of these states, large and small, are reliably Democratic or reliably Republican in presidential elections. These states are also largely ignored by candidates.[26] Democratic candidates will spend little time or attention on Texas because it is a lost cause. Republican candidates will do likewise, because they can take Texas' 38 Electoral votes for granted. Thus, the modern Electoral College forces the presidential campaign to focus on a relatively small number of Elector-rich swing states like Ohio and Florida,[27] while effectively ignoring many other voters around the country.[28] A common estimate is that roughly four-fifths of U.S. voters are ignored in this way in presidential elections.[29]

This isn't just a problem because of the wounded pride of voters in small or "safe" states who feel left out. It means the location-specific issues of special concern to battleground state voters get overemphasized in the campaign, while similar local issues inside small or safe states get overlooked. Because campaign promises correlate (though hardly

---

of large states. But even if this is true as an empirical matter, it is also problematic to criticize the undemocratic nature of the Senate in one breath and celebrate the concededly undemocratic Electoral College in the next.

[26] In 2008, for example, Barack Obama campaigned in only 14 states, representing only 33% of the American people. John McCain campaigned in only 19 states. George C. Edwards III, WHY THE ELECTORAL COLLEGE IS BAD FOR AMERICA 3–5 (2d ed. 2011). In 2003–2004, the Bush campaign conducted no national polls, commissioning polls only in 18 perceived battleground states. Koda et al., EVERY VOTE EQUAL, *supra*, 12–14.

[27] The influential Cook Political Report lists 10 states as "up for grabs" in 2018: Illinois, Indiana, Michigan, Minnesota, Ohio, Wisconsin in the Great Lakes region, and Arizona, Colorado, Nevada, and New Mexico in the Southwest. Richard E. Cohen, *Two Nations*, Cook Political Report, available at https://www.cookpolitical.com/analysis/national/2018-almanac-american-politics-preview/two-nations. *See also* Richard Cohen et al., THE ALMANAC OF AMERICAN POLITICS 7–9 (2018).

[28] Some have argued that this is a good thing: Swing state voters, knowing their votes are more decisive, will pay closer attention to the presidential race, meaning that the race will be decided by a group of better-informed voters. Posner, SLATE, *supra*. This argument is a modern relative of the Founders' original claim that the people at-large are too ignorant to be trusted. Even granting that swing-state voters will be more informed than average, it is not at all clear that they are representative proxies for the people at-large, or that the relative ignorance of the rest of the country would tend to skew elections in one direction or another. Absent such evidence, it is safe to assume that an election decided by all voters equally nationwide would be more representative of the popular will overall than an election decided by voters in a few key swing states. Additionally, the focus on swing states can distort policy outcomes, as discussed below.

[29] *See* Koda et al., EVERY VOTE EQUAL, *supra*, 435.

perfectly) with governing emphases, substantive policy is skewed because of the game theory aspects of the Electoral College. According to the organization National Popular Vote, "battleground" states receive 7% more federal grants than other states, twice as many presidential disaster declarations, more Superfund enforcement exceptions, and more No Child Left Behind exemptions.[30]

Perhaps the Trump campaign would not have spent as much time focusing on the coal industry had Pennsylvania, a major coal-producing state, not been a battleground state in 2016.[31] Indeed, when the Pennsylvania state legislature considered moving away from a winner-take-all method of allocating Electoral votes, both former Republican U.S. Senator Allen Specter and former Democratic Governor Ed Rendell protested, saying that Pennsylvania would get less federal funding for in-state projects because it would be less pivotal in the presidential election.[32]

So the original rationales for the College are largely moot today. There is no longer any need to preserve a balance with enfranchisement-poor Southern states in a modern, universal suffrage world. And even if a modern thinker still distrusted the common people to make the decision, that is largely moot in a system where Electors are legally bound to follow election results, and/or almost always do so by custom and norm.

D.   THE WEAKNESS OF MODERN RATIONALES FOR THE COLLEGE

Are there persuasive *modern* rationales for the Electoral College? Defenders posit several arguments, but few bear up under close scrutiny.

Electoral Certainty. Some argue that abolishing Electoral College makes it more likely for there to be ties, or margins of victory so razor thin that they lead to litigation and uncertainty.[33] If the statewide recount in Florida in 2000 was bad, this argument goes, imagine a *nationwide* recount. The

---

[30] *See* National Popular Vote, *Agreement Among the States to Elect the President by National Popular Vote*, https://www.nationalpopularvote.com/written-explanation.

[31] *See, e.g.,* Julie Cart, *Mountain States Feel the Neglect of Presidential Campaigns*, NEW YORK TIMES (June 6, 2000), describing how voters in mountain states consider their local issues, such as management of public lands, sprawl, and rural economic development, being ignored by presidential candidates.

[32] Mike Wereschagin and Brad Bumsted, *GOP Plan Could Jeopardize Pennsylvania's Political Clout*, PITTSBURGH TRIBUNE-REVIEW, Sept. 13, 2011, available at triblive.com/x/pittsburghtrib/news/regional/s_756446.html.

[33] *See* Posner, SLATE, *supra*.

Electoral College avoids this risk, the argument goes, by translating small popular vote margins into large Electoral margins.

It is true that the College tends to exaggerate margins of victory, making small popular majorities look like landslides in Electoral College votes. In 2012, for example, President Obama won 332 out of 538 possible Electoral College votes, or 61%, even though he only received 51% of the popular vote.[34]

But as a practical matter, if the goal is litigation-proof margins of victory so as to foster certainty and finality of result, a countrywide popular vote is the better alternative. As a system where there are only 538 votes, almost all coming in 51 winner-take-all "buckets" of 3 to 55 points each (i.e., the 50 states plus Washington, D.C.), the College is much more mathematically likely to achieve relatively close results in one or two key states holding the decisive bucket of votes. This happened in Florida in 2000, where the final certified margin of victory between Bush and Gore was only 537, representing only 0.01% of the combined vote between them (about 5.8 million). But nationally there were over 105 million votes cast in that election. Statistically, it is *much* less likely that a 0.01% margin would occur in a pool of votes of 105 million votes than 5.8 million. It is not clear who actually won Florida in 2000, but it is very clear who won the national popular vote. Legitimate questions have been raised about the presidential election results in Ohio in 2004 and Pennsylvania in 2016, but no one doubts who won the national popular vote in those years (George W. Bush and Hillary Clinton, respectively).

By this same logic, it is easier to commit successful fraud under an Electoral College system. Wily hackers (foreign or domestic) need only switch tens of thousands of votes in Ohio, Florida, or Pennsylvania to change the election outcome. Under a national popular vote plan, they'd have to switch over a million, spread out over a dozen or more states, to avoid suspicion. So whether we're talking "natural" uncertain results à la Florida 2000, or deliberate uncertainty caused by election fraud or Russian hacking, a nationwide popular vote is the better alternative.

Majority Winner and Runoffs. One other argument supporting the current system is that the College eliminates the need for a runoff

---

[34] Some might say this is a good thing, in that the appearance of a landslide boosts public confidence in the newly elected President, giving him or her the public mandate they need to govern. The actual value of this feature seems somewhat dubious, however. For one thing, the popular vote totals are widely and routinely reported, and most voters today are sophisticated enough not to be fooled by an artificial landslide. For another, to the extent that voters *are* so fooled, *quaere* the value to democracy of a mandate premised on widespread voter misunderstanding of the actual election results.

election in case no candidate achieves a majority of the vote. Under the Electoral College system, if no candidate receives a majority, the House of Representatives chooses among the top three Electoral vote-getters, each state getting one vote.[35] Certainly, a second, runoff nationwide election some weeks after the November election would be a logistically difficult undertaking, and one to be avoided if possible. But it is by no means clear that a runoff would be necessary under a national popular vote system, nor that the Electoral College's solution to the problem of a plurality-only winner is preferable to the alternatives.

First, a national popular vote system could simply allow a plurality winner. This would at least ensure that a candidate with fewer votes did not take office over someone with more votes. Second, the House could be given the same selection responsibility under a popular vote system if there was no majority winner.[36] Third, *quaere* whether having politicians in the House make the final decision is the best, or most democratic, method. If given the choice between (i) having the plurality winner, the person with the most actual votes, win, or (ii) allowing coalitions of congressmen on a state-by-state basis choose someone with fewer votes, most people would select the former. History does not look back too kindly on the House's decision in 1824 to award the presidency to John Quincy Adams over Andrew Jackson. Jackson won the popular vote by a 10-point margin (41% to 31%) but lost in the House thanks to what has now been called a "corrupt bargain," an alleged deal between Adams and third-party candidate Henry Clay, who threw his support behind Adams in the House deliberations and later was appointed Secretary of State.[37] At any rate, a reform discussed

---

[35]   U.S. CONST. Amen. 12. This has happened twice in our history, in the 1800 election of Thomas Jefferson and the 1824 election of John Quincy Adams. In the case of Adams, the House passed over the candidate with the highest popular vote, Andrew Jackson.

[36]   As currently formulated, the National Popular Vote Interstate Compact recommended at the end of this chapter allows a plurality winner of the national popular vote to become President, to avoid the logistical difficulty of a second, nationwide runoff election. While the NPV compact is certainly an improvement over the current system, a runoff system of some kind is generally preferable to a mere plurality win, for reasons discussed later in Chapter 7. But using a House-based selection process in case no candidate gets a nationwide majority would require a federal constitutional amendment, and in any event is less preferable than a voter-driven final selection process. Ultimately, states could adopt Instant Runoff Voting to elect presidents, ensuring a majority winner. See *infra* Section I. If only some states adopted Instant Runoff Voting, a nationwide *majority* winner would not be certain, but it would be much more likely.

[37]   *See* R. R. Stenberg, *Jackson, Buchanan, and the "Corrupt Bargain" Calumny*, 58(1) THE PENNSYLVANIA MAGAZINE OF HISTORY AND BIOGRAPHY 61–85 (1934).

later in this chapter, Instant Runoff Voting (IRV), would both ensure majority support and eliminate the need for a second runoff election.

Regional Diversity. By far the most persuasive modern argument in defense of the College is that it requires a candidate to have across-the-regions appeal and prevents a candidate loved in some (high-population) region(s) from winning despite being despised in other regions. To make this point, some have used the analogy of the World Series.[38] To win the World Series, the argument goes, you don't have to just amass the highest number of runs over the course of the 7 games. Instead, you have to score the most runs in 4 of the 7 games. So, too, with the Electoral College: it is fitting and proper that your support be spread over many regions of the country.

There is certainly some weight to this argument, depending on how you define regional appeal. To be sure, a system in which you have to win a majority in a requisite number of different states would, on average, tend to result in candidates' appeal being more geographically spread out than one in which you simply counted heads, including heads in densely populated areas. But the practical difference may not be as great as one might think.

No matter how you carve up the U.S. into regions—the U.S. Census has maps dividing the country into 4, 5, and 6 main regions—no one region by itself would be enough to carry the national popular vote, even if 100% of the voters voted for the same candidate.[39] (But no one region would command the necessary 270 Electoral votes needed to win, either.) A combination of a few main regions could do so. For example, a candidate decisively carrying the Northeast (New England and Mid-Atlantic states)[40] plus all of the West, including Pacific states[41] as well as Mountain states,[42] could conceivably win the popular vote. But again, such a candidate would win the Electoral vote as well.

---

[38]   The analogy seems to have first been used by MIT researcher Alan Natapoff. Anthony Ramirez, *Why The Election Is Like Baseball*, N. Y. TIMES (Nov. 6, 1996), available at http://www.nytimes.com/1996/11/03/weekinreview/why-the-election-is-like-baseball.html?pagewanted=all&src=pm.

[39]   *See* https://www2.census.gov/geo/pdfs/maps-data/maps/reference/us_regdiv. pdf; *see also* https://www.census.gov/popclock/data_tables.php?component=growth. This analysis assumes that voters in the various states register and turn out to vote at roughly the same rate. This is not necessarily true in practice, but this simplification will work for illustrating broad points about regional candidates.

[40]   New England plus New York, Pennsylvania, New Jersey, Delaware, and Maryland.

[41]   California, Oregon, and Washington.

[42]   Montana, Idaho, Wyoming, Nevada, Vermont, Colorado, Arizona, and New Mexico.

Many such regional combinations are implausible because, for many decades now, certain regions have reliably supported one party or another in presidential contests. So, for example, a Democratic candidate is likely to receive the support of the Northeast and Pacific states. If she were also to receive the votes of Virginia, North Carolina, and Florida, which are plausible assumptions, she would still need more votes to win the popular vote (as well as the Electoral vote). Similarly, a Republican candidate traditionally does well in the South, Mid-South (Tennessee, Arkansas, Kentucky), and Mountain states. Even if he were to get all these votes (including those in swing states like Virginia, North Carolina, and Florida), it would still not be enough to win the popular vote (or Electoral vote). Either way, a candidate is going to need some support from the Midwest to win the popular vote (or the Electoral vote). So, the prospect of a candidate winning the popular vote in one or two main regions, while getting no significant support elsewhere, does not seem a viable outcome—under either a popular vote system or an Electoral College system. At best, a regional candidate could play a spoiler role, denying any one candidate an Electoral majority, and throwing the election into the House.

So a one-region candidate can at most be a spoiler, and even a two-region candidate has virtually no chance of winning, under either a popular vote or Electoral College approach. But nonetheless, could a candidate in a popular vote system win in a race highly polarized along regional lines, even if it meant getting some support from more than two main regions?

The answer is yes, because it has happened frequently in our history, *even using the Electoral College system.* In 1860, for example, Republican Abraham Lincoln took the North and the Pacific Coast, while Democrat John Breckinridge swept almost all of the South, Maryland, and Delaware. Lincoln still won a decisive Electoral College majority. 1860 was the most regionally polarizing election in our history, and the election where regional polarization had the greatest (and most tragic) consequences for our nation, and yet the Electoral College had no preventive effect. In hindsight, of course, we should be glad of that, given Lincoln's greatness. But the point remains that the College is hardly the reliable circuit breaker for regionally polarized election victories imagined by supporters.

Nor is this an isolated example. For decades after the Civil War, the South voted Democratic, and the Northern states (both Northeast and Midwest) voted Republican, with the election being determined largely by the Pacific states. This was extreme regional polarization, despite the supposedly ameliorative effects of the College.

Indeed, that regional polarization exists today. For at least the last 6 presidential elections, the Democratic candidate has won the Northeast, Pacific, and most of the Midwestern states, while the Republican candidate has won the South and most of the "heartland" states.[43] A handful of swing states like Florida, Ohio, North Carolina, New Mexico, and Colorado are the only variation from this regional pattern (plus, at least one time in 2016, Pennsylvania, Michigan, and Wisconsin, where Republican Trump won in traditionally Democratic states).

So, yes, a national popular vote system might very well allow for a candidate to win in a regionally polarized environment. But if it does, it will be no different than the current system.

In fact, switching to a national popular vote plan would reveal how the Electoral College overstates the regional polarization of the country. We have all seen the Electoral College maps, with each state shaded red or blue for its statewide vote. But a far more accurate map would show the voting diversity within each state, like Figure 2.1, a county-based map shading levels of Republican and Democratic support for the 2016 election.[44]

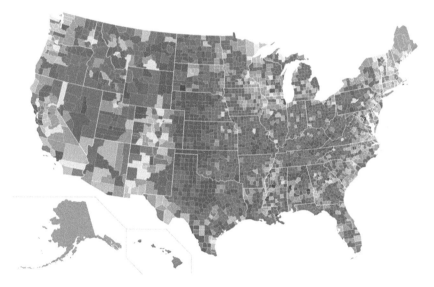

Source: Wikipedia Commons.

Figure 2.1   2016 presidential election results, shaded by county

---

[43]   *See* Richard E. Cohen, *Two Nations*, COOK POLITICAL REPORT (Aug. 4, 2017), available at https://www.cookpolitical.com/analysis/national/2018-almanac-american-politics-preview/two-nations.

[44]   Alicia Parlapiano, *There Are Many Ways to Map Election Results. We've Tried Most of Them*, NEW YORK TIMES (Nov. 1, 2016), available at https://static01.nyt.com/ne3555d3deb92e772f916/counties.png.

Figure 2.1 shows red areas within blue states, blue areas within red states, and pockets of pink and purple everywhere. An even more detailed, interactive map by *precinct* shows the same kind of variation within counties themselves.[45] This would be the campaign dynamic in a popular vote election: candidates crossing the country competing for votes in all regions, not just a few swing states. If anything, it would lead to a *less* regionally polarized perspective.

Another way of evaluating whether a popular vote election would really lead to a winner with regionally isolated appeal would be to look at state-wide elections held in large states with different regions, like California and Texas. These states elect their governors and federal Senators state-wide using a popular vote system. There is no "mini-Electoral College" for these elections. Nonetheless, one does not see such regionally isolated appeal. Instead, you see candidates who campaign across the entire state, and who receive support from across the state (although of course each candidate will receive higher and lower support depending on location).

And as far the World Series analogy? As any true baseball fan knows, the World Series is not the best way to determine which team is best over-all; one's season record over 180 games is a much better measure. What the World Series does is provide entertainment and drama for those who love the game, even if it means the occasional wild card draw lucks into the playoffs and becomes a champion with an uncharacteristically good (or lucky) post-season performance. Think of the 2011 St. Louis Cardinals, who were a whopping 10 games out of first place in their division in August, but who, thanks to the wild card system and some improbable come-from-behind performances in the post-season, won the seventh and final World Series game. This makes for great drama and competition, and is perfectly fine for baseball. But when we pick a President, presumably we value the will of the people over drama. As Yale Law's Akhil Reed Amar stated in congressional testimony when presented with this World Series analogy by an Electoral College defender, "All runs are not created equal. But . . . all men and women are created equal."[46]

Voter Participation. An additional advantage of popular vote is that it addresses a potential participation-suppressing effect of the current system

---

[45] Upshot Staff, *Political Bubbles and Hidden Diversity: Highlights from a Very Detailed Map of the 2016 Election*, NEW YORK TIMES (July 25, 2018), available at https://www.nytimes.com/interactive/2018/07/25/upshot/precinct-map-highlights. html .

[46] Osita Nwanevu, *The Democrat Who Loves the Electoral College*, SLATE (Nov. 26, 2016), available at http://www.slate.com/articles/news_and_politics/ politics/2016/12/the_democrat_who_loves_the_electoral_college.html.

caused by the winner-take-all manner of allocating Electoral College votes. Democrats in Texas, and Republicans in California, have little incentive to vote for President. They know that no matter how many of them and their like-minded neighbors turn out, all of the state's Electoral votes will end up being awarded to the candidate of the other party.

To be sure, no voter can plausibly think that their one vote will be outcome-determinative in any significantly large race;[47] many of us nonetheless vote anyway. But psychologically, most people would think their vote "counts" more if it is cast for the winning candidate, even if it was not by itself outcome-determinative. The psychological sense of futility is stronger when one is convinced that one's candidate has no chance of winning.

Data supports this psychological intuition: in 2012, for example, voter participation in non-battleground states was 11% lower than that in battleground states.[48] For the last several decades, at least, the national presidential election contest has been perceived as much closer than the race for President in individual states, except for the handful of battleground states.

E.   THE IMPLAUSIBILITY OF A FEDERAL CONSTITUTIONAL FIX

If the Electoral College truly does need to be reformed, how best to accomplish it? The College itself is provided for in the U.S. Constitution. The most direct and obvious course would thus be to amend the Constitution to abolish it. Such an approach could allow for a plurality winner, or could allow for a separate runoff election some time after the November general election but before the inauguration. Both approaches have been proposed in Congress in recent decades, with bipartisan sponsors, co-sponsors, and congressional support. But none have achieved the necessary two-thirds majority in both Houses of Congress necessary for a constitutional amendment to be considered for ratification.[49]

---

[47]   This is not necessarily true in local races, however, especially low-turnout primaries, runoffs, and special elections. As an example, in the same County Commission district to which the author was elected (about 80,000 in total population, 40,000 in registered voters), in the election immediately preceding, a candidate won the Democratic nomination by a one-vote margin in election day voting. A different result in the Democratic primary could very well have changed the general election outcome.

[48]   Koda et al., EVERY VOTE EQUAL, *supra*, 37.

[49]   *See id.* at 141–155 (describing the major proposals since 1969). In 1969, a

Even if such a proposal did receive the necessary two-thirds vote in both the House and the Senate—a very implausible scenario in the foreseeable future, given the partisan rancor and ideological differences present in Congress—it would still be unlikely to pass. The Constitution requires that any amendment not only receive a two-thirds vote in both Houses, but also that it be ratified by three-fourths of the state legislatures.[50]

This would be a tall order for any proposal, but particularly one which changes the mode of election, for each state would view itself as having a direct political stake in the outcome. Doubtless some "safe" states, tired of being pushed to the sidelines during presidential races, would support it. But legislatures in swing states would have every political incentive to oppose it. Since that means anywhere from 9 to 12 states[51] would naturally oppose, and 13 states opposing (slightly over one-fourth of 50) would be enough to prevent ratification, such an amendment starts out virtually dead on arrival.

Worse, even support among non-swing states could be doubtful. Since the two instances in recent decades in which the popular vote winner lost (Bush 2000, Trump 2016) involved Republican candidates benefiting from the Electoral College, state legislators may perceive the popular vote proposal as benefiting Democrats, dooming it among many Republican state legislators even in "ignored" states.[52] Even if a substantial majority of Americans favor this amendment, and that support is reflected by the support of a substantial majority of state legislatures, it is highly unlikely that it would receive the necessary three-fourths support.

So, while a constitutional amendment calling for a nationwide popular vote would be the best solution, it is politically non-viable. More plausible reform options come at the state level. Under the Constitution, each state

---

proposal involving runoff elections received the necessary two-thirds support in the House, only to be filibustered in the Senate.

[50] *See* U.S. CONST. Art. V.

[51] The well-respected Cook Political Report assesses 11 states (Minnesota, Illinois, Michigan, Iowa, Indiana, Wisconsin, and Ohio in the Midwest, and Nevada, Arizona, New Mexico, and Colorado in the Southwest) as "up for grabs" in presidential elections in 2018. But even that source acknowledges that its designation of two states (Florida and Virginia) as "safe" seats is controversial, with both reasonably considered still to be swing states. Cohen, *Two Nations, supra.* Cohen et al., THE ALMANAC OF AMERICAN POLITICS, *supra.*

[52] This perception is very likely incorrect. While in the last two anomalous presidential elections (2016 and 2000), the College happened to have favored the Republican candidate, that dynamic could very well be reversed in future elections, for the simple reason that America is so evenly split between Democratic and Republican-leaning voters.

legislature has plenary authority over how to allocate Electoral College votes in a presidential election.[53]

Indeed, most of the fundamental changes in the way we elect Presidents in the U.S. occurred through state legislative action. At the time of the Founding, very few states used elections to decide which candidate(s) received Electoral votes, and not all which did allocated them on a winner-take-all basis. Now, all 50 states plus D.C. use elections, and all but Maine and Nebraska allocate on a winner-take-all basis. Similarly, early in our republic's history, it was common to use a long presidential ballot listing each of the Elector candidates separately, with voters voting for Elector candidates rather than the presidential and vice-presidential nominees themselves. Now, almost all use "short ballots," where the voter simply selects the candidate for President and Vice President directly.[54] None of these fundamental changes in how we choose a President was accomplished through a federal constitutional amendment or even federal legislative action. Instead, each was achieved piecemeal on a state-by-state basis through the actions of state legislatures.

What kind of state-by-state reforms could be adopted to improve the presidential election process? There are three which have received significant attention. I discuss each, from least helpful to most helpful.

F. LITIGATION STRATEGIES

If a state were to replicate the Electoral College system for statewide elections, courts would never permit it. Imagine a county-based, "mini-Electoral College" within a state, where each county's winner-take-all election counted for one Mini Electoral Vote to elect the governor. Or, to make the analogy to the College more exact, one where each county would be allocated Mini Electoral Votes based partially on population, but with each county getting 2 Mini Electoral Votes regardless of size. Such a system would clearly violate the "one person, one vote" principle of the Fourteenth Amendment's Equal Protection Clause, which mandates that each individual vote counts equally.[55] The Supreme Court has already so ruled, invalidating county-based winner-take-all methods in the analogous context of state legislative elections.[56]

---

[53]   U.S. Const., Art. II, § 1; McPherson v. Blacker, 146 U.S. 1, 74 (1892).
[54]   Koda et al., Every Vote Equal, *supra*, 5–6.
[55]   *See* Reynolds v. Sims, 377 U.S. 533 (1964).
[56]   *See* Gray v. Sanders, 372 U.S. 368, 379–381 (1963) (invalidating a "county

Of course, no such legal challenge would succeed against the state-based allocation of Electoral College votes, for the simple reason that the Constitution spells out the Electoral College system. If something is spelled out in the Constitution, it can't be unconstitutional.

However, the fact that almost all states have decided to allocate their Electoral Votes on a *winner-take-all basis* may be challengeable. Allocation methods within a state are *not* spelled out in the Constitution. All the Constitution says is that "Each State shall appoint, in such Manner as the Legislature thereof may direct, a Number of Electors," said number being equal to the number of Senators and Representatives.[57]

Recently, a group of election reformers led by Harvard Law Professor Lawrence Lessig and famed litigator David Boies have filed suits in 4 states challenging the winner-take-all allocation of Electoral votes. The suits argue that such a "unit rule" allocation from among the states essentially throws away the presidential votes of voters within a state who end up voting for the minority-supported candidate, stifling Republicans in California and Democrats in Texas. It also incentivizes presidential candidates to ignore voters in non-swing states. This violates the "equal weight for equal votes" principle of the Equal Protection Clause. This undervaluing of minority voters, the lawsuits argue, also impairs their Free Association rights under the First Amendment. The suits seek replacement of the winner-take-all allocation method with either (i) a national popular vote model or else (ii) a proportional allocation of Electoral votes—where, say, 40% of the state's vote for a Republican candidate would yield approximately 40% of the state's Electoral votes. The complaints specifically reject allocation by congressional district because that simply replicates the winner-take-all distortions on a smaller scale—a "unit rule" by congressional district rather than by state.[58]

These suits are intriguing and have at least surface plausibility. The "one person, one vote" flaws of winner-take-all are obvious. And the Supreme Court has recognized the fatal inequality of the "unit rule"

---

unit" system for electing Georgia state legislators because it gave differing weight to different voters' votes).

[57]   U.S. CONST. Art. II, § 1, cl. 2.

[58]   *See, e.g.*, Complaint for Declaratory and Injunctive Relief, Rodriguez et al v. Jerry Brown et al, Case No. 2:18-cv-01422 (C.D. Cal. Feb. 21, 2018), paras. 1–12, 32–49, 60, available at https://equalvotes.us/wp-content/uploads/2018/02/complaint-california.pdf. The coordinated suits in Texas, Massachusetts, and South Carolina make similar arguments. *See* Equal Votes, *Legal Documents*, available at https://equalvotes.us/wp-content/uploads/2018/02/complaint-california.pdf.

in the presidential election context, striking down a county-based unit rule for gathering petition signatures necessary to placing a presidential candidate's name on a state ballot.[59]

But these claims also have substantial legal hurdles. One hurdle is that the Supreme Court has said that state legislatures have "plenary authority" in allocating Electoral votes.[60] Of course, that does not mean that states can employ presidential election rules that violate Equal Protection, as *Bush v. Gore* made clear in invalidating a state legislature-directed presidential vote-counting process.[61] More difficult for the plaintiffs are the repeated past instances where similar arguments have been made, only to be rejected by lower federal courts and dismissed without a hearing by the Supreme Court.[62] The plaintiffs try to distinguish these older lower court cases by pointing out they required a showing of improper discriminatory purpose, a requirement eliminated by the more recent case of *Bush v. Gore*.[63] But not all of the lower court decisions relied on that requirement; some rejected the challenge for independent reasons.

More fundamentally, a state-based "unit rule" method is explicitly endorsed by the Constitution for when the House chooses a President when no candidate achieves an Electoral College majority. Each state's House delegation counts as one vote. Additionally, by the same logic, the use of single-member districts to elect the House of Representatives, which allows the party winning a nationwide majority of votes to yield a minority of seats, could arguably be challengeable under the same theory. While invalidation of district-based House of Representative elections might be a welcome result for both these plaintiffs and other advocates

---

[59]   Moore v. Ogilvie, 394 U.S. 814 (1969).

[60]   McPherson v. Blacker, 146 U.S. 1, 35 (1892); *see also* Bush v. Gore, 531 U.S. 98, 104 (2000).

[61]   *See* Bush v. Gore, 531 U.S. at 110–111 (2000).

[62]   *See* Delaware v. New York, 385 U.S. 895 (1966) (summarily denying Delaware permission to file a complaint raising a similar claim about the unequal weight of small and large states); Penton v. Humphrey, 264 F. Supp. 250, 251–252 (S.D. Miss. 1967) (three-judge court) (rejecting "unit rule" challenge on the merits, and interpreting *Delaware v. New York* as doing the same) Williams v. Virginia State Board of Elections, 288 F. Supp. 622, 627 (E.D. Va. 1968) (three-judge court) (rejecting identical argument on the merits), *summarily aff'd*, 393 U.S. 320 (1969); Hitson v. Baggett, 446 F. Supp. 674, 675–676 (M.D. Ala. 1978) (rejecting claim based on unequal weight of votes in large and small states, and that the use of at-large voting dilutes the votes of minority voters), *summarily aff'd*, 580 F.2d 1051 (5th Cir. 1978), *cert. denied*, 439 U.S. 1129 (1979).

[63]   *See* Complaint, Rodriguez v. Brown, *supra*, at paras. 39–40 (distinguishing *Williams, supra*, at 627, and citing *Bush*, 531 U.S. at 104–106).

of proportional representation, it might be too radical an implication for the current Supreme Court to countenance, thus dooming the Electoral College challenge as well.[64]

Even if these cases were to overcome the imposing legal hurdles, it is not clear how much they would actually improve the presidential election system. To be sure, if they resulted in the adoption of a national popular vote model, they could miraculously transform an undemocratic process to a fair one. It would be the most transformative election-reform litigation since the "one person, one vote" cases of the 1960s. But if they merely prompted states to allocate Electoral votes by congressional district (which the lawsuits understandably reject) or even proportionally (which the lawsuits embrace), representational problems would still remain, for the reasons discussed immediately below. Ultimately, perhaps the lawsuits' best contribution is to raise awareness of the College's flaws, and nudge state legislatures toward voluntary adoption of reforms like the NPV Compact discussed below.

G. STATE-BASED, DISTRICT ALLOCATION OF ELECTORAL VOTES

One reform proposal which has already been implemented in a few states is to change the method by which states allocate Electoral votes from a winner-take-all approach to a district approach. Maine and Nebraska currently allocate Electoral votes by which candidate wins each congressional district. The winner of the state overall gets the 2 Electoral College votes awarded each state that correspond to its 2 votes in the Senate.

Such a reform would not necessarily decrease substantially the chance that a nationwide popular vote winner would still lose. A recent study of close presidential elections since 1972 shows that this approach would

---

[64] The Electoral College plaintiffs could potentially distinguish (i) House of Representative elections because the district results are not aggregated nationally to elect a single candidate, as with the Electoral College. Thus, the "unit rule" results for House elections are not aggregated *in the same election*, as with the College. But that distinction would not apply to (ii) the use of the unit rule by the House to choose a president when there is no Electoral College majority. Perhaps the court could conclude generally that unit rule inequalities are presumptively invalid, unless expressly authorized in the Constitution's text. Such a rule would distinguish (ii) the use of the House where there is no Electoral College majority, but not (i) the use of single-member districts in the House, the latter being provided for by federal statute but not spelled out in the text of the Constitution.

actually have a significant tilt toward Republican candidates. For example, it would have awarded the presidency to Mitt Romney in 2012, despite Romney losing the national popular vote by over 5 million votes. This is due partly to the winner-take-all nature of the 2 Electoral votes per state each state would still get, and partly due to the bias toward Republicans in congressional districting—the latter both the result of gerrymandering, and the demographic reality that Republican voters are more strategically spread out among congressional districts, while Democrats tend to over-cluster in a few urban areas.[65]

On a related and more fundamental level, even if the resulting partisan bias eased over time, using congressional districting to determine the bulk of Electoral vote allocation would simply replicate the problematic gerrymandering that currently exists in congressional redistricting. As outlined in Chapter 4, this gerrymandering is severe, very hard to avoid, and distorts the popular will significantly. The replication of House districting in presidential races would merely exacerbate the already existing incentives for map-drawers to engage in partisan gerrymandering because the stakes would be even higher.

Under the current congressional districting system, and, indeed, under *any* districting system, many districts would be noncompetitive districts in which one party or another would be perceived as having no chance. Thus, the evil of the current system discussed above—Democrats have no incentive to turn out in Republican states, and vice versa—would simply be reduced from the statewide level to the district level.

Further, since candidates would know which districts were "safe" for one party or another, and which districts were "swing" districts, they would once again be incentivized to ignore the safe districts and focus only on the swing districts. Since by most accounts there are fewer than 100 swing districts out of the 435 current House districts,[66] this means that once again, about four-fifths of voters would be ignored—about the same as under the current system.

Thus, while perhaps a slight improvement over the current winner-take-all system used in 48 states and D.C., a district allocation of Electoral votes still leaves much to be desired.

---

[65] *See* Chapter 4.
[66] *See, e.g.*, the assessment of the Cook Political Report, Amy Walter, *The Map Has Changed, but the Math Remains the Same* (Jan. 18, 2018), available at https://www.cookpolitical.com/analysis/national/national-politics/map-has-changed-math-remains-same.

H. STATE-BASED, PROPORTIONAL ALLOCATION OF ELECTORAL VOTES

Generally. A better way for a state to allocate Electoral votes would be proportionally. For example, if a state had 20 Electoral votes, and the 2 major party candidates split the vote 60–40, one candidate would get 12 votes (60%) and the other would get 8 (40%). If the ratios did not match up perfectly for a state's given number of Electors, one would round to the nearest whole number. So, if in the above example the Republican candidate received 54%, the Democratic candidate 44%, and the remaining 2% of the vote was split among several third-party or independent candidates, then the Republican candidate would get 11 Electoral votes, the Democratic candidate 9, and the remaining candidates 0, for no single one of those remaining candidates received the minimum threshold necessary (5%, or, using rounding, at least 2.6%) to receive 1 out of 20 Electoral votes. Colorado considered this approach in a 2004 referendum, but the referendum did not pass.

This system would make it a little less likely that a nationwide popular vote winner would lose to a candidate with fewer nationwide votes. It would still be possible, both because of the 2 Electoral votes each state receives regardless of population and also because of errors introduced by rounding, but it would be less likely. But it would still incentivize candidates to ignore the vast majority of voters, privileging voters in a few large, key swing states.

The Continued Dominance of Large States. This is because the presidential vote in any given state is only going to swing so far in one direction or another. Historically, a candidate's share of the vote in a given state will not increase or decrease more than 8 percentage points over the course of a campaign. For most states, this would translate to at most one extra Electoral vote under this proportional allocation system. Here's why.

The median number of Electoral votes is 7. Thus, for half the states, each Electoral vote requires at least 14% (100/7) of the statewide vote. The average number of Electoral votes is 11, meaning that each Electoral vote would be worth at least 9% (100/11) of the statewide vote. For all these states—the smallest 38 states—even the most aggressive campaign effort will at most change the Electoral score by one vote. (Given that there is rounding, an 8-point swing would be more than half of the 9 or 14 points needed to change the Electoral count by one vote.) Some commentators have dubbed this reform a switch from a winner-take-all system to a "winner-take-one" system.[67]

---

[67] Koda et al., EVERY VOTE EQUAL, *supra*, 159–160.

In fact, the only states where this proportional allocation system could make more than one vote's difference are states with at least 20 Electoral votes. In such states, each Electoral vote would be worth 5%, and an 8-point swing (itself quite a feat) could be worth slightly more than 1.5 Electoral votes, rounding up to 2. There are only 6 such states: Illinois, Pennsylvania, Florida, New York, Texas, and California. Not coincidentally, they are the biggest states by population. So, arguably, the proportional Electoral vote allocation system would continue to encourage campaigns to pay attention to a few key states and ignore the rest.[68]

More important, either of these two approaches (state-level allocation of Electoral votes by district or proportionally using whole-number rounding), along with any other individual state-level approach that simply adjusts how a particular state(s) allocate(s) its Electoral votes, continues to create significant inequalities in the mathematical weight individual voters have. Recall that because of the extra 2 Electoral votes each state gets by virtue of its automatic representation in the Senate, smaller states are disproportionately benefited. A Wisconsin voter's presidential vote continues to count more than three times as much as a Californian's. This is not a subjective, pragmatic evaluation of modern campaign dynamics; it is literally the case that as a mathematical matter, the votes are not weighed equally.

To ensure that each vote weighs the same, and that the nationwide winner becomes President, while also discouraging candidates from writing off entire swaths of the country, one needs to move away from intrastate allocation tinkering and mandate that winning the national popular

---

[68] There is another, less crude way of allocating Electoral votes proportionally within a state that would avoid most of these problems. One could eliminate actual live Electors entirely and allow for fractional allocation of Electoral votes, an approach not possible at the state level if one retains individual live human Electors (who obviously cannot be divided into fractional subparts). In 1971, the Senate considered (but did not adopt) a constitutional amendment which would allow a state's Electoral votes to be proportionally divided up to three decimal places. In Ohio in 2000, for example, based on their respective share of the statewide total vote, Al Gore would have received 9.862 Electoral votes to George W. Bush's 10.606, with Ralph Nader receiving 0.532. Under a variation of this proposal, a candidate would not receive any Electoral votes without netting some minimum percentage of the vote—say, 5%. Under this approach, Gore would have received 10.118 Electoral votes in Ohio to Bush's 10.882. This method is even less likely to defeat a nationwide popular vote leader, but it can still happen; indeed, under either variation, Bush would still have won the election, despite receiving about 500,000 fewer votes nationally. Koda et al., EVERY VOTE EQUAL, *supra*, 56–58 (Figs. 3.1 and 3.2). It would also continue to give unequal weight to votes in small states as compared to large states.

vote is the only way to win. Fortunately, there is a way to do this without clearing the near-impossible hurdle of a federal constitutional amendment.

I. NATIONAL POPULAR VOTE INTERSTATE COMPACT

Generally. That solution is the National Popular Vote Interstate Compact, a growing movement among states interested in reforming our broken presidential election system. Under the NPV system, states agree to allocate all of their Electoral votes to whichever candidate gets the most votes nationwide.[69] Because each state legislature has plenary authority to allocate Electoral votes as it sees fit, NPV does not require a federal constitutional amendment.

Actually, any state at any time can do this. The problem is one of unilateral disarmament: Who goes first? If you are a Democratic state like California, it would hurt your candidate's chances to risk the 55 solid Electoral votes she is sure to receive under the current winner-take-all system. If you are a Republican state like Texas, you are similarly reluctant to risk the otherwise assured 38 votes for the GOP nominee. As states gradually phased in to the national popular vote commitment, there would be a transitional period in which the pioneering states would be hurting the cause of the candidate supported by the strong majority of its voters. This is of course a recipe for inaction.

The genius of the NPV Compact is the delayed triggering mechanism. The Compact only becomes effective when enough states have signed on to control 270 Electoral votes, the minimum needed to determine the outcome of the election. So far, 12 states, representing 172 Electoral votes, have passed the measure between 2007 and 2014.[70] Thus, NPV is over 64%

---

[69] The Compact requires that all signatory states continue to conduct popular elections for President, and to continue to use the "short presidential ballot," in which a voter casts a vote directly for the presidential candidate rather than for individually named Electors. Moving away from popular election, or from a short ballot, would make it difficult to determine the precise number of voters in the state in question who supported an individual candidate, thus creating uncertainty in the national vote total. In the unlikely event that a non-signatory state decides to eliminate popular elections entirely or depart from the short ballot, that state's vote would not be counted in the national popular vote "denominator" for purposes of the NPV Compact. *See* http://www.nationalpopularvote.com/written-explanation.

[70] They are California, Connecticut, D.C., Hawaii, Illinois, Massachusetts, Maryland, New Jersey, New York, Rhode Island, Vermont, and Washington.

of the way toward becoming effective. It needs only 98 more Electoral votes. In states representing 95 more Electoral votes, it has already passed at least one legislative chamber.[71] As of 2018, NPV proposals were pending in 9 states, representing 142 Electoral votes.[72]

Majority v. Plurality. As currently constituted, the NPV Compact contemplates that any candidate with a plurality of the popular vote wins, even if they do not receive a majority. While this is not ideal, it is not a reason to prefer the Electoral College. Under our current system, Presidents often get elected with only a plurality of the popular vote. It has happened 14 times in our history, almost 1 in 5 times, including with Presidents Lincoln, Truman, and Kennedy. It happened twice each for Grover Cleveland and Woodrow Wilson. It has also happened recently, with Bill Clinton and George W. Bush.

While the Electoral College system does require a majority winner, it only addresses the scenario in which a candidate fails to achieve a majority of *Electoral* votes. As explained above, though, its solution is to allow the House to select the President from the top three vote-getters, meaning that political deal-making could result in a second- or third-place finisher winning over the first-place choice of the people.

Worse, the House vote is not based on a pure majority of all 435 House members voting, but rather on a state-by-state basis. This state-based, winner-take-all system can replicate the anomalous results of the Electoral College itself. The vote of a House member in a small state weighs more than one in a large state. A candidate winning just bare majorities in a large number of states can prevail over one with more House members' support overall, but who inefficiently racked up large majorities in a smaller number of states. Given the choice, a plurality system based on the will of the people is more democratic, and arguably preferable, to the current system.

At any rate, there is nothing in the language of the NPV Compact that would preclude a later amendment to it to provide for a majority vote requirement. For their part, the NPV organization explicitly acknowledges being open to such a later refinement. As discussed below, while a provision for a nationwide runoff election some weeks after the general election would be one mechanism to achieve this goal, a better one might involve using IRV.

---

[71] *See* National Popular Vote, *Status of States*, www.nationalpopularvote.com/state-status.

[72] *See* National Conference of State Legislatures, *National Popular Vote: Current Status* (Feb. 22, 2017), available at http://www.ncsl.org/research/elections-and-campaigns/national-popular-vote.aspx#Current Status of the Compact.

J.   OBJECTIONS TO NPV INTERSTATE COMPACT

As with a federal constitutional amendment providing for a direct
nationwide popular vote, critics have raised objections. Many of these
objections echo those made to outright abolition of the College, such as
those discussed above. There are other objections.

Rural Areas Ignored? Some have argued that under NPV, campaigns
would ignore rural areas and focus only on vote-rich urban areas. But
actual campaign experience does not bear this out. Within battleground
states, presidential campaigns focus on all areas of a state, urban, subur-
ban, and rural. To be sure, more attention is focused on areas with more
voters within the state, but no areas are ignored. For instance, candidate
events take place in areas in rough proportion to their share of the state's
population. NPV advocates use as an example the battleground state of
Ohio in 2012. In that state, about 50% of the state's population were in
the 4 major Metropolitan Statistical Areas (MSAs); about 25% were in
'second-tier,' lower MSAs; and 25% were in rural areas. Campaign events
in those 3 main areas during the 2012 general election roughly mirrored
those percentages.[73]

Other Objections. Other common objections to NPV suffer from a
common misconception that it would change the presidential election
process in any way other than how to make the final decision. Some
critics have suggested that it could cause chaos because of state-by-state
differences in voter eligibility or election administration, or require an
undesirable new federal election bureaucracy to help administer it.[74] But
under NPV, presidential elections would continue to be administered as
they are today, by each state using its own rules re: election administration
and voter eligibility.

Similarly, some have suggested that the possibility of faithless Electors
could doom NPV's implementation.[75] But again, there is no relevant
change to the administration of the election. Faithless Electors have been
too rare to change the outcome of any past election, and will continue to
be so. Individual states have passed laws to curb the impact of faithless
Electors; those laws will still be in place. Nothing changes.

---

[73]   Koda et al., EVERY VOTE EQUAL, *supra*, 407.
[74]   *See* National Popular Vote, *Answering Myths*, available at http://www.
nationalpopularvote.com/answering-myths.
[75]   Andrew Rudalevige, *The Electoral College Has Serious Problems. So Do Any
Alternatives*, WASHINGTON POST: MONKEY CAGE (Nov. 15, 2016), available at https://
www.washingtonpost.com/news/monkey-cage/wp/2016/11/15/should-the-u-s-keep-
or-get-rid-of-the-electoral-college/?utm_term=.44391e1f623c.

Finally, some critics have praised the Electoral College's potential for handling a crisis in which a candidate elected in November dies, withdraws, becomes disabled, or is discovered to be ineligible between the election and the meeting of the Electors.[76] NPV lacks this virtue, goes the argument. Again, this aspect of the system does not change under NPV. NPV does not abolish the Electoral College.

Winners and Losers. Who would win and who would lose under NPV? Both large states and small states which are not swing states would stand to gain; they would no longer be ignored by campaigns and deemphasized in policy. To be sure, large concentrations of voters would receive more attention than more diffuse concentrations of voters, but not disproportionately so, and no one would be completely ignored. Similarly, voters in large states would be benefited in a different way in that their vote would no longer be arbitrarily weighed less than voters in small states as a mathematical matter. The losers would be the swing states, which would no longer enjoy their current disproportionate and unfair attention during the campaign and in the governing afterward. Voters in large swing states would receive the compensation of the significant campaign and policy attention that would flow from their large population size.

On the subject of who wins and loses under NPV, one final (and candid) argument from Republican critics is that NPV would favor Democrats. To be sure, during recent elections, there were 2 instances in which the popular vote winner lost in the Electoral College (Bush 2000, Trump 2016), and both times the College helped the Republican nominee. This perception (accurate or not) may explain why Republican-leaning states have so far not adopted NPV.[77]

There are several responses to this argument. First, it is not clear whether NPV really does favor Democrats. Since World War II, 5 Republican Presidents have received the most popular votes countrywide

---

[76] *Debate: Should We Dispense with the Electoral College?*, 156 U. PA. L. REV. PENNumbra 10, 20.

[77] Or, it may stem from an inherent conservatism among Republican policy-makers—a higher respect for the status quo, a fiercer reverence for the wisdom of the Founders, a greater sensitivity to potential unintended consequences, and/or a general resistance to change. In recent decades, most significant election reform innovations, even those without obvious partisan advantages, have been sparked by movements among liberal activists and policymakers rather than conservative, Republican ones. This is true for such innovations as early voting, a voter-verified paper trail, cumulative voting, and Ranked Choice Voting, to name a few. *See* Michael P. McDonald, *A Brief History of Early Voting,* THE HUFFINGTON POST (Sept. 28, 2016), www.huffingtonpost.com/michael-p-mcdonald/a-brief-history-of-early_b_12240120.html.

(Eisenhower, Nixon, Reagan, George H.W. Bush, and George W. Bush in his second term), and 6 Democratic presidential candidates have done so (Truman, Carter, Bill Clinton, Gore, Obama, and Hillary Clinton). This is not a decisive disparity. Nor is there a disparity if one counts elections won by these candidates: 2 each for Eisenhower, Nixon, and Reagan, plus 1 each for each Bush, totaling 8 elections, versus 2 each for Bill Clinton and Obama, plus 1 each for Truman, Carter, Gore, and Hillary Clinton, also totaling 8 elections. It is simply too difficult to say with confidence how an NPV approach would affect the partisan analysis going forward.

This is particularly true because Republicans lost the popular vote in 2000 and 2016 at a time when they were playing under Electoral College rules and running an Electoral College campaign. If NPV were passed, both parties would change the way they campaigned. Both George W. Bush and Donald Trump made this argument post-election, claiming that they could have won under a national popular vote system because they would have changed their campaign tactics. Any partisan advantage under a popular vote system might conceivably be ameliorated or eliminated rather quickly as candidates and campaign strategists adapted to the new environment.

Nonetheless, there might be something to this argument. The College undeniably gives disproportionate weight to smaller, rural states. These rural states tend to vote Republican.[78] Democratic voters, meanwhile, tend to cluster heavily in urban areas, running up huge margins in heavily urban, blue states—but doing so inefficiently because the logic of the College rewards slight majorities in many states over overwhelming majorities in a few states.[79] To the extent this is true, it is yet another reason to favor abolition of the Electoral College—not out of a desire for advantage for one party, but out of principled opposition to any election system which arbitrarily skews the result away from the will of the people.

At the end of the day, Republican state legislators in non-swing states have a choice. They can choose principle, or naked partisanship. Or, more pragmatically, they can decide between a theoretical, uncertain, slight partisan disadvantage which might temporarily ensue under NPV, or the certain, mathematical, demonstrable, significant disadvantage, both in terms of campaign attention and emphasis during governance, which comes from the current system. Republican legislators in large non-swing

---

[78] *See,* Jon Huang et al., *Election 2016: Exit Polls,* New York Times (Nov. 8, 2016), available at https://www.nytimes.com/interactive/2016/11/08/us/politics/election-exit-polls.html.
[79] *See* Chapter 4.

states have the further incentive of remedying a system which inherently, mathematically, devalues their state's voters compared to voters in small states.

Ultimately, NPV makes policy sense for the same reason that abolishing the College makes policy sense. Under NPV, every vote in every state mathematically weighs the same; candidates are not incentivized to privilege swing state voters and ignore safe state voters; and a candidate with fewer nationwide votes cannot prevail over a candidate with more votes.

K. LEGAL OBJECTIONS

Perhaps the most significant objections to NPV are not policy objections but legal ones. Critics have posited a number of legal difficulties with NPV.

1. Compact Clause

Some critics of NPV claim it violates the Compact Clause of the Constitution, which provides in pertinent part that "No State shall, without the Consent of Congress, . . . enter into any Agreement or Compact with another State, or with a foreign Power."[80]

Congressional Consent. An initial objection from NPV critics is that the NPV Compact cannot become effective without the affirmative consent of Congress, even if states representing 270 or more Electoral votes sign on.[81] The plain language of the Compact Clause certainly seems to suggest this is the case.

However, in a series of cases, the Supreme Court has interpreted the Clause more narrowly than that. The overall theme is that the Clause only applies to those agreements which increase the signatory states' power to the detriment of federal power. In an 1893 case upholding a boundary agreement between Virginia and Tennessee, the Court, in *dicta*,[82] reasoned that the Clause could not possibly require that every single

---

[80] U.S. CONST. Art. I, § 10, cl. 3.
[81] Derek T. Muller, *The Compact Clause and the National Popular Vote Interstate Compact*, 6 ELECTION L.J. 372, 393 (2007).
[82] "Dicta" are statements made in a court's opinion that are not necessary to a resolution of the actual controversy before it. They do not have the precedential value of an actual holding necessary to resolve the case, but can nonetheless provide guidance to lower courts in future cases. *See* Cohens v. State of Virginia, 19 U.S. 264, 399 (1821).

agreement between states—a contract for services, boundary agreements, or other agreements which could not reasonably concern the federal government—be held in abeyance pending an Act of Congress. Such an overly broad and unworkable result could not have been the intent of the Founders. Therefore, the Clause "is directed to the formation of any combination tending to the increase of political power in the states, which may encroach upon or interfere with the just supremacy of the United States."[83] That is the kind of interstate agreement which might concern Congress.[84] The Court explicitly affirmed and applied that test, using the language quoted above, in a 1976 case, ruling that an interstate boundary agreement between New Hampshire and Maine did not require congressional approval.[85] Indeed, no court has ever invalidated an interstate agreement on this ground.

The modern test comes from a 1978 case, *U.S. Steel Corporation v. Multistate Tax Commission*. In that case, the Court upheld an interstate compact among many states creating a commission setting uniform corporate tax rules. The Court reaffirmed the *Virginia v. Tennessee* rule requiring congressional consent only for those interstate agreements which increase signatory states' power in such a way as to "encroach or interfere with the just supremacy of the United States." In applying this test, the Court emphasized that the uniform corporate tax compact it upheld did not: (i) authorize the states to exercise any powers which they did not already have; (ii) delegate any sovereign state power to a third party; (iii) unduly burden interstate commerce; or (iv) eliminate the freedom of a state to voluntarily enter into or withdraw from the agreement.[86]

The same analysis on the same factors above applies with respect to NPV. First, as to (i), NPV does not give any state a power regarding allocating Electors which it did not already have, or enhance that power in any way as to detract from federal power. The Constitution expressly grants this power of Electoral selection to the state legislatures. The Supreme Court held in *McPherson v. Blacker*, and reaffirmed over 100 years later

---

[83]   Commonwealth of Virginia v. State of Tennessee, 148 U.S. 503, 519 (1893).

[84]   Later Court decisions upheld a number of interstate agreements which did not have congressional consent, although they did not explicitly analyze them under the Compact Clause or apply the *Virginia v. Tennessee* test. *See* St. Louis. & S.F.R. Co. v. James, 161 U.S. 545 (1896); Hendrick v. Maryland, 235 U.S. 610 (1915); Bode v. Barrett, 344 U.S. 583 (1953); New York v. O'Neill, 359 U.S.1 (1959).

[85]   New Hampshire v. Maine, 426 U.S. 363 (1976).

[86]   U.S. Steel Corp. v. Multistate Tax Commission, 434 U.S. 471, 472–478 (1978).

in *Bush v. Gore*, that the Constitution "conferred on the state legislature plenary power to prescribe the method of choosing electors."[87]

As a general matter, there can be no Compact Clause violation or need for congressional approval when the Compact concerns "areas of jurisdiction historically retained by the states."[88] The selection of Electors is quintessentially an area of jurisdiction retained by the states—indeed, granted *exclusively* to the states—throughout the history of the republic.

The only power given to *Congress* regarding the Electors is the power to decide when they would be chosen and when they would meet.[89] Congress continues to have that same power after the NPV becomes effective.

Nor does NPV (ii) transfer sovereign power of any state over to a third party. Each state's legislature is the only entity making the decision about how to allocate Electoral votes. And (iii) there is no credible argument that NPV unduly burdens interstate commerce.

Finally, (iv) each state is free to enter into the Compact and to withdraw from it as it sees fit. The Compact does limit the ability of a state to withdraw at the eleventh hour and make the withdrawal effective for that same election cycle. Article IV, Section 2 of the NPV Compact provides that "[a]ny state may withdraw from the agreement" unless such a withdrawal occurs within 6 months of the end of the current presidential term. In such an event, the withdrawal would not become effective "[u]ntil a President or Vice President shall have been qualified to serve the next term."[90] It is true that the state's ability to withdraw is slightly restricted within the last 6 months before an election. This is the strongest legal argument against the Compact--although even if the argument succeeded, it might serve only to invalidate that particular withdrawal restriction, rather than the Compact as a whole. On balance, though, this withdrawal restriction is likely not problematic.

First, it does not permanently bar a state from withdrawing, but merely requires that it do so in a timely fashion for it to be effective right away. Second, there are sound reasons of certainty, predictability, and election

---

[87] McPherson v. Blacker, 146 U.S. 1, 35 (1892); Bush v. Gore, 531 U.S. 98, 104 (2000).

[88] McComb v. Wambaugh, 934 F.2d 474, 479 (3d Cir. 1991).

[89] *McPherson*, 146 U.S. at 35 ("Congress is empowered to determine the time of choosing the electors and the day on which they are to give their votes, which is required to be the same day throughout the United States; . . . otherwise the power and jurisdiction of the state is exclusive").

[90] *See, e.g.*, Agreement Among the States to Elect the President by National Popular Vote, MD CODE ANN., ELEC. LAW § 8-5A-01, Art. IV (West 2018) (Maryland codification of the NPV Compact).

administration for foreclosing eleventh-hour withdrawals and preventing a nationwide game of "chicken" among participant states. For one thing, presidential campaigns need to know what kind of campaign they are to run: a national campaign versus a swing-state-focused Electoral College campaign. Indeed, courts generally take a dim view in election cases of states changing the rules in the middle of the game. Third, courts have recognized interstate compacts to be binding contracts among states. States can be constitutionally held to comply with a contract's terms.[91] Indeed, any legislative attempt to nullify the NPV Compact (outside the withdrawal parameters previously agreed to) would be an attempt to impair the obligation of a contract, and thus would be invalid under the Constitution's Contract Clause.[92]

Impact on Nonmember States. NPV opponents also argue that it violates the Compact Clause because it encroaches unduly on the rights of nonmember states.[93] The reasoning is that, by ultimately deciding the presidential election outcome, the member states have taken away decision-making power from the nonmember states.

However, from the plain terms of the NPV itself, this is not the case. Member states pledge to award their Electoral votes, and thus decide the outcome, on the winner of the *national* popular vote. For purposes of calculating this national total, *every* state's votes are counted, both member and nonmember.[94] A member state has no special influence over the outcome of the national popular vote as opposed to a nonmember. The same is true for individual voters within member and nonmember states. Each vote is counted the same.

Nonmember states may argue that there is nonetheless a practical effect that harms them, pressuring them to go along with a national popular vote approach even if they favor an Electoral College approach. But the

---

[91]   Commonwealth of Virginia v. State of Tennessee, 148 U.S. at 524 (1893).
[92]   "No state shall . . . pass any law impairing the Obligation of Contracts . . .", U.S. CONST., Art. 1, § 10, cl. 1; *See* U.S. Trust Co. of New York v. New Jersey, 431 U.S. 1, 17 (1977) (explaining that the Contract Clause of the Constitution limits the ability of states to modify their own contracts and regulate contracts between private parties, but does not affect the ability of a state to repeal or amend statutes).
[93]   *See,* Tara Ross, *Federalism & Separation of Powers: Legal and Logistical Ramifications of the National Popular Vote Plan*, ENGAGE: J. OF THE FED. SOC'Y PRAC. GROUPS 37, 41 (Sep. 2010), available at https://fedsoc.org/commentary/publications/legal-and-logistical-ramifications-of-the-national-popular-vote-plan.
[94]   The only exception would be if a state decided to end popular elections for president within its borders. *See, e.g.*, MD CODE ANN § 8-5A-01, ART. III (West 2018).

Constitution does not guarantee an Electoral College outcome where it differs from a national popular vote outcome. All it guarantees is that each state shall have a number of Electoral votes equal to its Senators and Representatives, and that each state's legislature will have plenary authority over how to allocate those Electoral votes. NPV does not interfere with any of that.

This practical concern, too, was addressed in *U.S. Steel*. There, those challenging the multistate corporate tax agreement claimed that as a practical matter, nonmember states would have no choice but to end up abiding by the standards set by the multistate commission, if their corporations were to avoid double taxation. The Court rejected this argument, reasoning that even if such informal or practical pressure existed, it was not "an affront to the sovereignty of nonmember States," and did not "implicate" the "federal structure."

Nor can nonmember states argue that they are being ganged up on. The Court in *U.S. Steel* specified that the number of parties to an agreement is irrelevant if it does not "impermissibly enhance state power at the expense of federal supremacy."[95] It also held that even if the practical effect of the multistate tax compact was to cause "some increase in the bargaining power of the member States" regarding the corporations under their taxing authority, that was not fatal.[96]

Individual versus Collective State Action. Finally, everyone concedes that each state individually has the power to declare that all its Electoral votes will go to the national popular vote winner. This is clear from the Supreme Court case which declares that under Article II, each state legislature has plenary authority in determining the manner in which it will allocate Electoral votes.[97] For this reason, the Compact does not give any member state a power it didn't already have, thus satisfying that part of the *U.S. Steel* test. The question is then whether doing so *collectively* is somehow unconstitutional. There is no compelling reason why that should be the case.

2. Other Legal Arguments

Critics of NPV have raised other legal objections, less worthy of detailed discussion. For example, some have claimed that it would violate the federal Voting Rights Act, which forbids unfair dilution of the voting

---

95 *U.S. Steel*, 434 U.S. at 472.
96 *Id.* at 473.
97 *McPherson*, 146 U.S. 1, 35 (1892).

strength of racial, ethnic, and language minorities.[98] But since every vote is equal under the NPV, for this to be the case, it would have to be true that the current Electoral College system provides minorities more than their nationwide proportionate share of influence on the presidential election. There is no evidence that this is true. In fact, the practical ability of minority voters to determine the outcome of the presidential elections has been declining in recent decades. For example, in 1976, 73% of African-Americans were in a potential "swing voter" position: they lived in battle-ground states (partisanship within 2.5 points of being a 50–50 tie), and made up a significant share (at least 5%) of the overall state population. By 2000, that percentage of black swing voters decreased to 24%. In 2004, it fell to just 17%.[99]

Others have claimed that NPV would violate Article II in that it gives some other entity, besides a particular state's legislature, decision-making power over how to allocate Electoral College votes.[100] But as explained above, NPV retains power in each state legislature. That state legislature decides to enter the NPV Compact and can withdraw at any time. The only argument remaining under Article II would be an argument that by entering NPV, a state legislature is somehow delegating its electoral allocation power to another entity—perhaps the NPV member states collectively, or the national electorate—and that this delegation is unconstitutional because it is no longer the "legislature" making the decision.

A recent Supreme Court decision answered a very analogous question. In that case, Arizonans had adopted a ballot initiative that transferred redistricting power for U.S. House races from the state legislature to an independent redistricting commission. Challengers argued that this arrangement violated the Elections Clause of the Constitution, which says that "The Times, Places, and Manner of holding Elections for Senators and Representatives shall be prescribed in each State by the Legislature thereof . . .".[101] If referendum voters take redistricting power away from the legislature and vest it in a commission, the challengers argued, it is no longer the "Legislature" prescribing election procedures.

The Court rejected this argument. Essentially, the Court said that the legislature could make whatever prescriptions it wanted in this area. If it passed laws which established a citizen initiative process, and that process

---

[98]   52 U.S.C. § 10301(a) (Westlaw through P.L. 115–90).

[99]   FairVote, *2006 Presidential Elections Inequality: The Electoral College in the 21st Century*, available at http://www.fairvote.org/media/perp/presidentialin equality.pdf.

[100]   *See* Tara Ross, *supra* note 93, at 38.

[101]   U.S. Const. Art. I, § 4.

changed redistricting procedures, that would be valid. The Court declined to take a rigid or narrow view here.[102] Given this non-rigid view of the word "legislature" in the Constitution, it seems reasonable to say that a state legislature can decide that it will abide by the result of the largest citizen initiative of all—a nationwide election for President.

Finally, one other basis for challenging the NPV raised by opponents is the Guaranty Clause.[103] The argument is that NPV violates Article IV, Section 4, Clause 1 of the Constitution, which provides that the U.S. "shall guarantee to every State in this Union a Republican Form of Government." There is no accepted definition of what a "Republican" form of government is for this purpose, nor any reason to think that a direct popular election of the President would violate it. Indeed, the people did a statewide direct popular election of the chief executive (i.e., the governor) of multiple states in the Union at the time of the Founding.[104] That was not considered to be in violation of the Guaranty Clause. More importantly, validity under the Guaranty Clause has been held to be a nonjusticiable political question, meaning that it cannot be challenged in court.[105]

L. INSTANT RUNOFF VOTING

One nagging thought about NPV is its willingness to award the presidency to a mere plurality winner. To be sure, we've seen plurality winners ascend to the presidency 14 times in our history, and the current system's method of assuring majority support—throwing the election into the House of Representatives—leaves much to be desired.

But, nonetheless, a plurality winner is not an ideal solution. That is because whenever a mere plurality is enough to win an election, there is a risk that votes among multiple candidates popular with the majority will be split, and a plurality winner will sneak by with, say, 39% of the vote, despite being the least-preferred candidate of the majority. That

---

[102] Arizona State Legislature v. Arizona Independent Redistricting Commission, 135 S. Ct, 2652, 2671–2672 (2015).

[103] *See, e.g.*, Kristin Feeley, *Guaranteeing a Federally Elected President*, 103 NORTHWESTERN L. REV. 1427, 1450, 1460 (2009).

[104] Michael J. Dublin, UNITED STATES GUBERNATORIAL ELECTIONS 1776–1860 xx (2003).

[105] Luther v Borden, 48 U.S. 1, 42 (1849) (holding that it is for Congress to decide what government is established in a state and to determine whether it is a republican one under the Guaranty Clause of the Constitution).

happened with Donald Trump in the early Republican primaries in 2016. In the first half of those primaries, the key earliest 25 which made him the front-runner and then presumptive nominee, Trump rarely scored above 38%, and never a majority. Contemporaneous polling showed that Trump would have lost in those states in a head-to-head match against either Marco Rubio or Ted Cruz, depending on the state.[106] And, there was a robust, organized, public "Never Trump" movement among Republicans, with no corresponding "Never Cruz" or "Never Rubio" movement. Thus, it is fair to assume that a plurality, or even a majority, of Republican primary voters in those states would have ranked Trump very far down their preference list. Nonetheless, he emerged as their party's nominee.[107]

This is the "spoiler" effect in action. It is why political scientists rank plurality, winner-take-all elections as one of the worst in terms of accurately reflecting the popular will.[108] For this reason, if we could adopt an NPV movement while simultaneously avoiding plurality voting, we should do so.

As discussed above, running a separate presidential runoff election nationwide would pose logistical problems and would be expensive. Also, turnout in runoff elections is often significantly lower than in regular elections,[109] which means that an even smaller percentage of the electorate would make the final decision than the already relatively low turnout we see in the U.S.[110] Fortunately, there is another method of ensuring

---

[106]   *See* Rob Richie, *Trump Moves into Majority Position in GOP Nomination Contest*, FAIRVOTE (Mar. 23, 2016), available at http://www.fairvote.org/trump_moves_into_majority_position_in_gop_nomination_contest. Indeed, this dynamic calls for reform of the presidential preference primaries as well. Most states have some form of proportional allotment of presidential delegates on the Democratic nomination side. But winner-take-all methods continue to dominate on the Republican side. If winner-take-all continues, IRV should be used. Even better would be to move toward proportional methods of allocating delegates. *See* Chapter 8.

[107]   Indeed, this experience underscores the need for more proportional allocation of delegates in presidential preference primaries, and a move away from blanket winner-take-all contests. The Democratic Party pretty uniformly uses the former, and the Republican Party predominately the latter.

[108]   *See* S.J. Brams and D.R. Herschbach, *The Science of Elections*, 292 SCIENCE 1449 (2001), available at http://www.sciencemag.org/cgi/content/summary/292/5521/1449.

[109]   *See, e.g.*, Steven G. Wright, *Voter Turnout in Runoff Elections*, 51 JOURNAL OF POLITICS 385 (1989), available at http://www.journals.uchicago.edu/doi/pdf/10.2307/2131348 (77% of all Democratic gubernatorial, senatorial, and congressional runoffs held from 1956 to 1984 saw declining turnout, although the extent of decline varied widely).

[110]   Turnout in U.S. presidential elections has traditionally been much lower than

a majority-support winner without the trouble and expense of a second election: Instant Runoff Voting, also known as Ranked Choice Voting (RCV).

Under IRV, the voters get to rank their preferences—1st, 2nd, 3rd, and so on. If no candidate receives a majority of 1st-place votes, the weakest candidate is eliminated, and the votes for that candidate are added to the totals of the remaining candidates based on the 2nd choice of those voters who had ranked that loser first. This process continues until one candidate has a majority and is elected. It resembles the process used in a two-round runoff election, except that instead of needing to vote a second time, voters indicate their back-up choices in case a runoff is needed, allowing it to occur "instantly."

This system would have the advantage of empowering third-party candidates. No longer would it be correct to say that a vote for an independent or third-party candidate would be "throwing away your vote." If your 1st-place candidate did not get enough votes, your vote would be transferred to your 2nd-place candidate. This is a salient effect at a time when a majority of Americans say they would welcome a viable third party.[111]

Similarly, no longer would voters who preferred third-party candidates have to worry that a vote for their candidate would backfire and actually help the candidate they liked the least. Liberal voters in 2016 were told that a vote for Jill Stein was really a vote for Donald Trump—and, in swing states at least, that was correct. Conservative or libertarian voters were told that a vote for Gary Johnson would end up helping Hillary Clinton—again, at least in swing states, there was truth to that claim.

---

comparable turnout in other developed democracies. According to a 2017 study by the Pew Research Center, the U.S. turnout rate was about 56% of the voting age population. Of the 35 member nations in the OECD (Organisation for Economic Co-operation and Development), the U.S. placed 28th, just above Slovenia. Drew Desilver, *U.S. Trails Most Developed Countries in Voter Turnout*, PEW RESEARCH CENTER: FACT TANK (May 15, 2017), available at http://www.pewresearch.org/fact-tank/2017/05/15/u-s-voter-turnout-trails-most-developed-countries/.

[111] *See, e.g.*, Lydia Saad, *Perceived Need for Third Major Party Remains High in U.S.*, GALLUP (Sept. 27, 2017), available at http://news.gallup.com/poll/219953/perceived-need-third-major-party-remains-high.aspx; Gallup, *Americans' Desire For Third Party Persists This Election Year* (Sept. 30, 2016), available at http://news.gallup.com/poll/195920/americans-desire-third-party-persists-election-year.aspx. Some commentators suggest that the "lock" on elections of the two-party system is a good thing, a bulwark of political stability. However, our direct election of an executive for a fixed term provides stability no matter how he or she is elected. And while a two-party system may also promote stability, it also does so at the expense of accurately reflecting the popular will.

The zero-sum logic of plurality, winner-take-all is that any vote given to a minor party candidate makes it more likely that the major party candidate of the opposite ideology will attain the plurality and win.

Under IRV, a liberal could confidently rank Jill Stein first, and then Hillary Clinton second, secure in the knowledge that if Stein did not secure sufficient votes, the voter's ballot would be transferred to the safer bet of Clinton. Similarly, a conservative could vote for Gary Johnson first, and Donald Trump second, similarly secure. This would lead to a more diverse and healthier democracy in which third-party alternatives to the two major parties would flourish and offer a real range of choices to voters. It would not usher in an era of electoral chaos or the election of "fringe" candidates, because IRV still requires that a majority of votes, (1st, 2nd, and 3rd round combined, if need be), elect the candidate. This would still tend to reward consensus candidates and freeze out fringe candidates.

And the empowerment of third-party candidates would be more than token. True, it may be the case that Jill Stein won't actually get enough votes to become President, and all initial votes for her may end up transferring to Hillary Clinton. But when third-party candidates get a larger share of the vote, they end up qualifying for more matching public financing dollars from the federal government.[112] And major party candidates will actively solicit 2nd and 3rd choice votes from third-party voters, encouraging them to take third-party issue positions more seriously. Indeed, IRV would enable third parties to bargain with major parties, offering to officially encourage their members to give a major party candidate a 2nd or 3rd place vote, if the major party will make certain policy concessions. This kind of deal-making, especially if made public, would be healthy for democracy, allowing a wider range of policy positions to be seriously considered, and giving third parties real leverage for the first time. This dynamic is at play in U.S. states which allow "fusion" tickets, where 2 parties cross-list on the ballot.[113] It is also at work in Australia, where IRV is used to select members of the lower house of the national legislature.[114]

---

[112]   Public Funding of Presidential Elections, FEC (updated Feb. 2017), available at https://classic.fec.gov/pages/brochures/pubfund.shtml#Primary.

[113]   Benjamin R. Kantack, *Fusion and Electoral Performance in New York Congressional Elections*, 70 POLITICAL RESEARCH QUARTERLY 291 (2017) available at http://journals.sagepub.com/doi/full/10.1177/1065912916689823; for a general discussion of fusion voting see Adam Morse and J.J. Gass, *More Choices, More Voices: A Primer on Fusion*, BRENNAN CENTER FOR JUSTICE: VOTING RIGHTS AND ELECTIONS SERIES (Oct. 2, 2006), available at https://www.brennancenter.org/publication/more-choices-more-voices-primer-fusion.

[114]   Interview with Paul Pirani, General Counsel, Australian Election Commission (Feb. 23, 2018) (notes on file with author).

Just as any state has plenary authority to allocate Electoral votes by district or proportionally, any state has plenary authority to adopt IRV as the election mechanism in presidential contests. States should consider doing so as a first step toward reforming our presidential election system. Even if NPV were not ultimately adopted, IRV would still be an improvement over the winner-take-all models currently used.[115] IRV will be discussed further in Chapter 7.

---

[115] If NPV were adopted, states using IRV would need to clarify how to count their IRV votes toward a nationwide total. They could either count all votes cast for the majority winner in the final round toward the nationwide total, or else just the votes cast for that winner in the first round. Either method is defensible, but it would be preferable for all IRV-using states to be consistent in this manner, and for all rules to be clarified *ex ante*.

3.   The Senate

A.   OUR UNDEMOCRATIC SENATE

Presidential elections are not the only area in which our election system is undemocratic. As noted in the Introduction, in the first three elections of the past decade (2010–2014), a majority of Americans voted for Democrats for Senate, yet Republicans won a majority. The "world's greatest deliberative body" also suffers fundamental structural problems.

At the time of the Founding, voters didn't even have the opportunity to choose their Senators. Instead, the Constitution gave state legislatures the power to select Senators, the way it did for the Electoral College—only worse, for the operative language, "two Senators from each State, chosen by the Legislature thereof,"[1] seemed more suggestive of direct choice by the legislature. The comparable language regarding Electors—"Each state shall appoint, in such Manner as the Legislature thereof may direct,"[2] opened the door for states to choose an election by the people. Unlike with presidential elections, state legislatures did not move toward popular election for the Senate during the first century of the Republic. It took ratification of the Seventeenth Amendment in 1913 to provide for popular election of Senators.

1.   The Senate's Rightward Skew

But another feature remains which is almost as undemocratic: the fact that each state gets two Senators, regardless of population. As a result, California, with 38 million residents, has as much of a say on ratification of treaties, confirmation of Cabinet and Supreme Court nominees, and passing legislation as Wyoming, with under 600,000 residents. Under this system, a Vermonter has 30 times the Senate voting power of a New Yorker just over the state line.[3]

---

[1]   U.S. CONST. Art. I, § 3, cl. 1.
[2]   U.S. CONST. Art. II, § 1, cl. 2.
[3]   Adam Liptak, *Smaller States Find Outsize Clout Growing in the Senate*, NEW YORK TIMES, available at http://www.nytimes.com/interactive/2013/03/11/us/politics/democracy-tested.html#/#smallstate.

Why do we have this dramatic disproportionality? Because of a dispute during the Constitutional Convention between small states like Delaware and New Jersey, and large states like New York and Virginia. Small states feared that they would be rendered irrelevant in the newly formed Congress, dominated by the large states. The original plan for Congress, the "Virginia Plan," called for a bicameral legislature, all apportioned based on population.[4] Small states countered with the rival "New Jersey Plan," which called for a unicameral legislature with each state getting the same representation. The "Connecticut Compromise," also called the "Great Compromise," split the baby, with House membership based on population but Senate membership made equal for each state.[5]

As noted above, the Great Compromise causes hugely unequal voting power among U.S. voters. Worse, the inequality has been growing. The underrepresentation of large-state voters and overrepresentation of small-state voters is much worse than at the time of the Founding.[6] The gap between the populations of small and large states has grown with this country's overall population. The result is a disparity in voting power between states measured at 66 to 1 (i.e., between California, the largest population state, and Wyoming, the smallest). And with current demographic trends, it will only keep getting worse: by 2040, two-thirds of Americans will be represented by 30% of the Senate.[7]

This has a direct effect on legislation. The Senate passes legislation opposed by a majority of U.S. voters, and rejects legislation supported by a majority of U.S. voters. This, too, is getting worse. In 2017, the "Senate was increasingly casting votes in which senators representing a minority of the population were defeating senators representing most of America." As a percentage of all passing votes as of April 2017, "far more [were] approved by less than half of the country's population . . . than in any year prior."[8]

---

[4] James Madison, THE PAPERS OF JAMES MADISON 12, 18 (Robert A. Rutland & William M. Rachel eds. 1977). Under the Virginia Plan, the state legislature would nominate Senate candidates, with the final selection being made by the House.

[5] Max Farrand, FRAMING OF THE CONSTITUTION OF THE UNITED STATES 84, 99 (1913).

[6] Liptak, *Smaller States Find Outsize Clout Growing in the Senate, supra.*

[7] Philip Bump, *By 2040, Two-Thirds of Americans Will Be Represented by 30 Percent of the Senate*, WASHINGTON POST (Nov. 28, 2017), available at https://www. washingtonpost.com/news/politics/wp/2017/11/28/by-2040-two-thirds-of-ameri cans-will-be-represented-by-30-percent-of-the-senate/?utm_term=.c5e950f88031.

[8] Philip Bump, *The Senate May Be Developing an Electoral College Issue*, WASHINGTON POST (Apr. 10, 2017), available at https://www.washingtonpost.com/

The bias is not just toward small states. Because rural, sparsely populated states tend to vote Republican, and highly urban, densely populated states tend to vote Democratic, the Senate skews rightward out of all proportion to actual American voter sentiment.[9] In recent decades, Democrats' biggest voter and population gains have been in California and New York, yet these states represent only 4% of the Senate. In effect, the clustering effect is naturally "packing" these state-size "districts" with too many Democratic voters, diluting the national Democratic Senate vote. Republicans, on the other hand, have seen gains in small rural states, shoring up and bolstering their disproportionate Senate power. According to polling and electoral analyst Nate Silver, in 2018 the Senate has the strongest pro-GOP bias since the start of direct Senate elections in 1913.[10] Based on recent polling data, "[e]ven if Democrats were to win every . . . Senate race for seats representing places that Hillary Clinton won or that Trump won by less than 3 percentage points . . . they could still . . . *lose* five Senate seats."[11]

The skew is just as strong viewed through the lens of race and ethnicity rather than partisanship. A 2015 study by the Pew Research Center concluded that Democrats have an up to 80% advantage in party identification among African-Americans. The Democrats are advantaged by almost 3 to 1 among Asian-Americans and by more than 2 to 1 among Hispanics.[12] But, according to research conducted in 2007, because racial minorities have a greater presence in high-population states than low-population states, both African-Americans and Hispanics are

---

news/politics/wp/2017/04/10/the-senate-may-be-developing-an-electoral-college-issue/?utm_term=.af6d71653e6c.

[9] Nate Silver, *The Real Problem with the Senate's Small-State Bias*, FIVETHIRTYEIGHT (Aug. 3, 2009), available at https://fivethirtyeight.com/features/real-problem-with-senates-small-state/.

[10] *Id.* The rural-state overrepresentation did not always advantage Republicans. In the early 20th century, Democrats controlled most of the rural states and enjoyed this representational advantage. *See* Lindsay Rogers, THE AMERICAN SENATE 99–100 (1926) (Democratic Senate majority represents a nationwide minority due to Democratic dominance of smaller states).

[11] David Wassweman, *The Congressional Map Has a Record-Setting Bias against Democrats*, FIVETHIRTYEIGHT (Aug. 7, 2017), available at https://fivethirtyeight.com/features/the-congressional-map-is-historically-biased-toward-the-gop/; *see also* Ed Kilgore, *Republicans Are Playing with a Stacked Deck in the Senate*, NEW YORK MAGAZINE, DAILY INTELLIGENCER (Aug. 7. 2017), available at http://nymag.com/daily/intelligencer/2017/08/republicans-are-playing-with-a-stacked-deck-in-the-senate.html.

[12] Pew Research Center, A *Deep Dive into Party Affiliation* (Apr. 7, 2015), available at http://www.people-press.org/2015/04/07/a-deep-dive-into-party-affiliation/.

substantially underrepresented in the Senate.[13] Based on 2004 population estimates, the researchers concluded that African Americans were under-represented by 2.44 seats and Hispanics by 5.26 seats.[14] Although black voters' or Latino voters' candidate of choice would not necessarily have to be black or Latino respectively, it is telling that blacks make up 12% of the U.S. population but only 3% of Senators, and that Latinos make up 18% of the population yet only 4% of Senators.

In fact, if the 2-Senators-per-state rule were not enshrined in the text of Article I, it would clearly be unconstitutional under the "one person, one vote" principle established by the Supreme Court. Disparities of 60 to 1 in voting power would be easily challengeable, and any defenses thereto would be laughed out of court.

2.   Justifications for the Skew

To justify such a strong pro-GOP, pro-white bias, we would need a pretty compelling policy rationale. None exists. The historical justification was that the Great Compromise was necessary to ensure adoption and ratification of the Constitution. That rationale hardly seems compelling today. If we were to move toward a more representative Senate election system, small states would certainly object and oppose, but they would not secede. The Union would survive.

The modern justification is that states continue to be separate, quasi-sovereign entities deserving of respect and equal representation. We are a union of states, after all; it's in our country's name.

As discussed in Chapter 2 regarding the Electoral College, U.S. states are much less distinct polities today than they were at the time of the Founding. Interstate travel, commerce, communication, migration, and resettlement are now effortless, common, and constant. Daily commutes across state lines are unremarkable. Federal law is more comprehensive, pervasive, and uniformizing. States have voluntarily agreed to join uniform law compacts in many areas.[15] In terms of psychological identity, state residence is far

---

[13]   Neil Malhorta and Connor Raso, *Racial Representation and the U.S. Senate*, 88 SOCIAL SCIENCE QUARTERLY 4, 1045 (December 2007).

[14]   *Id.* at 1043.

[15]   For example, the Uniform Commercial Code, developed as a "unified coverage" of commercial law, has been adopted in all 50 states and D.C. U.C.C. § 1-104 (AMERICAN LAW INSTITUTE & UNIFIED LAW COMMISSION 2017). Similarly, the Uniform Child Custody Jurisdiction and Enforcement Act, developed in part to address the problem of interstate custody, has been adopted by 49 States, the D.C., and the Virgin Islands. PREFATORY NOTE, UNIFORM CHILD CUSTODY

down the priority list for most people, falling well behind nation, race, ethnicity, party, ideology, and religion, to name just a few, in terms of major loyalties.[16] The notion that Delaware or Colorado is a sovereign entity deserving of loyalty on a par with loyalty to the U.S. is laughable today.

In fact, it's not even clear how much the states were viewed as sovereign entities at the time of the Founding itself. While advocates for the small states sometimes made this claim during the Constitutional Convention, they sometimes just relied on their fear of being swamped by the large states. And several notable and influential Founding Fathers rejected the idea entirely. Alexander Hamilton, the most prolific author of the influential Federalist Papers, argued in the Constitutional Convention that states were artificial entities made up of individuals rather than independent sovereign entities deserving representation in their own right.[17] Massachusetts' Elbridge Gerry (for whom the gerrymander was named—see Chapter 4) argued during the Convention that "we never were independent states, were not such now, & never could be even on the principles of the [Articles Of] Confederation." He mocked the small-state advocates as "intoxicated with the idea of their sovereignty."[18] There certainly are provisions of the Constitution explicitly protecting state sovereignty,[19] but they concern the ability of a state to govern itself in local affairs. States' equal role in *national* representation—in the Electoral College and the Senate—can plausibly be

---

JURISDICTION AND ENFORCEMENT ACT (NATIONAL CONFERENCE OF COMMISSIONERS ON UNIFIED STATE LAWS 1997). The Universal Bar Exam, which allows the transfer of scores between participating states, has been adopted by 28 states, D.C., and the Virgin Islands. NATIONAL CONFERENCE OF BAR EXAMINERS, ADOPTION OF THE UNIFORM BAR EXAMINATION WITH NCBE TESTS ADMINISTERED BY NON-UBE JURISDICTIONS (2017) available at http://www.ncbex.org/exams/ube/.

[16] Studies documenting the great salience of non-geographic demographic factors abound and span the decades. *See, e.g.*, Charles S. Bullock and Bruce A. Campbell, *Racist or Racial Voting in the 1981 Atlanta Municipal Elections*, 20 URBAN AFFAIRS QUARTERLY 149 (1984) (race); Bruce E. Cain and D. Roderick Kiewiet, *Ethnicity and Electoral Choice: Mexican American Voting Behavior in the California 30th Congressional District*, 6 SOCIAL SCIENCE QUARTERLY 315 (1984) (ethnicity); Pew Research Center, *Wide Gender Gap, Growing Educational Divide in Voters' Party Identification*, www.people-press.org/2018/03/20/wide-gender-gap-growing-educational-divide-in-voters-party-identification/ (March, 2018) (gender and education).

[17] Alexander Hamilton, THE PAPERS OF ALEXANDER HAMILTON, JANUARY 1787–MAY 1788 220 (Harold C. Syrett ed., 1962).

[18] Yale Law School, *Madison's Notes on Constitutional Debates, June 29, 1787*, THE AVALON PROJECT, available at http://avalon.law.yale.edu/18th_century/debates_629.asp3.

[19] *See, e.g.*, U.S. CONST. Art. IV, § 3 (guaranteeing territorial integrity of every state).

viewed as concessions to a minority of small-state representatives necessary to ensure the supermajorities needed for adoption and ratification.

3. Potential Fixes of the Skew

Unlike the Electoral College, there is no way to change the Senate system
without a federal constitutional amendment. The 2-Senators-per-state rule
is enshrined in Article I.

One could imagine a constitutional amendment which would reap-
portion Senators based on population. Some have argued for this.[20] One
method might be to draw 100 single-member districts of equal population.
To make them all truly equal would require that we ignore state boundaries entirely, which some may view as too radical. Drawing districts while
still recognizing state boundaries would ameliorate the inequality without
completely eliminating it. Alternatively, we could expand the size of the
Senate, let each state keep a minimum of 2 Senators, but allow those
states with more than 2% of the U.S. population to have more Senators
based on their population—a "mini-Great Compromise." Still another
approach might be to give each state one Senator, and apportion "extra"
Senators based on population. Under this approach, California would
get 7 Senators, Texas 5, Florida and New York 4 each, Pennsylvania and
Illinois 3 each, Georgia, North Carolina, and Michigan 2 each. A few
other states might keep a second Senator, but the rest would have only 1.
Again, these state-boundary-respecting approaches would not eliminate
the skew toward small states, but it would ameliorate it.

But the hypothetical effects on state representation in the Senate simultaneously demonstrate such proposals' merits and political impossibility.
Because only the top 10 states in population have over 2% of U.S. population, and only about 7 have roughly 2%, only 10 states would stand to gain
from such a population-based reform of the Senate, and 33 (50−17) would
actually stand to lose. Since it takes 38 states to ratify, such a proposal
would be a political nonstarter.

And that's assuming it could even get to the states. Since the normal
route for proposing a constitutional amendment requires a two-thirds vote
by both House and Senate, it seems unlikely that this route would yield
results; about 66 of the 100 Senators (i.e., the Senators from the 33 states
with less than 2% of the U.S. population) would be effectively voting to

---

[20] *See, e.g.*, Frances E. Lee & Bruce I. Oppenheimer, SIZING UP THE SENATE:
THE UNEQUAL CONSEQUENCES OF EQUAL REPRESENTATION 23 (1999) (discussing
such proposals).

reduce their own power. Indeed, when reformers tried to get direct popular election of Senators passed, it took decades and repeated attempts over Senate opposition. Reformers had to use the other route to amend the Constitution, that of getting state legislatures to propose a Constitutional Convention.[21] Only when state legislature resolutions calling for such a Constitutional Convention neared the necessary two-thirds of states did Congress reluctantly act.[22]

Worse, it is not even clear that such a reform would be possible, even if reformers could get a constitutional amendment passed. In a few little-discussed provisions of the Constitution, the Constitution purports to specify that certain constitutional clauses can never be amended. They have to do with state sovereignty. One of them provides that no state can be denied its "equal suffrage in the Senate" without its consent.[23] If this is correct, it means that all 50 states must unanimously agree to any change to the 2-Senators-per-state rule. There is an argument that this provision *itself* could be amended through the normal amendment process, which would then set the stage for a reform amendment to be adopted and ratified. Both aims theoretically could even be accomplished in the same amendment.[24] But even if successful, such an argument merely moves this election reform from "legally impossible" to "impossible for all practical purposes."

B.   THE FILIBUSTER

The news about the Senate is even worse. Not only can a minority of voters elect a majority of Senators. Not only can legislation pass over the objection of Senators representing a majority of the people. In addition, internal Senate Rules provide that no legislation can pass without three-fifths of the Senate voting. That internal Senate Rule is the filibuster.

The filibuster is a procedural device which allows a minority to prevent a bill or nomination from coming to a vote on the Senate floor. It keeps it in limbo indefinitely, effectively killing it.

---

[21]   *See* U.S. Const. Art. V.

[22]   Gordon E. Sherman, *The Recent Constitutional Amendments*, 23 Yale Law Journal 129, 148 (1913).

[23]   U.S. Const. Art. V. The other guarantees the territorial integrity of a state's boundaries. U.S. Const. Art. IV, § 3.

[24]   Michael B. Rappaport, *Reforming Article V: The Problems Created by the National Convention Method and How to Fix Them*, 96 Virginia Law Journal 1509, 1514 (2010).

1. The "Talking" Filibuster's History

The filibuster has a checkered history. There is good reason to think it originated as an unintended consequence rather than a reasoned decision that it was necessary for democracy. At the time of the Founding, the Senate did not have a filibuster rule. The first Senate could use the standard parliamentary motion of the "previous question," by which a majority vote could end debate and proceed to an immediate vote on the substantive topic.[25] Although the previous question motion was infrequently invoked, this majority-oriented practice continued to be the rule for 17 years until 1806, when the Senate eliminated the "previous question" rule at the suggestion of then-Vice President Aaron Burr.

But the motivation for the change was merely a perception that it was unnecessary. Senators assumed (naively) that true gentlemen would not engage in intentionally dilatory action, and the infrequent use of the previous question motion seemed to bolster this view. As political scientist Norman Ornstein has testified, "unlimited debate was a historical accident, not an objective of the Framers."[26]

With the previous question motion eliminated, there was no procedural way to prevent endless, dilatory debate. But there was little occasion to miss it, either, because it simply didn't come up. Although actions intended to delay a vote may have occurred beforehand,[27] a formal "filibuster" to kill a bill did not occur in the first 50 years of the Republic, and filibusters were rare up until the early 20th century.[28]

In 1917, after Senate filibustering frustrated President Wilson's efforts to prepare for World War I, the Senate adopted its first "cloture" rule,

---

[25] *See* John V. Sullivan, H.R. Doc. No. 108-241, *Constitution, Jefferson's Manual, and Rules of the House of Representatives of the United States*, 109TH CONGRESS 240–242 (2005) (discussing Thomas Jefferson's authoritative manual on Senate Rules).

[26] Examining the Filibuster: *The Filibuster Today and Its Consequences: Hearing Before the S. Rules Comm.*, 111TH CONG. 168–174 (2010) [hereinafter 2010 Filibuster Hearings] (statement of Norman J. Ornstein, American Enterprise Institute), available at http://www.aei.org/docLib/20100519-Ornstein-Testimony.pdf.

[27] Catherine Fisk & Erwin Chemerinsky, *The Filibuster*, 49 STANFORD LAW REVIEW 181, 188 (1997) (describing a deliberate attempt in 1790 to postpone debate on a measure).

[28] Emmet J. Bondurant, *The Senate Filibuster: The Politics of Obstruction*, 48 HARVARD JOURNAL ON LEGISLATION 467, 473 (2011). Some commentators argue that because the previous question saw such infrequent use, it provides little evidence for an anti-filibuster view. *See, e.g.*, Fisk & Chemerinsky, *The Filibuster*, *supra*, 188. At a minimum, however, it shows that the formal Senate rules at the time of the Founding were inconsistent with the notion of a filibuster.

providing a formal procedural mechanism to end debate through a super-majority vote requirement. Even then, both filibusters and cloture motions continued to be rare until the late 20th century. In the 30 years after the adoption of the cloture rule in 1917 (1918–1949), there were 60 filibusters (an average of 2 per year), and a total of 27 filibusters (an average of 1.4 per year) during the next 20 years (from 1950–1969).[29] A key 1975 rule change triggered a spike in filibuster use which continued, decade after decade, leading to the modern, dysfunctional, anti-democratic dynamic.

2. The "Silent" Filibuster

The original filibuster stemmed from the Senate's custom of unlimited debate. So, if a Senator or group of Senators was willing to put the time in and keep talking on the Senate floor, they could delay a vote indefinitely until the sponsors relented and withdrew it.

Most of us are familiar with this "talking filibuster." Grade school civics classes used the shorthand "talking a bill to death." It conjures up images of Jimmy Stewart in *Mr. Smith Goes to Washington*, the lonely, heroic Horatio at the Gate.

The reality is far less romantic. First, starting in the mid-20th century, the filibuster became notorious for its use by segregationists during the civil rights era. Senators used it in attempts to block measures prohibiting everything from lynching to race discrimination.

Second, Senators now have a lazy cop-out version of the filibuster, effecting maximal obstruction with minimal effort. In response to the civil rights filibusters, the Senate instituted a "two-track system" for floor debate, leading to the development of the "silent filibuster."[30] The two-track system allows the Senate to consider one measure while another is held pending.

This proved to be a double-edged sword, with one edge a lot more dangerous. Unlike an old-fashioned, *Smith Goes to Washington*-style fili-buster, which brings the Senate's work to a standstill, the silent filibuster allowed the Senate to continue important work. However, by doing so, it made filibusters easier to do, and as a result more frequent.

Indeed, the "silent filibuster" became so easy to use, all a Senator had to do for it to become effective was simply to indicate a willingness to use it. Thus, if "a senator or group of senators signal an intention to filibuster a measure, the majority leader typically does not bring the measure up for

---

[29]   2010 Filibuster Hearings, *supra*, 2–3.
[30]   Fisk & Chemerinsky, *The Filibuster*, *supra*, 188.

live debate at all . . .".[31] By means of the track system, "a senator could filibuster an issue without uttering a word on the Senate floor."[32]

This has been the rule since 1975.[33] Nowadays, a single Senator can hold up a piece of legislation without having to even show up on the Senate floor. Just filing a paper indicating his intent to filibuster will suffice. This single Senator represents only 1% of the Senate; if he comes from a small state, he may represent well less than 1% of the U.S. population.

At first, Senators used this silent filibuster rarely but they have resorted to it more and more in recent decades. While specific data on the use of the silent filibuster is difficult to tabulate, U.S. Senate sources estimate that between the change to the cloture rules in 1975 and the year 1990, Senators employed the filibuster approximately 120 times, an average of 8 times per year. However, the pace picked up dramatically during the Clinton Administration. Judging by the number of cloture motions, there were 80 filibusters in the 103rd Congress (1993–1994) alone, a 500% increase.[34] This stepped-up pace continued, as did a slow but steady rise in filibuster usage up to the present day. Another study, focusing not just on cloture motions, but on any instance where a threatened filibuster blocked or significantly delayed legislation, has estimated that this happened to about 8% of major legislation in the 1960s, and about 70% of major legislation in the 2000s.[35]

3. Cloture

The cloture rule evolved in various stages from its 1917 origin. In 1975, as the Senate created the silent filibuster, it also changed the cloture rule. In that year, the Senate changed the cloture threshold from two-thirds to three-fifths of the full Senate, except on amendments to change the Senate Rules.[36] This lowered the "numerator" required from 67 votes (two-thirds of 100 Senators) to 60 votes (three-fifths of 100). Ever since, as a practical

---

[31] Benjamin Eidelson, *The Majoritarian Filibuster*, 122 YALE LAW JOURNAL 980, 989 (2013).

[32] Fisk & Chemerinsky, *The Filibuster*, *supra*, 201.

[33] Resolution to amend Rule XXII of the Standing Rules of the Senate, 94 S. RES. 4 (1975); 121 CONG. REC. 4108-71, 5251 (1975).

[34] *U.S. Senate Cloture Motions*, SENATE.GOV, available at https://www.senate.gov/pagelayout/reference/cloture_motions/clotureCounts.html.

[35] Ezra Klein, *The Rise of the Filibuster: An Interview with Barbara Sinclair*, WASHINGTON POST, Dec. 26, 2009, available at http://voices.washingtonpost.com/ezra-klein/2009/12/the_right_of_the_filibuster_an.html.

[36] Christopher M. Davis and Betsy Palmer, Cong. Research Serv., PROPOSALS TO AMEND THE SENATE CLOTURE RULE (Nov. 14, 2003).

matter, for a controversial measure to pass, a simple majority will not suffice: 60 votes are needed.

Currently, a filibuster is used over 100 times every legislative session, about 12 times more often than prior to the silent filibuster's advent. The filibuster takes an undemocratic institution and makes it even more undemocratic. Coupled with the natural rightward skew of the Senate, the filibuster is pernicious.

4.   Abolishing the Filibuster

Can it be eliminated? Yes, easily. Even more easily than the Electoral College.

The word "filibuster" does not appear in the Constitution, nor does our Founding document provide any specific authority for it. The fundamental source of authority for the filibuster is the Constitution's general authority of each chamber of Congress to "determine the Rules of its Proceedings."[37] As such, the Senate can change it whenever it wants.

Some have argued that it takes a supermajority vote in the Senate to accomplish this. Rule 22 specifically requires a two-thirds majority of those present and voting to change the Senate Rules.[38] Others have argued that this provision is not binding and that a simple majority may change the Rules, based on a number of theories. These theories include the notion that a past Senate cannot bind a later Senate on how to conduct its internal affairs; and that each Senate sworn in after a biennial election is a new Senate and can amend its Rules using the default rule of majority vote. A variation of this latter theory points to the practice of adopting the Senate's Rules at the beginning of each new Senate's session after being sworn in; until that happens, some argue, the Rules do not apply. The Robert's Rules default provision for a simple majority to pass an amendment apply instead, allowing a simple majority amendment at least during this early stage.[39]

The above legal, theoretical back-and-forth is largely moot, however. As a practical matter, a determined Senate majority can amend Senate Rules by calling for a point of order, and has done so several times to water down the filibuster. Under Senate Rule 20, any Senator can raise a

---

[37]   U.S. Const. Art. I, § 5, cl. 2.

[38]   While it is often the case that the number of Senators present and voting on a particular measure will be far fewer than the full 100, on an important matter like changing the filibuster rule, one could expect close to a full house. Thus, two-thirds of [almost 100] will likely be even greater than 60.

[39]   *See* Fisk & Chemerinsky, *The Filibuster, supra*, 210–215.

procedural point of order at any time. The Chair—whoever is presiding over the Senate at the time—then makes a ruling. Any Senator can then appeal such a ruling, which can be overturned by a simple majority vote.[40]

The Senate's Democratic majority used this loophole in 2013 to scale back the filibuster through the use of the so-called "nuclear option." Senate Majority Leader Harry Reid called for a point of order to change Rule 22 to allow for cloture by simple majority for all presidential nominations, except for Supreme Court nominations. The Chair denied the point of order and it was successfully appealed, allowing for amendment of the Rule.[41]

The Republicans used their own nuclear option more recently to expand the "simple majority for cloture" rule to Supreme Court nominations. Senate Majority Leader McConnell raised a point of order to change the vote of cloture on *all* nominations to a simple majority. The Chair denied it and, as in 2013, the Majority Leader appealed the ruling. The appeal succeeded.[42]

Now, all that remains of the filibuster is ordinary legislation. But that is precisely where the filibuster's effect has been the most pernicious.

5. Filibuster Pros and Cons

Unlike other objections to our governing structure discussed in this book, the filibuster debate has no obvious partisan tint. Both Democrats and Republicans have decried its use when they have been in the majority and defended it as a treasured custom when they have been in the minority. Commentators calling for its abolition spring from both the left and the right.[43]

---

[40] *See* Government Printing Office, 113th Congress, 1st Sess., Doc. 113-18, STANDING RULES OF THE SENATE (Nov. 2013), Rule XX, available at https://www.gpo.gov/fdsys/pkg/CDOC-113sdoc18/pdf/CDOC-113sdoc18.pdf.

[41] *See* 159 S. REC. 8417 (2013); Jeremy W. Peters, *In Landmark Vote, Senate Limits Use of the Filibuster*, NEW YORK TIMES, Nov. 21, 2013, available at https://www.nytimes.com/2013/11/22/us/politics/reid-sets-in-motion-steps-to-limit-use-of-filibuster.html.

[42] *See* 162 CONG. REC. S2390 (daily ed. Apr. 6, 2017); Matt Flegenheimer, *Senate Republicans Deploy 'Nuclear Option' to Clear Path for Gorsuch*, NEW YORK TIMES (Apr. 6, 2017), available at https://www.nytimes.com/2017/04/06/us/politics/neil-gorsuch-supreme-court-senate.html.

[43] *See, e.g.*, Paul Krugman, *A Dangerous Dysfunction*, NEW YORK TIMES (Dec. 20, 2009), available at https://www.nytimes.com/2009/12/21/opinion/21krugman.html?_r=1; Timothy Noah, *Abolish the Filibuster!*, SLATE (Feb. 1, 2005), available at http://www.slate.com/articles/news_and_politics/chatterbox/2001/02/abolish_the_fi

Arguments against the filibuster center around its counter-majoritarian effect.[44] Forty-one Senators have the ability to block legislation supported by 59 Senators. Worse, these 41 Senators could represent far less than 41% of the U.S. population, if they come disproportionately from smaller states. According to the critics, this is "an intentional abuse of the privilege of unlimited debate," used not to inform or persuade, but to "obstruct the proceedings of the Senate by preventing the majority from taking action opposed by a minority of senators."[45]

Indeed, even the word "filibuster" betrays its suspect nature. It is derived from a Dutch word meaning "freebooter," and was used in colonial times to refer to pirates or piracy, or other meanings associated with unauthorized warfare and pillage.

Supporters of the filibuster argue that this obstructionism is a feature, not a bug. Laws *should* be difficult to pass, the argument goes. They restrict liberty so there should be a bias against passing them unless absolutely necessary. Further, making laws difficult to pass also has the salutary effect of forcing long and careful deliberation, enhancing the quality of the final legislative product. It also ensures stability of policy, preventing policy from switching back and forth with every temporary change in public mood.

Indeed, that was one of the original purposes of having Senate terms of 6 years instead of the 2 years used in the House. The Senate was designed to be the *deliberative* body, and deliberately less responsive to public mood than the more egalitarian House—the analogue to the U.K. House of Lords as opposed to the House of Commons. This would facilitate cool,

---

libuster.html; William Kristol, *Break the Filibuster*, THE WEEKLY STANDARD (May 9, 2005), available at https://www.weeklystandard.com/Content/Public/Articles/00 0/000/005/551vzoao.asp; Randy Barnett, *What's Wrong with the Filibuster*, SIGNIFYING NOTHING (Sept. 5, 2003), available at https://blog.lordsutch.com/archi ves/669?entryid=669.

[44]   *See, e.g.*, Gerard N. Magilocca, *Reforming the Filibuster*, 105 NORTHWESTERN UNIVERSITY LAW REVIEW 303 (2011). There are those who argue that the filibuster is not only unwise, but also unconstitutional. *See, e.g.*, Josh Chaffetz, *The Unconstitutionality of the Filibuster*, 42 CONNECTICUT LAW REVIEW 1003 (2011) (making this argument); Fisk & Chemereinsky, *The Filibuster*, *supra*, 239–250 (discussing arguments for and against); *but see* Michael J. Gerhardt, *The Constitutionality of the Filibuster*, 21 CONSTITUTIONAL COMMENTARY 445 (2004) (arguing for the filibuster's validity). Given the filibuster's long provenance, the lack of clear authority against it in the Constitution's text or in Supreme Court case law, and the many procedural obstacles (such as standing, immunity, and the "political question" doctrine) to actually having the Court rule on the merits of the question, it seems likely that only the political process can eliminate it.

[45]   Bondurant, *The Senate Filibuster, supra*.

dispassionate debate. As George Washington put it, the Senate was the "saucer" that "cools" the legislation of the House.[46]

A further argument for the filibuster is that it protects minority rights. "Minority" here obviously does not refer to racial or ethnic minorities: the filibuster's history with civil rights legislation shows that the filibuster has been no friend to those sorts of minority rights. But the minority political party, or even the temporary minority of Senators on one side of a particular issue, deserves to have a voice, to avoid what Founder James Madison called the "tyranny of the majority." It may be inconvenient when your side is in the majority, but you will come to depend on it when you are in the minority and staring down the barrel of horrible legislation.

Assessing this pragmatic argument requires a practical estimate of how often proposed legislation is bad and how often good, regardless of which party is in power. This in turn depends on your satisfaction with the status quo. If you think the current state of the laws is good, and government generally functions the way it ought to, you may be willing to tolerate the filibuster, on the theory that most laws represent a net change for the bad. However, most Americans, regardless of party, think that the current state of government is unsatisfactory and there is great need for change.[47]

This sort of analysis is similar to the evaluation of "false positives" and "false negatives" common in medicine. Just as the Food and Drug Administration screens potential drugs both for their actual ability to help as well as their potential side effects, reformers should estimate the likelihood of laws helping and hurting, all other things being equal. Requiring supermajority requirements makes sense when the cost of screwing things up is high and the cost of failing to act is low. We require jury verdicts to be unanimous because the cost of convicting an innocent man is high. Ditto for amending the Constitution, because the cost of screwing up the Constitution is high. But this logic does not apply to every piece of ordinary, garden-variety legislation. Supermajority requirements should

---

[46] Amy Steigerwalt, BATTLE OVER THE BENCH: SENATORS, INTEREST GROUPS, AND LOWER COURT CONFIRMATIONS 75 (2010). The quote comes from a possibly apocryphal conversation between Washington and Jefferson.

[47] Art Swift, *Americans Name Dissatisfaction with Government as Top Problem*, GALLUP (May 18, 2018), available at http://news.gallup.com/poll/208526/adults-name-government-dissatisfaction-important-problem.aspx. Jessie Hellmann, *Poll: Americans Dissatisfied with Government*, THE HILL (May 18, 2018), available at http://thehill.com/blogs/blog-briefing-room/276559-poll-americans-dissatisfied-with-government.

be the exception, not the rule. They were originally contemplated to be the rare exception but now have become the rule.

Additionally, with the fast-paced developments in technology and commerce in an increasingly interconnected world, there is arguably now more than ever a need for government to be able to act nimbly. Gumming up the works is costlier in the age of climate change and the global financial crisis than it was in the age of the clipper ship and the general store.

As for the "tyranny of the majority," it is indeed a concern. Majority voting blocs can trample on individual rights. However, the filibuster is hardly the best remedy against that. For that, we have the courts and a long tradition of robust judicial review.

Some have even argued counterintuitively that the filibuster can, in fact, support majority rule. A study of 1991–2010 cloture votes showed that in roughly one-third of the successful filibusters defeating a failed Senate majority vote for cloture (i.e., 51–59 votes for cloture), the successfully filibustering minority was actually representing a group of states holding a majority of the nationwide population. These "majoritarian filibusters" might legitimately be viewed as "good" filibusters, a needed corrective to the inherent anti-majoritarian bias in the Senate's structure. They could thus "function as a democratic backstop, obstructing narrow Senate majorities that represent only a minority of Americans."[48] However, if this occurs only one-third of the time, filibusters continue to be a net negative from a representational standpoint.

Indeed, the same study underscores the pernicious nature of the filibuster as used in the 21st century, as it interacts with and reinforces the pro-Republican bias of the Senate's two-votes-per-state rule. These more defensible, "majoritarian" filibusters are more likely to defeat Senate majorities when the Republicans control the Senate. This is precisely because GOP dominance of smaller, rural states means that GOP Senate majorities are less likely to represent a majority of the U.S. population. Of the 59 "majoritarian" filibusters occurring in the 1990s and 2000s, only 2 were used against a Democratic majority, and a whopping *57* (96%) were used against Republican majorities.

Thus, the filibuster clearly exacerbates the already existing anti-Democratic bias of the Senate. Given that its effect is so clearly tilted in one direction, filibuster defenses based on the rights of a nominally abstract "minority" ring especially hollow.

---

[48]   *See* Eidelson, *The Majoritarian Filibuster, supra,* 985.

6. Proposed Filibuster Reforms

Proposed reforms take several shapes. The most obvious is outright abolition, which has already occurred with presidential appointments.[49] We see from the action on presidential appointments that the Senate can accomplish abolition with a simple majority vote overruling an adverse ruling from the Chair on a point of order—the final explosion of the "nuclear option." For the reasons stated above, such abolition would be salutary.

Failing that, another alternative would be simply to lower the threshold for cloture from 60 to a lower number, perhaps 55. Some Senators have discussed this possibility as a compromise measure. It would still allow for protection of minority interests but would be less obstructionist. In fact, it might be significantly more majoritarian than one would think at first glance. The study of "majoritarian filibusters" found that about three-fourths of these more defensible filibusters succeeded where the majority's vote for cloture was 54 votes or under. By contrast, only about one-third of bad, "counter-majoritarian" filibusters involved failed cloture votes of 55 votes or higher. In other words, lowering the cloture threshold to 55 would preserve most of the good, majoritarian filibusters while eliminating most of the bad, counter-majoritarian filibusters.[50]

---

[49] Ironically, the filibuster may be more justified with judicial confirmations (where it has been abolished) than with ordinary legislation (where it still applies). At least with ordinary legislation, consent of the House is required. So, if a Senate majority representing less than a nationwide majority passes a nationally unpopular bill, the population-based House can provide a majoritarian check. (Although, given gerrymandering and demographic clustering, that is no longer a safe assumption: see Chapter 4.) No such House of Representatives safeguard exists with judicial confirmations because the Constitution gives the Senate the only role in confirming presidential appointments. Thus, a nationwide majority strongly opposing a judicial nominee has no recourse if a Senate majority made up of lots of small states confirms. A similar argument exists regarding non-judicial presidential appointments but is weaker because of the need to defer to the President regarding the makeup of his own executive branch—a deference not due when a President appoints members of the coequal judicial branch, over which both the executive and the legislature can legitimately have equal say.

[50] Eidelson, *The Majoritarian Filibuster*, *supra*, 985–989. There is some doubt as to whether this reform could be accomplished with a simple majority vote, as occurred with eliminating the filibuster for presidential appointments. Some have argued that this would require a formal amendment to Rule 22, which would take a 2/3 vote—that is, that the more moderate compromise proposal might actually be harder to achieve, ironically enough. Louis Jacobson, *Could the Nuclear Option Get Rid of the Filibuster Entirely? Checking Trump's Tweet,* POLITIFACT (May 18, 2018),

Yet another alternative discussed by Senators was a sliding-scale approach to the cloture threshold. Under a 1990s proposal by Senators Tom Harkin and Joe Leiberman, adopted a decade later by Republican Senate Majority Leader Bill Frist, a first cloture attempt would require 60 votes; a later, second cloture attempt would require only 57 votes; a still later, third attempt 54 votes; and thereafter a simple majority. This would allow a filibuster to significantly delay but not outright kill a bill.[51] This approach would preserve the deliberative nature of the Senate—the "saucer that cools the milk"—but still allow a determined simple majority to pass laws. Any of these approaches would be an improvement over the current system.

Ten years ago, none of the above reforms would have been considered politically plausible. The tradition of the filibuster was too ingrained and each party in power considering a move feared the inevitable consequences when they lost the majority and the tables were turned. But the increasingly frequent abuse of the filibuster since the 1990s made the unthinkable thinkable, and we now live in a post-filibuster confirmation process world. There is no reason the Senate could not make that the case for legislation as well.

available at http://www.politifact.com/truth-o-meter/article/2018/jan/22/nuclear-option-senate-fiibuster-donald-trump/.

   [51] *See* John C. Eastman, *Filibuster Preservation*, NATIONAL REVIEW (May 15, 2003), available at https://www.nationalreview.com/2003/05/filibuster-preservation-john-c-eastman/.

4. House gerrymandering

A. GENERALLY

The United States is unusual among modern democracies in that we allow partisan legislators to draw district lines, including the very lines in which they personally will run. Almost all other Western democracies using single-member districts, including the U.K., Canada, Australia, and France, delegate this function to independent commissions of some type.[1]

Every 10 years, at the beginning of a new decade, the latest U.S. Census figures come out. They usually show that because of population shifts, congressional and state legislative districts have become significantly uneven in population. Because the Constitution's "one person, one vote" principle requires that districts be substantially equal in population,[2] legislators redraw the state legislative and congressional lines in the first few years of every decade.[3] Since this gives the party temporarily in charge of the state legislature at that time the ability to draw lines in its favor, we have gerrymandering.

Gerrymandering has been with us since the beginning of the Republic. The term comes from Elbridge Gerry, a Founding Father from Massachusetts who as governor signed a redistricting bill featuring a long and winding state senate district drawn to favor his party, the Democratic-Republicans, over the rival party, the Federalists. As the oft-told story goes, when one prominent Federalist saw a drawing of the snake-like district, he remarked that it looked like a salamander. Another Federalist replied, "No, a Gerrymander," and the term was born.[4] The district did

---

[1] *See* Nicholas Stephanopoulos, *Our Electoral Exceptionalism*, 80 UNIVERSITY OF CHICAGO LAW REVIEW 769, 771 (2013); Richard H. Pildes, *The Constitutionalization of Democratic Politics*, 118 HARVARD LAW REVIEW 28, 78 (2004).

[2] *See* Reynolds v. Sims, 377 U.S. 533, 558 (1964).

[3] Some states have begun to use nonpartisan redistricting commissions to draw state legislative lines, U.S. House lines, or both. See Chapter 6. But the above description is accurate for the vast majority of states.

[4] Erick Trickey, *Where Did the Term Gerrymander Come from?*, SMITHSONIAN MAGAZINE (Jul. 20, 2017), available at https://www.smithsonianmag.com/history/

its job, providing Democratic-Republicans a state senate majority even though Federalists won a statewide majority of the vote.[5]

Gerrymandering has continued ever since, and in recent decades has only gotten worse, as court-imposed "one person, one vote" requirements made redistricting occur decennially, and as computer-drawn maps become ever more sophisticated and granular in their fine-detailed partisan craftsmanship. These technological innovations allowed more fine-tuned line-drawing based on multiple layers of overlapping demographic data—party registration, race, income, etc. With the rise of "Big Data," the oceans of consumer data and specialized political databases, redistricters can drill down below the voting precinct level, which had often before been considered the lowest level building blocks for drawing districts.[6] And the growing predictability of voters' major party preferences[7] has made it all the easier to rely on those preferences to create reliably safe districts.

From a line-drawing perspective, there are three main ways to accomplish a gerrymander: cracking, packing, and stacking. Under "cracking," the lines slice up concentrations of the opposite party's voters so that they don't constitute a majority in any one district. "Packing" is the

---

where-did-term-gerrymander-come-180964118/. To hear his first biographer (and son-in-law) tell it, the name is unfair. Governor Gerry reportedly signed the bill reluctantly, concerned about the unfair line-drawing, but unwilling to veto it because of the then-prevalent view that governors didn't veto laws unless they deemed them unconstitutional.

[5]   This wasn't even the first gerrymander attempt in American history. That award goes to Virginian Patrick Henry, who in 1788 drew a Virginia congressional district designed to defeat his rival James Madison. Through political savvy and tireless campaigning, Madison managed to prevail in the 1789 election over his gerrymander-favored opponent, James Monroe, in the only time in history two future presidents ran against each other. Thomas Rogers Hunter, *The First Gerrymander? Patrick Henry, James Madison, James Monroe, and Virginia's 1788 Congressional Districting*, 9 EARLY AMERICAN STUDIES 781 (Fall 2011), available at https://www.jstor.org/stable/23546676?seq=1#page_scan_tab_contents. Since the Constitution wasn't ratified until 1789, American gerrymandering literally pre-dated the founding of the Republic.

[6]   *See* Micah Altman & Michael McDonald, *The Promise and Perils of Computers in Redistricting*, 5 DUKE JOURNAL OF CONSTITUTIONAL LAW & PUBLIC POLICY 69, 73–75 (2010) Vann R. Newkirk II, *How Redistricting Became a Technological Arms Race*, THE NEW YORKER magazine (Oct. 28, 2017), available at https://www.theatlantic. com/politics/archive/2017/10/gerrymandering-technology-redmap-2020/543888/.

[7]   Drew Desilver, *Split-Ticket Districts, Once Common, Are Now Rare*, PEW RESEARCH CENTER (Aug. 6, 2016), http://www.pewresearch.org/fact-tank/2016/08/0 8/split-ticket-districts-once-common-are-now-rare/ (discussing the declining instances of voters voting for one party for President and another for Congress).

converse: line-drawers stuff districts with overwhelming majorities of the opponent's party (70, 80, 90%) into one or a few districts, such that, while they could have numerically formed a majority in, say, 6 districts, they only do so in 3. "Stacking" can refer to several things, but for our purposes here, think of it as putting 2 or more incumbents of the opposing party into the same district so that they must run against each other. No matter what happens, there will be 1 less incumbent of that party after the election.

At this early point it should be noted that while flagrant and obvious instances of cracking, packing, or stacking may lead any fair observer to conclude that a redistricting plan is a gerrymander, there is no universally accepted definition of a "gerrymander." One man's gerrymander might very well be another man's legitimate redistricting effort which just happens to benefit one party. One common, but by no means exclusive measure, is how oddly shaped the district is.

Figure 4.1 illustrates a typical example of the obvious gerrymander. It is Pennsylvania's 7th Congressional District, drawn by the Republican-controlled state legislature during the post-2010 round of redistrict-

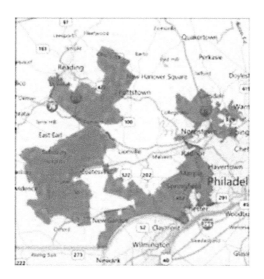

Source: Joint Ex. 12, *LWV v. Commonwealth*, 178 A.3d 737 (Penn. 2018).

Figure 4.1   Pennsylvania's 7th Congressional District: the "Goofy Kicking Donald Duck" gerrymander

ing, and struck down under the state constitution by the Pennsylvania Supreme Court.[8] It has come to be known as the "Goofy Kicking Donald Duck" district. It was part of a redistricting plan which increased the votes–seats disparity from about 5 percentage points (to the Democrats' disadvantage) in 2006 to 23 points (also to the Democrats' disadvantage) in 2012. It was clearly a gerrymandered district. But we are not always lucky enough to have gerrymanders so visually obvious, or to have a state supreme court aggressively police gerrymandering.

B. THE PROBLEM WITH "COMPACTNESS"

Indeed, while odd shape might be a red flag suggesting that a district is a gerrymander, it is not the best measure, even if easiest for the courts to spot or the public to grasp. A sophisticated gerrymanderer can crack, pack, and stack even in regularly shaped districts.

Figure 4.2 is a good example. It shows the evolution of the Wisconsin State Assembly redistricting plan. In 2008, under a court-drawn plan (shown on the left), Democrats won 56% of the votes and 53% of the seats. In the Tea Party wave election of 2010, Democrats won 43% of the votes, and 39 % of the seats. Not perfect in either case, but relatively small partisan bias, with each plan meeting the basic "majority wins control" criterion. But in 2012, after the Republican-controlled redistricting, Democrats won 53% of the votes yet only 39% of the seats—a 14-point partisan bias failing the majority control criterion. This is the plan (shown on the right) reviewed by the U.S. Supreme Court in the *Gill* case. In terms of its actual voting skew, it is a pretty substantial gerrymander. Yet the districts are relatively compact. Indeed, it is hard to see dramatic declines in compactness from the court-drawn plan and the politician-drawn plan.

And, sometimes, fair districts which properly represent the overall racial, political, and socioeconomic makeup of a jurisdiction might need to be oddly shaped. This might be because they follow natural boundaries like mountains or rivers, or respect political subdivision boundaries like cities or counties, or simply because they follow the irregular housing patterns of a racial minority. A district might need to be oddly shaped in order to make districts competitive, ensure racial fairness, and/or avoid overrepresenting one party or another, etc., all the while keeping the

---

[8] League of Women Voters v. Commonwealth, 178 A.3d 737, 741–742 (Pennsylvania 2018).

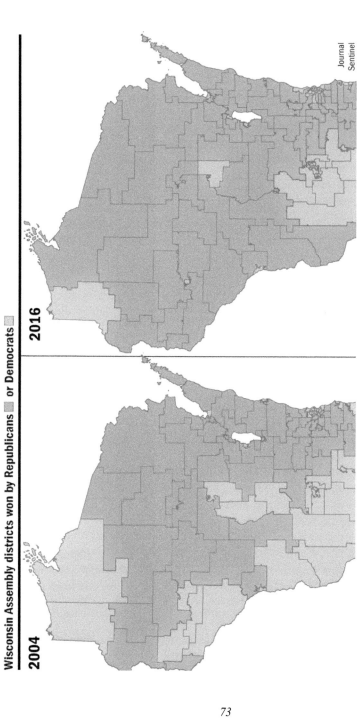

Wisconsin Assembly districts won by Republicans ▢ or Democrats ▢

2004

2016

Journal
Sentinel

Source: Milwaukee Journal-Sentinel (with permission).

Note: These two maps show the presidential vote by Assembly district in 2004 and 2016, two races where the statewide vote for president was a virtual toss-up. But the GOP edge in districts was much bigger in 2016, due to both a gerrymandered map and a decline in rural strength for Democrats. In 2004, 56 of 99 districts had a Republican makeup based on presidential vote. In 2016, 63 of 99 did.

Figure 4.2   Wisconsin State Legislative Maps, 2004 v. 2016: evolution of a compact gerrymander

district population equal to the mathematical "ideal" population required under "one person, one vote."[9]

So, a rigid focus on compact districts might be counterproductive from a redistricting policy standpoint. And it certainly is a crude tool for sussing out gerrymanders, because (i) a district can be compact and still be a gerrymander, and (ii) a district can be oddly shaped and *not* be a gerrymander.

More fundamentally, there does not seem to be a compelling case for considering compactness too high up on the hierarchy of redistricting criteria. There is no requirement under the Constitution or federal law that districts be compact.[10] All things being equal, it would be nice to have districts be small and regular in shape so that voters are less confused about which districts they are in. But respecting city and county boundaries would probably help voters know their district even better, even though that might be at odds with pure compactness.

Similarly, having districts relatively small, and round or square shaped, might make it easier for constituents to travel to see their representative. But both of these are slight advantages, marginal at best, especially in an age where constituents contact their representatives via the Internet and phone, or even in person with little difficulty in densely populated urban centers where districts are compressed together in relatively small areas. If compactness is at odds with ensuring racial or partisan fairness, or respecting political subdivision boundaries, would it not make sense for compactness to give way?

C.   VOTES VERSUS SEATS

There are many different ways of measuring the extent to which a districting plan deviates from the representational ideal. This chapter introduces one such measure, "partisan bias," the difference in percentage of a party's votes earned versus seats gained. This is a common measure used in political science.[11] Courts routinely use a version of it in racial gerrymandering cases to evaluate claims of minority vote dilution.[12] The measure makes

---

[9]   For more on the tension among these competing criteria, see Chapter 6.

[10]   *See* 2 U.S.C. § 2c (2018) (requiring use of single-member districts for U.S. House elections, but specifying neither compactness nor any other redistricting criteria).

[11]   *See, e.g.*, Matthew S. Shugart & Rein Taagepera, Votes from Seats: Logical Models of Electoral Systems (2017) (Votes From Seats).

[12]   *See* Thornburg v. Gingles, 478 U.S. 30, 84 (1986) (relying, in evaluating vote dilution claims, on "the proportion between the minority group and the

intuitive sense. If a political party gets 43% of the vote in a particular state, that party ought to control roughly 43% of the seats, give or take.

This measure can make allowances for rounding up or down— obviously, a party can't control one-third of a district, so if the ratio comes out to "Republicans should control 3.3 seats" there will have to be some variation. It also makes allowances for the fact that partisan populations aren't distributed evenly throughout a jurisdiction. So, since all districts have to be closely equal in population, if almost all the Democrats live in one corner of the state, it might be hard to draw reasonably compact districts that result in the right statewide ratio. But, allowing for some variation due to these considerations and similar partisan-neutral considerations like natural boundaries (rivers, mountains), political subdivision boundaries (counties, cities) and the like, we would normally expect not to see substantial variations between seats and votes.

Not everyone agrees that proportionality between seats and votes should be an ideal to strive for.[13] But large deviations from that proportionate share, unexplained by partisan-neutral considerations, should at least give one pause.

At a minimum, we would expect that if one major party received a majority of the vote in the jurisdiction, that party, and not another major party, should receive a majority of the seats.[14] The Supreme Court has endorsed this fairly intuitive principle in the analogous context of legislative apportionment.[15] Some Justices had suggested that failure to meet this relatively low bar would be strong evidence of unconstitutional partisan gerrymandering,[16] although the current Court has declined to make this a strict legal requirement.[17] One state constitution in Australia

---

electorate at large"); Johnson v. DeGrandy, 512 U.S. 997, 1019 (1997) (discussing "proportionality" analysis and explaining that underrepresentation may indicate vote dilution while overrepresentation could suggest the opposite); *id.* at 1025 (O'Connor, J., concurring) (proportional underrepresentation is always relevant and probative of vote dilution).

[13] *Cf.*, Vieth v. Jubilerer, 541 U.S. 267, 287–288 (2004) (plurality opinion) (emphasizing that the Constitution does not guarantee any politically cohesive group election in proportion to its numbers).

[14] *See* John F. Nagle, *Measures of Partisan Bias for Legislating Fair Elections*, Carnegie Mellon University Reprints (May 2015), available at https://arxiv.org/ftp/arxiv/papers/1505/1505.06749.pdf (making this observation).

[15] Reynolds v. Sims, 377 U.S. 533, 565 (1964). "Reapportionment" decides how many congressional seats each State gets, based on State populations. Once we know how many seats each State gets, "redistricting" determines exactly how the districts should be shaped.

[16] *See, e.g., Vieth*, 541 U.S. at 318 (Breyer, J., dissenting).

[17] *Id.* at 287–288 (plurality opinion).

had until recently enshrined this measure of gerrymandering in law, with constitutional text instructing the nonpartisan redistricting commission to make best efforts to ensure majority votes yield a majority of seats.[18] This book will term this "the majority criterion."

So, for example, in North Carolina, when Democrats won only 46% of the statewide vote in the 2010 election run under a Democratic-drawn map, they should not have won (but did win) 7 out of 13 congressional seats (a majority). Two years later, when they actually did win a majority (51%) of the statewide vote under a Republican-drawn map, they should not have won only 4 of 13 congressional seats (only 30%). In each case, gerrymandering made the difference. Democrats had gerrymandered the map in 2010, and Republicans in 2012. In fact, in 2012, the first election after the 2010 round of redistricting, 5 states—Arizona, Michigan, North Carolina, Pennsylvania, and Wisconsin—failed to meet even this minimal standard of fairness: the party with the most votes did not obtain a majority of seats.[19] As noted in Chapter 1, this "majority loses" scenario occurred on a nationwide level for the House in 2012. It has occurred at least 4 other times in the 20th century, including as recently as 1996.[20]

Besides the seats-to-votes curve, there are a number of other mathematical measures for gerrymandering.[21] One test yielding a lot of recent attention is the *efficiency gap*. This test measures the number of "wasted votes" in a plan—i.e., either votes which went to the losing candidate, or votes which went to a winning candidate over and above the minimum needed to win, which is the number of opposition votes plus one. The losing votes might be caused by cracking, and an overabundance of winning votes might be caused by packing. If a party's voters are forced into

---

[18] SOUTH AUSTRALIAN CONSTITUTION ACT 1934 § 83(1) (2017).
[19] *See* Sam Wang, *The Great Gerrymander of 2012*, NEW YORK TIMES (Feb. 2, 2013), available at http://www.nytimes.com/2013/02/03/opinion/sunday/the-great-gerrymander-of-2012.html?pagewanted=all.
[20] Richard Winger, *Only Four U.S. House Elections in the Last Hundred Years Gave One Party a House Majority, Even Though the Other Major Party Polled More Votes for U.S. House*, BALLOT ACCESS NEWS, Nov. 12, 2012, available at http://ballot-access.org/2012/11/12/only-four-u-s-house-elections-in-the-last-hundred-years-gave-one-party-a-house-majority-even-though-the-other-major-party-polled-more-votes-for-u-s-house/ (1914, 1942, and 1952); Robert H .Carle, STATISTICS OF THE PRESIDENTIAL AND CONGRESSIONAL ELECTION OF NOVEMBER 5, 1996 (1997).
[21] For a good discussion of the various tests, see Samuel S.-H. Wang, *Three Tests for Practical Evaluation of Partisan Gerrymandering*, 68 STANFORD LAW REVIEW 1263 (2016); as well as the Princeton Gerrymander Project, available at http://gerrymander.princeton.edu/info.

districts where they have no reasonable chance of winning (cracking), or if they are packed into a district where there are far more of those votes than needed to win (packing), this is a sign of gerrymandering. A large difference between those measures for Democrats versus Republicans shows up as a high "efficiency gap," indicating a likely gerrymander.

D.   RECENT EXACERBATION OF THE PROBLEM

By most evaluations, gerrymandering has gotten worse in recent decades. In the modern era, it began a significant rise in the post-2000 round of redistricting, and rose sharply in the most recent, post-2010 round. In past decades, the number of House seats gained through gerrymandering has increased from fewer than 5 in the 70s, 80s, and 90s to almost 20 today.[22] While gerrymandering's focus in decades past was often on protecting incumbents of both parties from challengers, today it has taken on a more hardball partisan color.[23] The pronounced effect, in recent years a pro-GOP bias, continued through the 2016 election.[24]

But Democrats have gerrymandered as well. The same studies show that Democratic-drawn maps in Illinois, Maryland, and Massachusetts in the same redistricting cycle generated a benefit to Democrats of anywhere between 2 and 4 seats per state.[25]

---

[22]   *See* Sam Wang & Brian Remlinger, *Slaying the Partisan Gerrymander*, THE AMERICAN PROSPECT (Sept. 25, 2017), available at http://prospect.org/article/slaying-partisan-gerrymander (summarizing results of redistricting analysis over recent decades); Laura Royden and Michael Li, *Extreme Maps*, The Brennan Center for Justice (May 9, 2017), available at https://www.brennan-center.org/publication/extreme-maps (summarizing substantial gerrymandering effects in first three elections after the 2010 round of redistricting, 2012–2016). Another analysis, measuring simply votes–seats deviations, shows merely that partisan bias was 3% and 7% for Democrats in the 1970s and 1980s, respectively; about 0 in the 1990s; and rising to 9% and 6% for Republicans in the 2000s and 2010s, respectively. Theodore S. Arrington, *Gerrymandering the House, 1972–2016*, UNIVERSITY OF VIRGINIA CENTER FOR POLITICS (Jan. 26, 2017), available at http://www.centerforpolitics.org/crystalball/articles/gerrymandering-the-house-1972-2016/. This suggests a rise in gerrymandering, but not a consistent, steady one. Either way, partisan bias continues to be a nontrivial problem.

[23]   Wang & Remlinger, THE AMERICAN PROSPECT, *supra*.

[24]   David A. Leib, *AP Analysis Shows How Gerrymandering Benefited GOP in 2016*, ASSOCIATED PRESS (June 25, 2017), available at https://www.denverpost.com/2017/06/25/gerrymandering-2016-election/.

[25]   *See, e.g.*, Royden & Li, *Extreme Maps*, *supra*.

Unsurprisingly, the bias in either direction was greatest among the states where one party controlled the redistricting process—i.e., it controlled both houses of the state legislature and the governorship.[26] This reinforces the natural inference that the partisan biases were at least partially the result of partisan gerrymandering as opposed to being merely some natural by-product of demographic clustering, discussed below.

Redistricters may have been emboldened by a 2003 Supreme Court decision suggesting that partisan gerrymandering, unlike racial gerrymandering, was not subject to court scrutiny.[27] As a result, redistricting for partisan advantage has become so much the norm that its practitioners brag about it.

In the several years immediately following the 2010 Census, the Republican State Leadership Committee embarked on its famed REDMAP initiative, which stands for "Redistricting Majority Project,"[28] a comprehensive and coordinated effort to gain control of state legislatures in key states expressly to dominate the post-2010 Census round of redistricting. REDMAP's website candidly boasted that in the 2012 election, only 49% of voters nationwide chose Republican House candidates, and yet, thanks to REDMAP's sophisticated redistricting strategies, Republicans ended up with 57.5% of the seats. The avowed and successful 2010–2012 goal was to "erect a Republican firewall through the redistricting process that paved the way to Republicans retaining a U.S. House majority in 2012."[29] The effort succeeded: depending on the estimate, it created a net benefit of 16–22 House seats for Republicans from 2012 to 2016, almost as many as needed to flip the House during this period.[30] Both parties have been trying it; recently, though, the GOP has just been better at it.

Republicans and Democrats alike have been frank about their gerrymandering aims.[31] In North Carolina, the Republican state House redistricting chair admitted that the plan's authors used political data in drawing the map "to gain partisan advantage." Referring to a revised version of the

---

[26]   *Id.* at 6–10.

[27]   *Vieth*, 541 U.S. 267 at 285–292 (plurality opinion).

[28]   The name also connotes, surely by design, that the maps would be turned red after Republican electoral success.

[29]   *See* Republican State Legislative Committee, *2012 REDMAP Summary Report*, REDMAP Redistricting Project, available at http://www.redistrictingmaj orityproject.com/.

[30]   Wang & Remlinger, The American Prospect, *supra*; Leib, *AP Analysis*, *supra*; Royden & Li, *Extreme Maps*, *supra*.

[31]   *See* Richard Pildes, *The Brazenness of Partisan Intent in the Court's Gerrymandering Cases*, Election Law Blog (May 15, 2018), available at http:// electionlawblog.org/?s=redistricting+brazen&x=0&y=0.

plan drawn after early court challenges, he said, "I acknowledge freely that [the 2016 Plan] would be a political gerrymander," which he claimed "is not against the law."[32] In Wisconsin, Republican plan-drawers "stress-tested" their maps to make sure they would yield a Republican majority under various scenarios.[33] Indeed, the email trail of redistricters in Michigan, Florida, and Ohio showed clearly that line-drawers were deliberately using partisan voter data to maximize the GOP's advantage, including staff in Michigan who referred to voters in Democratic counties as "Dem garbage" and reveled in "giving the finger" to a Democratic congressional incumbent.[34]

Democrats have been similarly frank. Back in the 1990s, one Democratic county legislator in Illinois infamously declared to his Republican opponents that "We are going to shove ... [this map] up your fucking ass and you are going to like it, and I'll fuck any Republican I can."[35] In the post-2010 round of redistricting, Democratic Maryland governor Martin O'Malley admitted that "[t]he goal of the Democrats" was to "ensure the election of another Democrat" in a particular congressional district.[36]

This increase in gerrymandering has also resulted in fewer competitive races. Studies of recent redistricting plans indicate that only about 10% of U.S. House seats are competitive. This is so whether you measure competitiveness *ex ante* by the Democratic–Republican ratio of registered voters in the district—say, anything more lopsided than 60–40 to be considered non-competitive[37]—or *ex post* by looking at whether the incumbent actually drew serious opposition in the general election. The lack of competitive districts explains why the incumbent reelection rate is

---

[32] Complaint for Declaratory Judgment and Injunctive Relief at 12, Common Cause v. Rucho, 279 F. Supp. 3d 587 (M.D.N.C. 2018).

[33] Whitford v. Gill, 218 F. Supp. 3d 837, 849–853 (W.D. Wis. 2016).

[34] David Daley, *Emails Are The Tools Of The Devil*, SLATE, July 28, 2018, available at https://slate.com/news-and-politics/2018/07/michigan-partisan-gerrymandering-newly-released-emails-reveal-the-intent-behind-republicans-redistricting-plan.html. In the Florida case, a state court in 2014 struck down the congressional plan and found that a "group of Republican political consultants or operatives did in fact conspire to manipulate and influence the redistricting process" with the intent to "favor the Republican Party." Romo v. Detzner & Bondi, Case No. 2012-CA-412, Final Judgment (2nd Judic. Cir. July 10, 2014), at 21.

[35] *See* Hulme v. Madison County, 188 F. Supp. 2d 1041, 1051 (S.D. Ill. 2001). This prediction proved incorrect: His Republican opponents did *not* like it, and successfully sued to invalidate the plan under "one person, one vote" and state law.

[36] Benisek v. Lamone, 266 F. Supp. 3d 799, 832 (D. Md. 2017).

[37] Political scientists generally consider any election margin over 60% to be a landslide. *See, e.g.*, Bill Bishop & Robert G. Cushing, THE BIG SORT: WHY THE CLUSTERING OF LIKE-MINDED AMERICA IS TEARING US APART 9–11 (2008) (THE BIG SORT) (discussing political science studies using this landslide measure).

so high, at around 90%.[38] And, as seen below, it is just as much the natural and inevitable result of "demographic clustering" as it is of intentional gerrymandering.

This lack of competitiveness doesn't just hurt the disadvantaged party in the district in question; it hurts all of us by hurting democracy itself. Lower competitiveness drives down turnout, increasing voters' sense of powerlessness and futility, fueling cynicism and apathy. It also means increasing polarization and less opportunity for across-the-aisle compromise. Perhaps most perniciously, it means that the only competition incumbents need to worry about is competition in the primary election from the extremes of their party—extreme left for Democrats, and extreme right for Republicans. To stay in office, incumbents are incentivized to drift ever further from the political center, paying heed not to the district voters as a whole but rather to the relatively small political fringe who are most active in party politics. Quoting the *amicus curiae* brief of a bipartisan group of federal politicians, Supreme Court Justice Elena Kagan recently wrote of the "cascade of negative results" of the new, high-tech partisan gerrymandering: "indifference to swing voters['] . . .views; extreme political positioning designed to placate the party's base and fend off primary challenges; the devaluing of negotiation and compromise; and the impossibility of reaching pragmatic, bipartisan solutions to the nations' problems."[39]

E.   "CLUSTERING"

Some experts have argued that the fault lies not in Democrats' redistricting stars but in themselves—specifically, their tendency to over-cluster in urban areas.[40] The 2008 book *The Big Sort* popularized this thesis. It documents how in the last few decades, Americans in an increasingly mobile society have tended to cluster with people who are ideologically like-minded. This has naturally caused increasing political polarization. Democrats, in particular, tend to gather in large urban areas. This makes

---

[38]   *See* FairVote, *Monopoly Politics 2002: Full Report*, available at http://archive.fairvote.org/index.php?page=490.

[39]   Gill v. Whitford, 138 S. Ct. 1916, 1940 (Kagan, J., concurring) (quoting Brief for Bipartisan Group of Current and Former Members of Congress as *Amici Curiae*, at 4, 10–23).

[40]   *See, e.g.*, Jowei Chen & Jonathan Rodden, *It's the Geography, Stupid*, NEW YORK TIMES (Jan. 26, 2014), available at https://www.nytimes.com/2014/01/26/opinion/sunday/its-the-geography-stupid.html?_r=0.

for natural "packing" of Democrats into supermajority districts, with fewer Democrats to go around to make up majorities in other districts, resulting in a "natural gerrymander" that is more the product of demographic clustering than politicians' mischief. John Ryder, the National Republican Committee General Counsel, who played a leading role in the GOP's post-2010 redistricting efforts, advances this more benign view of partisan redistricting efforts, stating that "[t]he current make up of Congress (and many legislatures) is more a product of spatial polarization/clustering than it is redistricting."

The "Big Sort" is real. There is more demographic clustering with like-minded people in the 21st century. For example, in the 1976 election, about 25% of Americans lived in "landslide" counties—counties where the margin of victory for one party or another was over 20%. By the 2004 election, that percentage rose to 50%. The trend continues: the median county in 2016 was won by more than 40 percentage points.[41] No one gerrymandered the county boundaries in the interim; instead, people's residency patterns changed organically.

A study by faculty at the University of Michigan and Stanford reached similar results, demonstrating the "unintentional gerrymandering" resulting from Democrats' over-concentration in urban areas. This concentration means that in many states, Democrats will naturally win less than 50% of the seats statewide even though they represent more than 50% of the statewide votes, regardless of the way the lines are drawn. Indeed, this "clustering" phenomenon is not limited to the United States. Similar studies have demonstrated a rightward votes-to-seats skew toward the more conservative party in the U.K., Australia, and New Zealand, due in part to the same phenomenon.[42]

But at the same time, "clustering" is not the only explanation for the undemocratic results of recent elections. One nonpartisan statistical study indicates that on the basis of clustering alone, Democrats would need to win the nationwide vote by a 2-point margin in order to control the House. This is a slightly uneven playing field for Democrats, caused entirely by demographic concentrations unrelated to gerrymandering. But the same study shows that thanks to the post-2010 round of redistricting, Democrats would have to win by about 8 points. This is an extra 6-point handicap, an effect larger than the "natural" handicap of demographic

---

[41] Bishop & Cushing, THE BIG SORT, *supra*, at 10.
[42] Jowei Chen & Jonathan Rodden, *Unintentional Gerrymandering: Political Geography and Electoral Bias in Legislatures*, 8 QUARTERLY JOURNAL OF POLITICAL SCIENCE 239, 265 (2013).

clustering. In some extremely gerrymandered states like North Carolina or Pennsylvania, that handicap is now up to 15 points.[43] Another study concluded that to take back the House in 2018, Democrats would need to gain 54–55% of the nationwide vote, more of a landslide than Barack Obama got in his decisive 2008 victory. This study pointed out that the urban clustering of Democrats was most concentrated in states where the redistricting plans were the least biased against Democrats, suggesting that clustering alone cannot be the only explanation.[44] And, certainly, if clustering were the only dynamic at work here, we would not expect to see the partisan bias of redistricting maps to be most extreme in states where one party controlled the entire districting process, as is in fact the case.

Clearly, demographic sorting is a real phenomenon, responsible for some of the partisan bias in current redistricting plans. And just as clearly, gerrymandering is substantially exacerbating a pre-existing problem, and needs to be addressed.

The most direct and final way to address it would be through the law. Certainly, one would think that democracy-defeating gerrymanders would be illegal once exposed. But that has not historically been the case with partisan gerrymanders. And even if that changes, it will be at best only a partial solution.

---

[43] Wang & Remlinger, THE AMERICAN PROSPECT, *supra*; *see also* Samuel S.-H. Wang, *Three Tests for Practical Evaluation of Partisan Gerrymandering*, 68 STANFORD LAW REVIEW 1263 (2016).

[44] Anthony McGann et al., *Why the Democrats Won't Win the House in 2018*, THE CONVERSATION (Feb. 15, 2018), available at http://theconversation.com/why-the-democrats-wont-win-the-house-in-2018-68037.

5.   Judicial policing of gerrymanders

While the question of whether and to what extent courts should police *partisan* gerrymandering is an ongoing and much-debated question, the comparable questions in the context of *racial* gerrymandering have long been settled. There are well-understood and long-accepted methods for determining whether a district is an unlawful racial gerrymander. They teach some useful lessons, both about judicial oversight of partisan gerrymandering, and the larger question of whether even robust judicial oversight can be a complete solution to the problem of fair representation.

A.   TRADITIONAL RACIAL GERRYMANDERS

The Supreme Court intervened to stop racial gerrymandering as far back as 1960. In *Gomillion v. Lightfoot*, the Court considered the racially gerrymandered boundaries of the city of Tuskegee, Alabama, drawn by the state legislature. The state redrew the city boundaries from a relatively square shape to an irregular 28-sided figure which excluded 395 of the city's 400 black voters from the city, without eliminating any white voters. Overruling a lower court ruling that federal courts had no authority to intervene in such a political decision, the Supreme Court reversed, holding that the above situation violated the right to vote on account of race in violation of the Fifteenth Amendment.[1] Later cases demonstrated that intentionally race-discriminatory districts could also be struck down under the Equal Protection Clause of the Fourteenth Amendment.[2] But the Constitution would only provide relief if a plaintiff could prove intentional discrimination.[3]

However, proving discriminatory intent on behalf of those who drew the lines or voted to approve the lines is difficult, and unfair racial gerrymanders escaped justice as a result. To address this problem, Congress

---

[1]   Gomillion v. Lightfoot, 364 U.S. 339, 346 (1960).
[2]   Whitcomb v. Chavis, 403 U.S. 124, 149 (1971); White v. Regester, 412 U.S. 755, 769 (1973).
[3]   City of Mobile v. Bolden, 446 U.S. 55, 66 (1979).

in 1982 amended Section 2 of the 1965 Voting Rights Act to clarify that proving a racially discriminatory *effect* would be enough to win a "minority vote dilution" case, including a case alleging a racial gerrymander. The language of the amended Section 2 "results test" was somewhat open-ended, requiring that courts examine "the totality of the circumstances" to see if minority voters have an equal "opportunity to participate in the electoral process and to elect representatives of their choice."[4]

In 1986, the Supreme Court announced a more specific, workable test for evaluating such otherwise open-ended "discriminatory effect" claims. According to this test, a plaintiff had to make a preliminary *prima facie* showing that (a) members of the minority group were sufficiently numerous and concentrated so as to allow the drawing of a compact majority–minority district; (b) the minority group members were politically cohesive (they tended to vote alike); and (c) the majority group members tended to vote as a bloc so as to defeat the minority voters' candidates of choice. Named for the Supreme Court case, these were the "*Gingles* preconditions."[5] A minority plaintiff who could not prove these conditions would lose. A plaintiff who could would then go on to produce evidence under the "totality of the circumstances."

To assist a judge in evaluating all the circumstances, the Court provided a list of factors taken from the statute's legislative history, called the "Senate factors." They included, among other things, any history of official discrimination against that minority in the jurisdiction affecting voting; the degree to which voting was racially polarized; any history of a lack of minority candidate electoral success; socioeconomic disparities on the part of the minority group members; and the extent to which the defendant's race-neutral explanation for the way the lines were drawn was tenuous.[6]

For the next several decades, minority voting rights advocates vigorously used the *Gingles* framework to challenge districting plans as dilutive of minority voting strength. Courts often ordered that the jurisdiction draw more single-member districts with a majority of minority voters.[7] This affirmative litigation effort under Section 2 of the Voting Rights Act substantially increased minority representation. It also dovetailed nicely

---

[4]   52 U.S.C. § 10301 (2012).

[5]   Thornburg v. Gingles, 478 U.S. 30, 55 (1986).

[6]   *Gingles*, 478 U.S. at 43–52 (citing Senate Report No. 97-417, 28–29 (1982), *reprinted in* 1982 U.S.C.C.A.N. 177, 205–207).

[7]   *See* Steven J. Mulroy, *Alternative Ways Out: A Remedial Road Map for the Use of Alternative Electoral Systems as Voting Rights Act Remedies*, 77 North Carolina Law Review 1867, 1874 (1999).

with Section 5 of the Voting Rights Act, which provided that in certain jurisdictions with a history of voting discrimination, no change in rules affecting voting could take effect unless it was "precleared" by either the U.S. Department of Justice or a specially convened federal three-judge district court.[8] Section 5 reviewers often did an analysis similar to that used in Section 2: measuring racial polarization in voting, evaluating whether redistricting maps featured a sufficient number of minority–majority districts. Together, Section 2 and Section 5 dramatically increased minority representation during this period.[9]

As a result of these decades of litigation, courts became veterans at evaluating racial gerrymander claims.[10] Well-established statistical methods to measure voting patterns, racial polarization levels, and the like were honed and confirmed.[11] Courts gained experience analyzing competing redistricting maps and evaluating population and voting statistics under those plans to predict the likely outcome in terms of minority electoral success. And courts commonly used a seats/votes comparison in evaluating these claims.[12]

However, in recent years, the ability to use the Voting Rights Act for minority empowerment has been substantially curtailed, and the pace of progress slowed. An early blow was the rise of the *Shaw v. Reno/Miller v. Johnson* "reverse racial gerrymander" claim, discussed below. Another was the advent of court rulings that disallowed claims for "crossover" districts, where the minority group was slightly below a majority in the proposed remedial district, but where minority voters would nonetheless be able to elect candidates of choice thanks to "crossover" voting by some whites.[13]

---

[8]   52 U.S.C. § 10304(a) (Westlaw through P.L. 115-90).

[9]   Chandler Davidson & Bernard Grofman, eds., *Quiet Revolution in the South: The Impact of the Voting Rights Act, 1965–1990* (1994); James C. Cobb, *The Voting Rights Act at 50: How it Changed the World*, TIME, Aug. 6, 2015, available at http://time.com/3985479/voting-rights-act-1965-results/.

[10]   *See, e.g.,* Samuel Issacharoff, *Judging Politics: The Elusive Quest for Judicial Review of Political Fairness*, 71 TEXAS LAW REVIEW 1643, 1688–1690, and nn. 227–233 (1993) (compiling cases to show that about one-third of all redistricting in the 1980s round was done under court supervision).

[11]   *See, e.g.,* N.A.A.C.P., Inc. v. City of Niagara Falls, N.Y., 65 F.3d 1002, 1012 (2d Cir. 1995); Teague v. Attala Co., Miss., 92 F.3d 283, 289 (5th Cir. 1996); Rural West Tenn. African-Am. Affairs Council v. Sundquist, 209 F.3d 835, 839 (6th Cir. 2000). The author participated in the *Attala County* case.

[12]   *See, e.g.,* Johnson v. DeGrandy, 512 U.S. 997, 1000–1014 (1994) (discussing "proportionality" of representation for Hispanics in South Florida under state legislative redistricting plan); LULAC v. Perry, 548 U.S. 399, 436–439 (2006) (same, for Hispanics in Texas congressional redistricting).

[13]   Bartlett v. Strickland, 556 U.S. 1, 13 (2009) (plurality opinion).

Such "coalition" districts are valuable not only to allow the drawing of more minority–majority districts (assuming racially polarized voting and underrepresentation), but also to encourage cross-racial coalitions, to make politics less racially polarized, and to lessen the tension between "descriptive representation" and "substantive" representation.[14] Perhaps the biggest blow was the 2013 Supreme Court decision in *Shelby County, Alabama v. Holder*, where the Supreme Court struck down as outmoded the "coverage formula" determining which jurisdictions would be covered under Section 5, thus ending Section 5 preclearance review.[15]

Aside from these legal developments, there were independent demographic developments making the traditional "minority districting" approach less effective in giving minority voters a realistic voice in the political process. In recent decades, minority groups have become more dispersed geographically, making it more difficult to draw compact single-member districts. African-Americans have moved from the cities to the suburbs in large numbers, scattering somewhat in the process.[16] And Hispanics, the fastest-rising, and now largest, minority group, have long been more geographically dispersed in their housing patterns, making the drawing of compact remedial districts difficult. Ironically, the improving situation with respect to racially segregated neighborhoods has worsened the prospects for politically empowering black and brown people through minority districting.[17] These demographic trends, along with the similar ideological "self-sorting" discussed above in Chapter 4, have combined to hamper the ability of minority groups to use Section 2 of the Voting Rights Act to influence the political process.[18] These hindrances stem from courts' inflexible devotion to single-member districts as remedies in these voting rights cases, when proportional and semi-proportional remedies are available.[19]

---

[14] *See* Chapter 8, Section D.3.

[15] Shelby County Ala. v. Holder, 570 U.S. 529 (2013).

[16] *See* Andrew Wiese, PLACES OF THEIR OWN: AFRICAN-AMERICAN SUBURBANIZATION IN THE TWENTIETH CENTURY 1 (2005); Dale Ho, *Two Fs for Formalism: Interpreting Section 2 of the Voting Rights Act in Light of Changing Demographic and Electoral Patterns*, 50 HARVARD CIVIL RIGHTS–CIVIL LIBERTIES LAW REVIEW 403, 407–409 (2015).

[17] *See* Steven J. Mulroy, *Coloring Outside the Lines: Erasing "One-Person, One-Vote" & Voting Rights Act Line-Drawing Dilemmas by Erasing District Lines*, 85 MISSISSIPPI LAW JOURNAL 1271, 1290 (making this point, and citing demographic studies showing Latino geographic dispersion).

[18] *See* Ho, *Two Fs for Formalism, supra*, 409–412.

[19] *See* Steven Mulroy, *Alternative, Nondistrict Vote Dilution Remedies Under the Voting Rights Act*, in Benjamin E. Griffith, ed., AMERICA VOTES! A GUIDE TO

B. "REVERSE RACIAL GERRYMANDERS"

Throughout the civil rights era, the phrase "racial gerrymander" unambiguously referred to a district drawn by a white majority to dilute the vote of black, Hispanic, or other minority voters. But in the 1990s, the phrase took on an alternate meaning: a majority–minority district drawn with "too much" emphasis on race, challengeable by white voters (usually) as a "reverse racial gerrymander." The theory here is similar to that used to challenge affirmative action plans.

The Supreme Court first recognized this new type of gerrymander in a 1993 case called *Shaw v. Reno* and a 1995 case called *Miller v. Johnson.*[20] *Shaw* held that a majority–minority district could violate the Fourteenth Amendment's Equal Protection Clause if the line-drawers used race too much. Significantly, this legal claim did *not* require a showing of any actual vote dilution—i.e., no showing that any group got X% of the vote but a substantially lower percentage of the seats. Indeed, in many of the early *Shaw*-style cases, white voters were *overrepresented* under a districting plan but still succeeded in getting a minority–majority district invalidated because it was oddly shaped.[21] According to the Court, the harm was not that white voting power was being diluted, but rather (i) such oddly shaped minority districts reinforced the "stigma" that all minority voters think alike ("stigmatic harm"); and (ii) they encouraged those elected to such districts to represent only their minority group rather than the district as a whole ("representational harm").[22]

Modern Election Law and Voting Rights (2012) (outlining the problems with single-member district remedies and arguing for alternative non-district remedies).

[20] Shaw v. Reno, 509 U.S. 630 (1993); Miller v. Johnson, 515 U.S. 900 (1995).

[21] Miller v. Johnson, 515 U.S. 900, 916 (1995); Bush v. Vera, 517 U.S. 952, 979 (1996); Shaw v. Hunt 517 U.S. 899, 900 (1996).

[22] *Shaw*, 509 U.S. at 647–648. These Court-identified harms were speculative at best. Whether prodded by Section 2 litigation, Section 5 preclearance objections, the threat of same, or similar policy concerns about minority vote dilution, such minority districts were almost always drawn after competent statistical evidence demonstrated racially polarized voting patterns, as discussed above. There is no "stigma" in recognizing this evident reality; if there were, all Section 2 and Section 5 enforcement actions would be unconstitutional. As to "representational harm," it is somewhat inconsistent and insulting to minority voters to suggest that their candidates of choice (who, after all, are just as motivated to ingratiate themselves to all voters in their district, the better to stay re-elected, as representatives in any other district) would ignore a significant minority within their district, but not to make that assumption about white-elected representatives in overwhelmingly white districts—or overwhelmingly Republican or Democratic districts, for that matter. More important, the representational harm would only make sense if the

Miller established the test used to determine whether a minority district ran afoul of the Constitution for these reasons. A (normally white) plaintiff seeking to challenge such a minority district had to make a preliminary showing, just as a minority plaintiff suing under Section 2 of the Voting Rights Act had to prove the *Gingles* preconditions. She would need to show that race was the "predominant factor" in drawing the district.[23] Although this could be done by showing direct evidence from the plan's legislative history—people saying on the record that their main goal with the district was to make sure it was majority-black, say—the more common method of demonstrating would be to prove that the challenged district's boundaries "subordinated [to race] traditional race-neutral districting principles," such as compactness, contiguity, respect for political subdivisions or communities defined by actual shared interests.[24]

As with the *Gingles* preconditions, if the plaintiff fails to prove this, she loses. If she does make this threshold showing, a court would then apply the stringent legal standard of "strict scrutiny" to the district. The redistricting plan would be presumptively unconstitutional and would survive judicial scrutiny only if the defendant jurisdiction could establish that the district boundaries were "narrowly tailored" to further a "compelling government interest." Although there is no final and comprehensive list of the governmental interests that would serve here, compliance with the Voting Rights Act is one such interest.[25] Remedying specific discrimination by the state in districting might be another. But an abstract desire to empower minorities because of historical societal discrimination would not.[26] To be "narrowly tailored" in this context means that race was used no more than necessary to further the relevant compelling government interest.

---

minority voters who elected these candidates pretty much thought alike—the very assumption the Court castigates as "stigma" in the first prong. *See Miller*, 515 U.S. at 929–931 (Stevens, J., dissenting) (making similar points). Given the problems inherent in unelected judges micromanaging the inherently political redistricting process, court intervention should be limited to instances where a concrete, tangible representational harm is proven—i.e. some mathematically measurable form of vote dilution.

[23]   The early cases dealt with black-majority districts, so the courts discussed the issue in terms of race. But the analysis would be the same for ethnicity, as with a district drawn to have a Hispanic majority.

[24]   *Miller*, 515 U.S. at 916–920. In later years, there was some confusion as to whether direct evidence of a predominant racial motive by itself would suffice, absent significant deviation from traditional race-neutral districting principles. But the Supreme Court recently clarified that it would suffice. Bethune-Hill v. Virginia State Board of Elections, 137 S. Ct. 788, 791–93 (2017).

[25]   *Bush*, 517 U.S. at 977.

[26]   *See Shaw*, 509 U.S. at 655–656.

This "strict scrutiny" standard is a tough one to meet. If a court adopts this standard, it will usually strike down whatever is being challenged. One oft-used formulation, not literally true but true enough to become an expression, is that this standard is "strict in theory but fatal in fact."[27]

Conservative opponents of this sort of districting affirmative action used the *Shaw/Miller* claim throughout the 1990s to strike down a number of minority–majority congressional districts.[28] The line of cases sharply curtailed the ability of legislators, litigants, and courts to create single-member districts providing racial and ethnic minority voters with a realistic chance to elect candidates of their choice.[29]

In the 21st century, the *Shaw/Miller* claim lost some of its salience. In part this was because plan-drawers adapted to the new regime, either drawing fewer minority–majority districts or drawing more nuanced minority-majority districts which would better pass judicial scrutiny. In part this was because of some relaxation of the strictness of the test on the part of the Court.[30] And in part this was because plan-drawers learned to characterize their plans as *partisan* gerrymanders rather than *racial* gerrymanders, thus immunizing them from judicial scrutiny.[31] *See infra*, Section C.

More recently, it has been Democratic plaintiffs, not conservatives, who have been using *Shaw/Miller* to challenge districts.[32] Republicans have learned how to draw minority–majority districts in such a way that they "bleach" surrounding districts, removing minority voters and making them majority conservative and Republican.[33] In some cases, Democrats

---

[27] *See* Gerald Gunther, *Forward: In Search of an Evolving Doctrine on a Changing Court: A Model for a Newer Equal Protection*, 86 HARVARD LAW REVIEW 1, 8 (1972–1973).
[28] *See, e.g.*, Abrams v. Johnson, 521 U.S. 74, 88–89 (1997); *Bush*, 517 U.S. at 957; *Shaw*, 517 U.S. at 920–921.
[29] *See* Mulroy, *Alternative Ways Out, supra*, 1876 (making this observation).
[30] *See* Lawyer v. Dept. of Justice, 521 U.S. 567, 580–583 (1997) (upholding majority-black state senate district under *Shaw* despite odd shape, noting that district was not more oddly shaped than white-majority state senate districts in recent redistricting plans). The author litigated this case at the trial level for the U.S. Justice Department.
[31] *See* Easley v. Cromartie, 532 U.S. 234, 259–267 (2001) (ruling that states could use race as a proxy for political party affiliation in drawing districts, avoiding invalidation under *Shaw*). This ability to avoid *Shaw* liability by using race as a proxy for party no longer applies. Cooper v. Harris, 137 S. Ct. 1455, 1481–1482 (2017).
[32] Erwin Chemerinsky, *Racial Gerrymander Can No Longer Be Justified as Proxy for Party Affiliation*, ABA JOURNAL (June 1, 2017), available at http://www.abajournal.com/news/article/chemerinsky_the_supreme_court_race_and_voting_districts.
[33] *See* Mulroy, *Alternative Ways Out, supra*, 1897–1898 (describing this phenomenon).

have alleged that Republican line-drawers have "packed" minority voters into a district to accentuate this effect, and they have challenged such districts under *Shaw/Miller* as using race more than necessary to draw the district.[34] Democrats recently won a significant victory in this vein, in a case apparently ending the Court-blessed practice of using race as a proxy for partisan gerrymandering.[35]

A more straightforward complaint by Democrats in this situation would be that the plans were an unfair partisan gerrymander. But since a 2004 Supreme Court case, a partisan gerrymander claim has been unavailable, forcing those wishing to challenge districting plans to focus on legal theories involving alleged racial gerrymanders (Section 2 of the Voting Rights Act, and *Shaw/Miller*).

Much of this sturm and drang of continued redistricting litigation, along with the uncertainty and constant partisan warfare it entails, would be avoided if jurisdictions used alternative electoral systems like the single transferable vote. These systems avoid minority vote dilution but raise none of the race-consciousness issues of *Shaw/Miller* because they do not involve race-based line-drawing. Indeed, they hardly involve line-drawing at all.

C.   PARTISAN GERRYMANDERS

An obvious potential remedy for partisan gerrymandering would be for the courts to intervene to stop it, as they have done extensively for decades in the case of racial gerrymandering. Indeed, in 1986, the Supreme Court ruled that partisan gerrymanders were unconstitutional and the courts could strike them down,[36] but the standard it set for liability was so high, and unclear, that no such legal challenge was ever successful.[37] In 2004, the Court reversed course, stating that partisan gerrymanders were a "nonjusticiable political question."[38] This referred to a little-used court doctrine, the "political question doctrine," reserved for those matters which are peculiarly appropriate for resolution by the political branches

---

[34]   *See* League of United Latin American Citizens v. Perry, 548 U.S. 399, 400 (2006); *see also* Alabama Legislative Black Caucus v. Alabama, 135 S. Ct. 1257, 1262–1263 (2015).

[35]   *Cooper*, 137 S. Ct. at 1481–1482.

[36]   Davis v Bandemer, 487 U.S. 109 (1986).

[37]   Vieth v. Jubilerer, 541 U.S. 267, 283–284 (2004) (plurality opinion) (discussing the lack of clarity in the *Bandemer* standard, and plaintiffs' lack of success under the standard).

[38]   *Id.*

(the executive and legislature) and peculiarly inappropriate for judicial resolution. In the modern era, this doctrine has been applied only to foreign policy and military matters.[39] The application to these areas is unsurprising, given that among the factors courts are to consider in deciding whether something is a "political question" are whether there is an unusual need for deference to the other branches, and/or an unusual need for uniformity among the branches[40]—both of which are often present when the federal government is working on the international stage in military actions or sensitive diplomacy.

But in an unusual move, *Vieth* applied the "political question doctrine" to partisan gerrymandering because of another of the recognized "political question" factors to be considered: the absence of "judicially manageable standards."[41] The issue here is, what objective, concrete, easily quantifiable standards can courts use to decide how much use of partisanship in a redistricting plan is too much? If it is instead merely to be a subjective judgment call, then that judgment call should be left to the elected representatives of the people rather than unelected, life-tenured judges. (Never mind that the elected representatives in question have a clear bias when they are drawing their own district lines, and a similar bias when they are deciding whether their party will benefit in U.S. House representation through the redistricting plan.)

Back when the Court first intervened in *apportionment* cases, addressing complaints that votes were diluted because some legislative districts were several times larger in population than other districts, a clear, simple, mathematical standard was available. The Court simply adopted the principle of "one person, one vote," requiring that district populations be roughly equal.[42] According to *Vieth*, no such ready standard was available for partisan gerrymandering.

This reasoning was highly questionable. The Court already had established judicially manageable standards for racial gerrymandering cases.

---

[39] *See e.g.*, Smith v. Obama, 405 U.S. 676, 684 (2016) (holding that whether military campaign in Iraq and Syria was illegal was a nonjusticiable political question). *See also* United States v. Prince, 398 F.2d 686, 688 (2d Cir. 1968) (same, for the legality of the Vietnam War); United States v. Hogans, 369 F.2d 359, 360 (2d Cir. 1966) (same).

[40] Baker v. Carr, 369 U.S. 186, 216 (1962) (listing factors to be considered).

[41] *Vieth*, 541 U.S. at 280.

[42] Reynolds v. Sims, 377 U.S. 533, 560–561 (1964). Actually, though, the Court rejected an argument that malapportionment cases were "political questions" years before it ever settled on the "one person, one vote" standard. *See Baker*, 369 U.S. at 260, suggesting that you do not need to have the mathematical formulae set in stone before you can recognize that court intervention is necessary.

Under the Voting Rights Act, plaintiffs showed that a politically cohesive minority group was underrepresented in a given districting plan from a votes-to-seats perspective,[43] and pointed to a history where their candidates of choice could not be elected. They then proffered illustrative alternative redistricting maps with compact minority districts, demonstrating that such underrepresentation was readily remediable. Under *Shaw/ Miller*, plaintiffs demonstrated how a district subordinated traditional race-neutral traditional districting principles to race, at which point the burden shifted to the government to demonstrate that the district's use of race was narrowly tailored to further a recognized compelling government interest.

The Court rejected the use of a *Shaw/Miller*-type test to suss out whether there was an *intent* to partisan-gerrymander. It reasoned that *Shaw/Miller* focused on a particular district, while a partisan gerrymander claim would necessarily have to focus on a statewide plan. But there is no reason why this needs to be the case. Even when assessing a statewide plan, one still needs to look at the contours of individual districts in that plan to assess the extent to which traditional districting principles have been subverted for partisan aims. Using a *Shaw/Miller* type of analysis could certainly assist in the process.

The Court also rejected a proposed test for a gerrymandering *effect*: i.e., that the plan prevents the majority party from controlling a majority of seats.[44] The Court responded that (a) there is no entitlement under the law to proportional representation, and (b) there was no clear way to determine which party was the majority party.[45]

This reasoning is even more suspect. It is undeniably true that there is no federal law guarantee that a political party can get proportional representation—i.e., control of a number of seats proportional to its share of votes. But that lack of proportionality can happen for benign or malign reasons, and courts are not powerless to distinguish between the two. If districts drawn with an eye toward compactness, fairness to racial/ethnic minorities, respect for political subdivision boundaries, ease

---

[43] While courts may not have used the exact phrase "votes to seats," they discussed a "proportionality" analysis comparing the minority's share of the electorate with control of districts under a challenged plan, which is effectively the same thing. *See Gingles*, 478 U.S. at 84; Johnson v. DeGrandy, 512 U.S. 997, 1000, 1014 (1994).

[44] *Vieth*, 541 U.S. at 286–287 (plurality opinion). This "majority votes/majority seats" test was proposed by the plaintiffs in the case. *Id.* The dissent proposed it as a possible test as well. *Id.* at 366 (Breyer, J., dissenting).

[45] *Vieth*, 541 U.S. at 288 (plurality opinion).

of incumbent–constituent interaction, etc. happen to result in a party getting one or two seats fewer than its proportional share, that is a more tolerable situation. That does not mean that a deliberate effort by the party in charge of redistricting to severely underrepresent a rival party, through demonstrable partisan-motivated district lines which significantly depart from that state's traditional party-neutral districting criteria, must be immune from constitutional scrutiny.

The exact analogous situation occurs regarding minority vote dilution. All acknowledge that racial and ethnic minority groups are not entitled to proportional representation. It is certainly true that the Constitution does not require such proportional representation. And the Voting Rights Act specifically provides that the Act does not entitle any group to proportional representation.[46] But while there was no rigid requirement of proportionality as a "floor," the Supreme Court acknowledged in *Gingles* that courts "must necessarily rely" on a measure comparing percentage control of districts to percentage of the electorate.[47] In *Johnson v. DeGrandy*, the Court rejected a Section 2 claim precisely because the existing plan provided "rough proportionality" to Latinos.[48] The Court stated that a lack of proportionality was "relevant" in evaluating a Section 2 claim and referred to "proportionality" repeatedly in explaining how to evaluate a vote dilution claim.[49] Significant underrepresentation from a vote-seats perspective would be an argument for liability, while overrepresentation would be an argument against. Writing for the Court, Justice Souter memorably explained that "one may suspect vote dilution from political famine," although not necessarily "from a mere failure to provide a political feast."[50] One can use a (non-rigid) proportionality measure as a red flag for gerrymandering cases without enshrining it as an absolute requirement.

The second notion, that a court cannot tell which is the majority party, is even more fanciful. In states where voters register by party, one can look at statewide registration figures as an initial estimate. They are often lopsided enough to give a clear indication of the majority party, even accounting for the fact that some voters may switch party allegiance between registration and the election, or register "insincerely" out of a desire to participate in another party's primary election. Only a small

---

[46] 52 U.S.C. § 10301(b) (Westlaw through P.L. 150-90).

[47] *Gingles*, 478 U.S. at 84.

[48] Johnson v. DeGrandy, 512 U.S. 997, 1000 (1994).

[49] *Id.*

[50] *Id.* at 1017. *See also id.* at 1025 (O'Connor, J., concurring) (proportionality is "always relevant," and lack of proportionality is "probative evidence of dilution").

percentage of voters overall do either of these two things. Where registration by party is not available, or is distrusted for the above reasons, one can look at past elections in the jurisdiction for that legislative body and tally up the total statewide number of votes cast for all Democratic candidates and all Republican candidates.[51]

Any judge's reluctance to intervene in the inherently political process of redistricting is understandable and commendable. Federal judges are unelected and life-tenured. For them to invalidate any legislative act is inherently undemocratic. That is why restrictions are placed on the ability of federal courts to act: there must be a live, ripe "case or controversy" brought to the court by parties with legal standing and which comes within the court's legitimate jurisdiction, and the court's ruling must be necessary to resolve the dispute between the parties.[52] This reluctance goes double for intervening in reapportionment and redistricting, which the Court once famously described as a "political thicket" which courts should not enter.[53]

But actually, gerrymandering is an area uniquely *suitable* for judicial intervention because it is a distortion of the political process. In a famous and oft-quoted footnote in an old Supreme Court case, the Court provided three categories of cases where judicial intervention was particularly appropriate, despite its inevitable anti-democratic nature. One was a clear departure from the Constitution's text. The other two described situations where the political process could not be trusted to act properly. One of those two was where the legislation "restricts those political processes . . . which might ordinarily be expected to repeal undesirable legislation."[54] Gerrymandering is a classic example of this. By rigging the electoral system, gerrymanderers prevent the political process from acting organically to address the problem of gerrymandering.

Vieth's judicial abdication is even more troubling when compared to the aggressive role played by courts in *Shaw/Miller* cases. Courts there intervene even when there is no demonstrable vote dilution, no seats–votes disparity, and even when whites are *over*represented in the plan in question. Under the current law, if you show a court an oddly shaped congressional plan drawn to provide black voters a chance to select a candidate of choice for the first time since Reconstruction, it is presumptively unconstitutional

---

[51]   *See Vieth*, 541 U.S. at 365 (Breyer, J., dissenting) (making this point).

[52]   Alexander M. Bickel, THE LEAST DANGEROUS BRANCH: THE SUPREME COURT AT THE BAR OF POLITICS 114–117 (1986).

[53]   Colegrove v. Green, 528 U.S. 549, 556 (1946) (Frankfurter, J., writing for a plurality).

[54]   United States v. Carolene Products, Inc., 304 U.S. 144, 152 n. 4 (1938).

and will almost certainly be invalidated. Show a court an identically oddly shaped district drawn to protect a Democratic incumbent or screw over the Democrats, and it is immune from judicial scrutiny.

Fortunately, *Vieth* was not the final word for judicial review of gerrymandering. The opinion discussed above was a plurality opinion only, joined by only four Supreme Court Justices. The crucial fifth, swing vote, Justice Kennedy, wrote a separate concurrence, candidly stating that although he was greatly concerned about the modern practice of gerry-mandering, he was at a loss to identify judicially manageable standards; however, he remained open to the possibility that some could be identified later. So, in his view, partisan gerrymandering was not subject to judicial review at the present time but might become so once again if a proper measurement for gerrymandering were proposed.[55] This sparked a hunt by academics and gerrymandering activists to find the elusive quantifiable measure of gerrymandering that would satisfy Justice Kennedy.[56]

The Court tantalized gerrymander reformers by taking two cases in 2018 which provided the potential for letting the courts correct partisan gerrymandering. Alas, in both cases, the Court punted.

In *Gill v. Whitford*, the Court dealt with a Republican-drawn Wisconsin state legislative redistricting plan where Republicans won 60% of the State Assembly seats with 48.6% of the vote. The three-judge district court below had found that Republicans had deliberately "packed and cracked Democrats throughout the state" in order to ensure Republican control for a decade.[57] Rather than relying solely on a discrimination-focused, equal-weight-for-equal-votes-type claim drawing on the Constitution's Equal Protection Clause, the plaintiffs also tried to advance the relatively novel theory that the partisan gerrymander represented retaliation against Democratic voters in violation of the First Amendment. Plaintiffs' experts relied on the statistical "efficiency gap" analysis (see Chapter 4, Section C) to prove a partisan gerrymander; the defendants' experts countered with evidence suggesting that the pro-GOP skew of the map was simply due to demographic clustering. The lower court found for plaintiffs, specifically

---

[55]   *Vieth*, 541 U.S. at 306–309, 310, 317 (Kennedy, J., concurring).

[56]   *See, e.g.*, Michael S. Kang, *When Courts Won't Make Law: Partisan Gerrymandering and a Structural Approach to the Law of Democracy*, 68 OHIO STATE LAW JOURNAL 1097, 1105–1106 (2007); Nicholas O. Stephanopoulos, *Partisan Gerrymandering and the Efficiency Gap*, 82 UNIVERSITY OF CHICAGO LAW REVIEW 831, 834 (2015); Benjamin Plener Cover, *Quantifying Partisan Gerrymandering: An Evaluation of the Efficiency Gap Proposal*, 70 STANFORD LAW REVIEW 1131, 1135–1141 (2018).

[57]   Gill v. Whitford, 218 F. Supp. 3d 837, 896 (W.D. Wis. 2016).

identifying as the plaintiffs' legal injury their compromised ability to translate their votes into seats.[58]

The Supreme Court reversed. It rejected the efficiency gap as a measure on the ground that it measured the plan's overall, statewide skew. Instead, the Court held, a court must focus on a district-specific analysis. This was because in order to show legal *standing* to sue—the doctrine that someone must suffer a concrete, particularized injury different from citizens as a whole in order to have the right to sue someone—an *individual* plaintiff who lives in a *specific* district must allege and prove that her particular vote in that district is diluted by cracking and/or packing.[59] However, rather than simply dismiss the case, the Court remanded it back to the lower courts for further proceedings consistent with its opinion.[60] This will allow the plaintiffs to develop more district-specific evidence of individualized injury and to try to replace the efficiency gap with another mathematical measure that is more district focused. It will also allow them to seek a narrower remedy if necessary, one proposing various fixes to individual districts and not necessarily a statewide redo of the map[61]—although the retirement of swing vote Justice Kennedy has now lessened significantly their chances of success.

In the second case, Maryland Democrats, who represent about five-eighths of the state's voters, drew themselves 7 out of 8 congressional districts. The Court there remanded for further proceedings in light of *Gill*.[62]

This is all very misguided and fundamentally misses the point about gerrymandering. Justice Kagan, writing in *Gill* for the Court's four liberal Justices in a concurring opinion, usefully explains why. According to Kagan, if plaintiffs on remand could more fully articulate and prove a burden on their First Amendment "associational rights," their right to associate with fellow Democrats to seek statewide Democratic control, then that separate theory might not require district-specific injury. A Democratic activist, party official, elected official, or perhaps even the party itself might have standing to complain of such a party-tampering

---

[58]   *Gill*, 1939 S. Ct. 1916, 1923–1926 (2018).

[59]   Plaintiffs did include among their number some who lived in problematic districts who alleged specific packing and cracking. But, according to the Court, they did not follow up their allegations with specific proof at trial. *Id.* at 1931–1932. They will have an opportunity to do so on remand.

[60]   *Id.* at 1932–1934.

[61]   Of course, under the right facts, a plaintiff could prove an individualized, district-specific injury by introducing (at least in part) statewide evidence; and, if the proven district-specific cracking and packing were widespread enough, it is possible that only a statewide redraw of the map could cure it. *See id.* at 1936–1938 (Kagan, J., concurring).

[62]   Benisek v. Lamone, 138 S. Ct. 1942, 1944–1945 (2018).

gerrymander, even if they happened to reside in a district left untouched by cracking and packing.[63] Kagan should have added that despite the majority's apparent rejection of a statewide votes-to-seats analysis as the proper measure, it is really impossible to avoid using this measure as the touchstone for analysis here.

Worse, even Justice Kagan seemed to suggest that any legally cognizable gerrymandering claim would involve some evidence that the line-drawers *intended* to gerrymander.[64] But the "unintentional gerrymandering" stemming from Democratic voter "clustering" raises a significant question as to whether intent should be required for a court challenge. For example, Democrats certainly "cluster" in big cities in Florida. Even though Democrats in Florida consistently had more registered voters statewide and more votes statewide for President from the 1990s until 2016, Republicans controlled state legislative and congressional seats between 60 and 70%. This kind of persistent dilution of one party's votes might arguably be a cause for judicial concern even if it were the product of "clustering" as opposed to intentional gerrymandering.[65] Amended Section 2 of the Voting Rights Act established that if the election system imposed a significant *racially* vote-dilutive effect, it is irrelevant if it was intentional; it needs to be fixed. So too could Supreme Court jurisprudence recognize that a redistricting map's demonstrated *significant* partisan bias was unconstitutional, irrespective of its cause. It should do that, but is unlikely to.

D. THE ULTIMATE INSUFFICIENCY OF JUDICIAL REVIEW

Regardless of the exact standard, if any, which the courts eventually adopt, the measure will never be enough. Judicial policing of gerrymandering, while welcome if it ever comes, will not fully address the problem. The Court, legitimately concerned about unelected judges interfering in the political process, will likely be very cautious in applying its judicial scrutiny, even if it decides to get into the "political thicket." Since the Supreme Court first began exploring the question of partisan gerrymandering in 1986, neither it nor any lower court has ever once struck down a

---

[63] *Gill*, 1939 S. Ct. 1916, 1936–1940 (2018). In other cases, of course, as in *Benisek*, it could be Republican activists and officials who could make this claim.

[64] *Id.* at 1937. The lower court in *Gill* had adopted a standard with such a requirement. *Id.* at 1925.

[65] *See* Ho, *Two Fs for Formalism, supra*, 413 (raising this question).

redistricting plan for being too partisan. Thus, the standard resulting from *Gill* would sniff out only the most severe gerrymandering.

During oral argument in *Gill*, Justice Breyer, one of the four most judicial-policing-friendly Justices, attempted such a formulation, which required, among other things, that any partisan leanings be both "persistent" and "extreme."[66] Similarly, leading experts formulating mathematical measures of partisan gerrymandering have proposed tests to see whether a challenged plan is an "extreme outlier."[67] The efficiency gap formula itself would have declared only 5 States' plans gerrymanders.[68] So even in the unlikely event that the Court rides in to the rescue, there will still be many gerrymanders left untouched by the federal courts.

Another reason to avoid depending on judicial policing of gerrymanders is that it is inherently reactive and takes too long to take effect. The Texas redistricting is a good example. The 2010 round of redistricting there, for both congressional and state legislative districts, is one of the most notorious of the last decade. Clear indications existed showing both intentional partisan gerrymandering and intentional racial discrimination in the plans, as lower courts repeatedly found. However, the cases have made their way up and down through the appellate court system several times, and are still unresolved. Because of the delay, it is unlikely that a remedial replacement redistricting plan can be put into effect before 2020, the last elections before the next round of redistricting—meaning that the plans will have been litigated for a full decade.

Indeed, as of this writing, 8 years into the 2010 decade, and 2 years before the next Census triggers another redistricting round, electoral maps in 8 states are still tied up in redistricting litigation. The litigation includes one lawsuit each in Maryland, Michigan, Texas, and Wisconsin, as well as 2 separate lawsuits in Georgia, 3 in North Carolina, and 4 in Pennsylvania.[69]

---

[66]   Transcript of Oral Argument at 12, Gill v. Whitford, 138 S. Ct. 52 (2017) (No. 16-1161), 2017 WL 4517131, at 11, 12.

[67]   Bruce E. Cain et al., *An Unreasonable Bias Approach to Gerrymandering: Using Automated Plan Generation to Evaluate Redistricting Protocols*, 59 WILLIAM & MARY LAW REVIEW 19 (forthcoming 2018) available at http://cho.pol.illinois. edu/wendy/papers/WMredist.pdf; Erica Klarreich, *Gerrymandering Is Illegal, But Only Mathematicians Can Prove It*, WIRED (April 16, 2017), available at https:// www.wired.com/2017/04/gerrymandering-illegal-mathematicians-can-prove/.

[68]   Nate Cohn & Quactrung Bui, *How the New Math of Gerrymandering Works*, NEW YORK TIMES: THE UPSHOT (Oct. 3, 2017), available at https://www.nytimes. com/interactive/2017/10/03/upshot/how-the-new-math-of-gerrymandering-works-supreme-court.html.

[69]   For a summary of the various cases with links to the pleadings, see Michael

A more effective long-term reform would be to take districting out of the hands of partisan state legislator incumbents who are naturally tempted to try to maximize the advantage for themselves and their personal colleagues (when they draw their own state legislative district lines) or their party generally (when they draw congressional lines). We could follow the course of almost all developed democracies, and follow the lead of several pathbreaking U.S. states, and transfer this function to nonpartisan redistricting commissions. If it worked as planned, this proactive approach would prevent the gerrymanders from occurring in the first place, which would certainly be better than providing an after-the-fact remedy for those with the resources and patience to file and follow through with years of litigation.

The questions would then become, how to structure it, and, would it be enough by itself to solve the problem?

Li, Thomas Wolf, & Alexis Farmer, *The State of Redistricting Litigation*, BRENNAN CENTER FOR JUSTICE, available at https://www.brennancenter.org/print/17671.

6. Nonpartisan redistricting commissions

A. INTERNATIONALLY

Among all the advanced democracies using single-member districts (SMDs) at the national level, all except the U.S. use redistricting commissions to draw the lines. This is part of a growing global consensus. Most of these countries used to draw districts the way we did prior to the "one-person, one-vote" judicial revolution, with legislators drawing their own district lines relatively free from judicial oversight. Notably, Canada, the U.K., and Ireland did so until court decisions in the 1960s through 1980s caused the invalidation of redistricting plans and strict judicial oversight. A similar pattern occurred in countries as diverse as France and Japan. In all these instances, the countries gave up the litigation-heavy model of politician-drawn maps for one of independent redistricting commissions. These plans can be challenged in court but are subject to highly deferential review; most court challenges are unsuccessful, and therefore very rare.[1]

Under the best version of this model, the commissions are truly independent from partisan political control. They are made up of nonpartisan government officials, judges, academics, or other experts who are appointed to the position. Some countries allow elected members of the legislature to be members of the commission but many do not. As another sign of independence, the commissions' plans ideally go into effect without the need for legislative approval, as in Australia, India, and New Zealand. Even where commission-drawn plans must be approved by the legislature to go into effect, as in the U.K., Canada, and France, the approval is *pro forma*, with legislative objections rare.[2]

In the various countries using these commissions, the actual drawing of the lines typically is left to individual experts like demographers, car-

---

[1] Nicholas Stephanopoulos, *Our Electoral Exceptionalism*, 80 UNIVERSITY OF CHICAGO LAW REVIEW 769, 773–83 (2013).

[2] Christopher S. Elmendorf, *Representation Reinforcement through Advisory Commissions: The Case of Election Law*, 80 NEW YORK UNIVERSITY LAW REVIEW 1366, 1388 (2005).

tographers, and statisticians. There are multiple opportunities for public notice and comment. After the plans come out, there is surprisingly little litigation because the courts have proven to be very deferential to this non-political process, much more so than with prior plans drawn by legislators. Litigation challenges to commission-drawn districting plans have failed in England, Canada, Australia, India, New Zealand, Ireland, and France, with the courts making their deference express by either praising the superior expertise of the commissions or explicitly calling for deferential legal standards of review.[3]

Most useful as models for the U.S. are federated nations like our own, where there is a national commission drawing maps for the national legislature and state or province commissions drawing maps at the lower level. In Australia, for example, there is a national, nonpartisan Australian Electoral Commission made up of a retired judge, a professional statistician, and another government official, all appointed posts.[4] Working with other professional nonpartisan appointed officials like the Surveyor-General and Auditor-General, they decide on a first draft of the House district lines, without using political data. They allow for public notice and comment before finalizing the maps. Electoral Commissions with roughly the same structure exist in each state for drawing state legislative districts.

The plans that emerge from the commission processes have less partisan bias, as measured from a votes-seats perspective. Quebec's 1972 adoption of commission districting reduced its partisan bias by almost half.[5] The Australian states of South Australia and Queensland saw pronounced drops in partisan bias levels once they adopted the commission approach, from almost 20 percentage points to about 6 points.[6] A 2013 study by University of Chicago law professor Nicholas Stephanopoulos, the co-developer of the "efficiency gap" measure of gerrymandering (see Chapter 5), found that Australian district plans generally (all now commission drawn) had partisan bias about one-third lower than American plans. This result also obtained when one looked at the efficiency gap as an alternative measure of partisan fairness.[7] More recent national House elections in

---

[3] *See* Stephanopoulos, *Our Electoral Exceptionalism*, *supra* 785–787 (citing cases).
[4] Commonwealth Electoral Act 1918 s. 5 (Aust.).
[5] Alan Siaroff, *Electoral Bias in Quebec Since 1936*, 4 CANADIAN POLITICAL SCIENCE REVIEW 62, 66–67 (2010).
[6] *See* Simon Jackman, *Measuring Electoral Bias: Australia, 1949–93*, 24 BRITISH JOURNAL OF POLITICAL SCIENCE 319, 345 (1994).
[7] Nicholas Stephanopoulos, *The Consequences of Consequentialist Criteria*, 3 UNIVERSITY OF CALIFORNIA IRVINE LAW REVIEW 669, 704 (2013).

Australia show that the share of seats by the two major parties, Labor and Liberal, match closely to their respective shares of the two-party vote.[8] In the last 10 years, the deviation has averaged 1.75 percentage points, never going above 9.8 percentage points.

Note, though, that while these studies show that commissions can reduce partisan bias, they do not tend to eliminate it completely. Occasionally, the deviation of seats from votes spikes to levels which most fair observers would find troubling. This underscores that disproportionate results are inherent in a districting system. A deviation of 5 or 6 percentage points is not uncommon, sometimes more. While this may at first not seem like much, it can make a real difference in two-party systems, where the major parties' respective total vote percentages are frequently within this range.

Indeed, even the national Australian Electoral Commission, pretty much the gold standard when it comes to nonpartisan, professional redistricting, has drawn plans which failed the basic "majority rule" criterion. In 1990, the Liberal Party won a majority of the two-party vote in its SMD House election, yet the Labor Party took a majority of the seats. In 1998, that situation reversed. This failure to even avoid minority rule is especially problematic for a parliamentary system like Australia's, where the majority of seats determines who will run the executive branch as well. This "majority loses" scenario happened recently in South Australia, even though its state constitution had explicitly provided that redistricting plans should meet the majority rule criterion. As commendable as Australia's system is, it cannot escape the inherent disproportionalities caused by carving a jurisdiction up into SMDs.

B.   IN THE U.S.

Currently, 37 state legislatures draw their own district lines, and 42 state legislatures draw congressional district lines.

A few reform-minded states have created independent redistricting commissions to draw the lines. These commissions have no legislators or other public officials as members, just a group of citizens balanced by party who are prohibited (at least for a set number of years) from taking advantage of the redistricting plan they create by running for office in such a district. Arizona, California, Idaho, Montana, and Washington have such commissions.

---

[8]   In systems like Australia where third parties can play a nontrivial role, a more helpful measure of the "majority rule" criterion is to measure the controlling party's share of the two-party vote.

There are hybrid models in between. For example, some states have commissions or boards which allow elected officials to be members. Arkansas, Colorado, Missouri, and Pennsylvania do this only for their own state legislative district lines, while Hawaii and New Jersey do this for both their own lines and U.S. House district lines. As another variation, 5 states (Iowa, Maine, New York, Rhode Island, and Vermont) have advisory commissions that report to the state legislature. Seven states (Connecticut, Illinois, Maryland, Mississippi, Oklahoma, Oregon, and Texas) have backup commissions which take charge of redistricting if the state legislature fails to do so by the relevant deadline. (This would happen most typically if the two chambers and governor were not all of the same party and they were hopelessly deadlocked.)[9]

Redistricting commissions seem to be an increasingly popular model. Ohio in 2018 added requirements of bipartisan support for congressional districting, and had already been using a commission with elected official members to draw state legislative lines. The November 2018 ballot saw citizen initiatives in 4 states which would adopt citizen-only nonpartisan redistricting commissions, which would replace traditional legislative redistricting (Michigan and Utah) or elected official-member commissions drawing state legislative districts only (Colorado and Missouri) with citizen commissions for congressional as well as state legislative line-drawing. And movements are afoot to pass similar measures in Pennsylvania and Virginia.[10]

Commissions which allow an equal number of Democratic and Republican appointees, along with some number of non-aligned tiebreaker members, are "bipartisan" commissions. By contrast, "nonpartisan" commissions require all members to be unaffiliated with a political party.

Iowa is the U.S. poster child for the independent redistricting approach. Since 1980, maps have been drawn by a nonpartisan group of technical civil servants working for the Legislative Service Agency (LSA).[11] These are legislative staff who in non-redistricting years do research and draft legislative language for legislators of both parties. They report to an advisory commission made up by 2 Democrats and 2 Republicans appointed by legislative leaders, and a final member selected by the first 4 members.

---

[9] Justin Levitt & Michael P. McDonald, *Taking the "Re" Out of Redistricting: State Constitutional Provisions on Redistricting Timing*, 95 GEORGETOWN LAW JOURNAL 1247, 1275 (2007).

[10] Alexis Farmer & Annie Lo, *Citizen And Legislative Efforts To Reform Redistricting in 2018*, BRENNAN CENTER (June 20, 2108), available at https://www.brennancenter.org/analysis/current-citizen-efforts-reform-redistricting.

[11] *See* IOWA CODE § 2B.12 (2014).

The commission holds public hearings, takes public input, and advises the LSA, but it is only the LSA that draws maps—the commission does not see drafts prior to them being made public. The staff drawing the plan must strive for equality of district population, compactness, and respect for county and city boundaries. They cannot look at political data or incumbent residences.[12]

Once the LSA and advisory commission finalize a plan, the legislature must approve their effort. If it does not, it can require the staff to send them a second, and if necessary a third, plan, but each successive plan's districts must be more equal in overall population. If the legislature rejects the third plan, the state supreme court has authority to act.

Since 1980, the process has worked relatively free form partisan rancor and with a high degree of trust by political leaders and the public. The legislature has never gone past the "third plan" stage, and has usually accepted the first or second submitted plan. In the 4 redistricting cycles since then, the state legislative plans varied from partisan bias of 1 or 2 percent (1982 & 2002) to bias of 5 or 6 percent (1992 & 2012). In the last 3 redistricting cycles, the bias has been pro-Republican.[13] An improvement over purely political line-drawing, to be sure, but still occasionally a nontrivial deviation from popular will.

C.   ONE-AND-A-HALF CHEERS FOR U.S. REDISTRICTING COMMISSIONS

Our home-grown redistricting commissions do seem to be improving the landscape somewhat with respect to partisan bias, though not as dramatically as those overseas. One study, focusing only on California's 2012 state legislative and congressional elections, the first after its adoption of commission districting, found that partisan bias dropped from about 5% to almost zero. But later assessments of later elections showed

---

[12] While this ban on use of political data may seem salutary, there is reason to question it. Enforced blindness to the political implications of line-drawing can lead to unintentional partisan bias in maps. It also makes it harder to ensure that districts are competitive. *See* Eric McGhee, ASSESSING CALIFORNIA'S REDISTRICTING COMMISSION: EFFECTS ON PARTISAN FAIRNESS AND COMPETITIVENESS, Public Policy Institute of California 3 (2018) available at http://www.ppic.org/wp-content/uploads/r-0317emr.pdf (recommending that California's commission should use partisan data to help them produce competitive and fair maps).

[13] *Id.* (noting that U.S. House plans have higher partisan bias, and state legislative plans have lower competitiveness, than other states, including a 17-point bias favoring Democrats in 2014).

greater partisan bias, in some cases above the national average.[14] And in an earlier and more comprehensive study of 2002 election results in 50 state legislative chambers, 26 states showed a median partisan bias of 4.7 percentage points in commission states, compared to 8.6 points in non-commission states.[15] This is an improvement, to be sure, but one that still left partisan bias remaining. And a later study of the 1992–2012 electoral period found no significant effect on partisan bias in state legislative *or* congressional elections.[16]

The outlook is similarly muddy when we use the "efficiency gap" (see Chapter 5) rather than simple partisan bias as our measure of gerrymandering. Efficiency gap creator Nicholas Stephanopoulos' 2015 study showed a median efficiency gap of 12% for legislator-drawn plans using this measure, compared to 6% for commission-drawn plans. That same study concluded that commissions "have not helped much" when it comes to the redrawing of state legislative district lines.[17] These mixed results certainly suggest an improvement, but only a slight one, and one that leaves a nontrivial bias remaining.

How about competitiveness? Putting aside partisan fairness, do redistricting commissions at least increase the number of competitive districts? The answer is similarly muddled. Certainly, they help somewhat. Australian commission-drawn districts tend to be more competitive than their legislator-drawn American counterparts, for example.[18] In the U.S., several studies suggest that commission-drawn U.S. districts are more likely to be contested and less likely to be decided by a whopping landslide margin.[19]

---

[14] *See* PlanScore, Iowa State Houses, available at https://planscore.org/iowa/#!1984-plan-statehouse-pb.

[15] Bruce E. Cain et al., *Redistricting and Electoral Competitiveness in State Legislative Elections* 2 (Apr. 13, 2007), (unpublished paper) (on file with the UC IRVINE LAW REVIEW).

[16] Stephanopoulos, *The Consequences of Consequentialist Criteria, supra*, 710–711.

[17] Nicholas Stephanopoulos, *Arizona and Anti-Reform*, 2015 UNIVERSITY OF CHICAGO LEGAL FORUM 477, 482 (2016). These results obtained only when considering presidential election results as an indicator of partisan preference among voters. Using congressional election results, there was no statistically significant improvement of commission-drawn plans over legislator-drawn plans.

[18] Stephanopoulos, *The Consequences of Consequentialist Criteria, supra*, 704.

[19] Cain et al., *Redistricting and Electoral Competitiveness, supra*, 2–3 (using 10-point margin as measure of landslide); Jamie Carson & Michael Crespin, *The Effect of State Redistricting Methods on Electoral Competition in United States House of Representatives Races*, 4 STATE POLITICS & POLICY QUARTERLY 455, 461–462 (2004) (20-point margin). However, at least one study concluded the exact opposite. *See* Seth E. Masket et al., *The Gerrymanders Are Coming! Legislative*

But this does not seem to have actually decreased in any significant way the rates of incumbent reelection, which continue to be at eye-popping over-90% levels.[20] One can justifiably wonder how significant an improvement on competition we have if unseating an incumbent remains a freakish occurrence.[21]

Redistricting commission misfires aren't just limited to a 5% or so deviation from partisan fairness perfection. Just as in Australia, commission-drawn plans can still violate the majority control criterion. Arizona is a good example. By voter registration, the party is about 35% Republican, 30% Democratic and 34% independent. Democrats thus represent about 47% of the two-party vote. In the post-2010 redistricting, Arizona's 5-member commission (2 Democrats and 2 Republicans appointed by legislative leaders, and 1 independent selected by the other 4 members) created a map with 4 safe Republican seats, 2 safe Democratic seats, and 3 competitive seats. Its congressional delegation switched from 5–4 Democratic to 5–4 Republican from election to election, moving with national tides in partisan opinion. This would seem to be an improvement over the lopsided wins given Republicans in the late 20th century under legislator-drawn plans.

But the results overrepresented Democrats: in 2012, they earned fewer statewide votes than Republicans and yet won a majority of congressional seats.[22] Arizona Republicans charged, with some legitimacy, that at least 2 and arguably all 3 of the nominal "competitive" districts actually favored

---

Redistricting Won't Affect Competition or Polarization Much, No Matter Who Does It, 45 POLITICAL SCIENCE & POLICY 39, 41 (2012).

[20]   James B. Cottrill, *The Effects of Non-Legislative Approaches to Redistricting on Competition in Congressional Districts*, 44 POLITY 32, 45 (2012).

[21]   Some may say that incumbents' high rate of reelection simply reflects that incumbents know how to cater to constituent attitudes, and that constituents genuinely like them. Indeed, for years survey data has shown that Americans hold Congress as a body in contempt while reporting that they like their individual Representative. *See, e.g.*, Elizabeth Mendes, *Americans Down on Congress, OK with Own Representative*, GALLUP (May 9, 2013), available at http://news.gallup.com/poll/162362/americans-down-congress-own-representative.aspx; Noah Berlatsky, *Everybody Hates Congress. So Why Do Congressmen Almost Always Get Re-elected?*, THE WEEK, Mar. 31, 2016, available at http://theweek.com/articles/615133/everybody-hates-congress-why-congressmen-almost-always-reelected. Others may argue that it is incumbency benefits other than gerrymandering, like name recognition and campaign finance advantages, which explain the high retention rate. Whatever the explanation(s), redistricting commissions do not seem to have moved the needle in any real way on the extraordinary job security of the incumbent U.S. House member.

[22]   It is of course true that winning a majority of congressional seats in a state is not nearly as politically significant as winning a majority of seats in a state legislature. The latter actually matters in terms of which party controls a state's legislative agenda. The former is simply symbolic as control of the House will be based on which party wins more seats nationwide. However, as a means of measuring "partisan

Democrats. The controversy wound up in the courts halfway into the decade. While the courts ultimately upheld the plan, judges concluded that pro-Democratic partisanship did play a role in the creation of at least one congressional district.[23] The controversy uncovered evidence that Democratic commissioners were secretly consulting with Democratic Party officials. One victorious Democratic House incumbent publicly boasted on election night of deliberate efforts to pack Hispanic voters into a district to assist Democrats.[24] And Arizona is not the only such example: a commission-drawn plan violated the majority control criterion in New Jersey in 2013, under a plan with fewer competitive districts and lower turnout.[25] One-and-a-half cheers, indeed.

What to make of all this? Clearly, nonpartisan redistricting commissions are an improvement over our current politician-led method of redistricting. This is especially true where many or all of the members are nonpartisan representatives rather than partisan elected officials, and where specific redistricting criteria cabin the commissioners' discretion. Commissions can help to reduce the skew, but are not a complete solution. And, perhaps because of the greater extent of demographic clustering in the U.S., that lukewarm assessment is even more apt for U.S. redistricting commissions than their overseas counterparts.

Perhaps for that reason, commission-drawn plans fare somewhat better than legislator-drawn plans in court challenges, but not as dramatically so as overseas plans. Over the last half-century, U.S. courts upheld 76% of challenged commission-drawn plans—better than the 65% survival rate of other U.S. plans, but not as good as the rarely-invalidated foreign plans.[26]

---

fairness versus gerrymander" for a given state's congressional redistricting plan, it is useful to see whether the plan passes the basic test of the majority control criterion.

[23]   *Harris v. Arizona Independent Redistricting Comm'n*, 993 F. Supp. 2d 1042, 1046 (D. Ariz. 2014).

[24]   Dave Daley, RATF**KED 173 (2016) (citing Rebekah L. Sanders, *Arizona Election Adds to Debate Over Redistricting*, ARIZONA REPUBLIC (Nov. 23, 2012)).

[25]   Mark J. Magyar, *Redistricting Reform In New Jersey*, New Jersey Spotlight (Dec. 2011/Jan. 2012), at 3, available at http://www.njlmef.org/policy-papers/FoLG_v3_4_Magyar.pdf.

[26]   Stephanopoulos, *Our Electoral Exceptionalism*, *supra*, 780. The tendency of courts to be more skeptical of legislator-drawn plans is understandable, given the natural conflict of interest involved when partisan legislators draw their own districts, or draw districts affecting partisan control of Congress. In corporate law, this kind of "self-dealing" by corporate officers is subject to much stricter review. The normally deferential "business judgment rule" does not apply—unless the decision was ratified by a neutral body like the shareholders. By analogy, one can see the rationale for greater judicial deference for plans approved by legislatures if they were also drawn or approved by a nonpartisan redistricting commission.

Public opinion seems to reflect the overall (and sensible) view that redistricting commissions are better than the systems they replace, but still far from completely satisfying. Voters in commission states have more faith in the fairness of their system, but cynicism and skepticism remain. In one study, public faith that redistricting was carried out "fairly" was only at 25% in non-commission states, and almost doubled in commission states. But, at 45%, it was still less than half of respondents.[27]

D.   THE "GAP" IN COMMISSION-BASED REFORM

The failure of redistricting commissions to eliminate completely representational anomalies, or to restore entirely public faith in redistricting, is understandable. It's not just because the particular models of redistricting commission we have adopted in the U.S. have insufficiently insulated the decision-makers from partisan influences. If that were the case, then simply redoubling our efforts at perfecting the redistricting commission models, and/or the implementation thereof, would be all that we would need to consider.

Instead, we must consider two other factors. One is the demographic phenomenon of "clustering," discussed in Chapter 4. It is an undeniable reality that Americans have been sorting themselves ideologically in their migration patterns, with more and more progressives and Democrats moving into urban areas, and more and more conservatives and Republicans moving to rural and exurban areas. This drives a wedge between the redistricting goals of compactness and population equality, on the one hand, and partisan fairness, on the other.[28] As discussed in Chapter 4, there is a partisan imbalance in our redistricting plans that is not attributable to intentional gerrymandering, one partially attributable to the Great Sorting In-Migration of the last half-century.[29]

See D. Theodore Rave, *Politicians as Fiduciaries*, 126 HARVARD LAW REVIEW 671 (2013) (making this argument).

[27]   Joshua Fougere et al., *Partisanship, Public Opinion, And Redistricting*, 9 ELECTION LAW JOURNAL 325, 335 (2010).

[28]   *See also* Vladmir Kogan & Eric McGhee, *Redistricting California: An Evaluation of the Citizens Commission Final Plans*, 4 CALIFORNIA JOURNAL OF POLITICS & POLICY 1, 26–27 (2012) (describing the inherent tension between respect for racial/ethnic fairness and political subdivision boundaries, on the one hand, and competitiveness, on the other).

[29]   *Id.* ("self-sorting" limits the effectiveness of any redistricting process, "no matter how fair or nonpartisan").

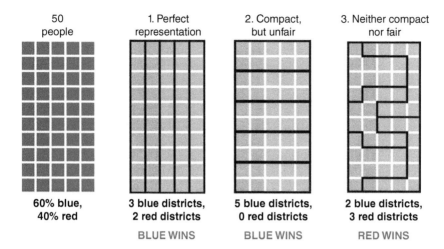

Figure 6.1   Gerrymandering, explained: three different ways to divide 50 people into 5 districts

Thus, while nonpartisan redistricting commissions, like judicial policing of gerrymandering, are certainly worthy things, they are not an adequate solution to the problem of fair representation. This is because they fail to address clustering, certainly. But it is also because they fail to address an even more fundamental underlying problem, one which would persist even if the "Big Sort" of the last 50 years were to evaporate: the inherently disproportionate nature of districting.

Figure 6.1 illustrates the point. In a hypothetical jurisdiction which is 60% Blue and 40% Red, there are various ways to draw the lines. Plan 3 on the far right is an obvious gerrymander: the lines zig and zag, Blue has 60% of the votes yet only 40% of the seats, and it fails the majority control criterion. But Plan 2 is really not much better: it satisfies majority control, but gives a 60% majority 100% of the seats and completely shuts out a significant 40% minority, masking the gerrymander with compact districts. Under the prevailing conventional wisdom, we are supposed to favor Plan 1, which yields proportional representation using compact districts.

But even this solution is far from perfect because it has zero competitive districts. Each general election will be a foregone conclusion. The only real competition will occur in the primary, meaning that candidates will be incentivized to play to the extremes of left and right, with no incentive to compromise. In the real world, no district will be 100% "Blue" or 100% "Red," but there can be districts which are over 65%, 70%, or 75% of one party. In such instances, the minority party voters within each district (e.g.,

Blue voters in the first 2 columns, Red voters in the last 3 columns) will have no incentive to participate, and no one to represent them. So even in the (highly unlikely) scenario where SMDs are drawn with such fairness, wisdom, and nuance as to eliminate all partisan bias, such partisan bias will be at war with true competition.

This is why redistricting commission rules which forbid consideration of partisanship in their criteria, or which would call for purely random redistricting, which some have actually proposed, would not work either. Sure, someone could program a computer to draw equipopulous districts, perhaps minimizing city/county splits and/or irregularity of shape, spin the roulette wheel, and let the chips fall where they may. But chances are you will end up with a plan that has either low competition, high partisan bias, or both. If you must draw a SMD plan, you are better off *not* being blind to partisan data, lest you create these problems.

At bottom, districting creates an unnecessary and intractable problem: that of "getting it right" representation-wise while balancing multiple, often conflicting criteria. Partisan fairness, competitive districts, contiguity, compactness, respect for political subdivisions—all are important, all point in different directions, and all must bow to the federal law imperatives of equality of population and racial/ethnic fairness. Something—usually several somethings—has got to give.

Indeed, there is an inherent incompatibility between drawing a "competitive" plan and a party-representative one. Reformers often complain (probably legitimately) about the fact that over 95% of House incumbents win reelection, even though voters view Congress unfavorably.[30] But if commissioners try to draw competitive, "swing" districts, there's a problem. If a state is 70% Democratic and 30% Republican, partisan fairness demands that roughly 70% of its congressional seats would be Democratic controlled and 30% of its seats GOP controlled. You can't do that and have competitive, 50–50 districts. The more you draw competitive districts, the more you will veer away from overall partisan fairness.

One's first instinct is to suggest a map that has a roughly proportional number of Democratic-leaning districts, a roughly proportional number of Republican-leaning districts, and then a few competitive swing districts. For example, in a state with 12 districts that is 60% Republican, one could draw 6 GOP districts, 4 Democratic districts, and 2 competitive

[30] Chris Cillizza, *People Hate Congress. But Most Incumbents Get Re-elected. What Gives?*, Washington Post (May 9, 2013), available at https://www.washingtonpost.com/news/the-fix/wp/2013/05/09/people-hate-congress-but-most-incumbents-get-re-elected-what-gives/?utm_term=.38637ec984d2.

districts. But it is almost never that simple. Since districts must be equal in population, contiguous, and normally *somewhat* compact (or at least not extremely bizarrely shaped), and since Democrats and Republicans tend to cluster, it becomes very difficult, if not impossible, to square that circle. Squaring the circle becomes more difficult as the number of districts gets smaller, because you have fewer districts to work with, and the mirroring of district-based results to statewide voter preferences becomes cruder. The average number of House districts in a state is 11; half the states have 7 or fewer. And even when you do square that circle, you still have only 1 or 2 competitive districts per state to show for it, which means no significant increase over the current system, which has about that number.

The same tension exists when you consider fair representation of minorities. As discussed in Chapter 5, the Voting Rights Act requires the drawing of minority–majority districts when certain conditions are met. Even when such districts are not legally required, they are a good thing for plan-drawers to strive for, in the name of diversity and fairness to racial and ethnic minorities, especially where voting patterns are racially polarized. But drawing such districts often means sacrificing partisan fairness, or compactness of districts, or both.[31] Drawing a plan that would be racially/ethnically fair, free of partisan bias, and full of non-bizarrely shaped equipopulous districts featuring at least a few competitive districts, would be quite a feat. At day's end, something always has to give.[32]

We know this because many people have tried. In 2018, for example, experts at FiveThirtyEight's Gerrymandering Project drew 7 nationwide House maps, using a different set of criteria as the primary guide. These included maps driven by such criteria as partisan proportionality, competitive districts, majority–minority districts, compactness, and compactness plus respect for county boundaries. The maps varied significantly in configuration, as well as their scores using the rival criteria. But all showed similar tensions. As the number of competitive districts increased, so did partisan bias, over and above the "natural" pro-GOP bias of 7 seats which the Project arrived at (acknowledging demographic clustering). Increasing the number of districts controlled by racial and ethnic minorities also

---

[31]   *See, e.g.*, Aaron Bycoffe et al., *The Atlas of Redistricting*, FIVETHIRTYEIGHT (Jan. 25, 2018), available at https://projects.fivethirtyeight.com/redistricting-maps/ (illustrating this point with examples). *See also* Kogan & McGhee, *Redistricting California, supra*, 26–27 (maximizing respect for racial/ethnic fairness and political subdivision boundaries makes achieving other goals like competitiveness difficult to achieve; "self-sorting" limits how much the redistricting process can achieve).

[32]   *See* Kogan & McGhee, *Redistricting California, supra*, 26–27 (even with professional nonpartisan redistricting, "there will always be winners and losers").

increased the pro-Republican partisan bias. Minimizing partisan bias reduced opportunities for racial and ethnic minorities. The contrasts were most dire when compactness was considered. Drawing a map dedicated to compact districts increased the number of competitive districts from the current 72 to a far healthier 104, but at the cost of increasing the pro-GOP bias from 7 seats to 29.[33]

These tensions are seen in the real world as well as in simulations, and can illustrate the problems with redistricting reforms which attempt to impose party-neutral criteria like compactness, contiguity, and respect for political subdivision boundaries. For example, voter initiatives in Florida, Amendments 5 & 6, took this approach. A coalition of left-wing interest groups concerned about pro-Republican electoral bias in redistricting placed these measures on the ballot in 2010, and they passed. But they have not worked out as hoped, due at least in part to the inherent pro-Republican bias of the compactness requirement in Florida caused by the over-concentration of Democratic voters in urban areas.[34] Florida is Ground Zero for the Big Sort.

And the Big Sort is responsible for a lack of competition as well as partisan bias. FiveThirtyEighty contributors have noted the overall decline in the number of competitive districts over the past 20 years, but concluded that only 17% of that decline was the result of redistricting decisions. The rest was a natural by-product of demographic clustering.[35]

This chapter goes through this exercise at some length to illustrate that redistricting is like trying to smooth a plastic cover over a table when you've got air trapped inside. Push down one part to smooth it out, and a bubble pops up elsewhere. Something always has to give.

Finally, even if lightning struck, and you managed to draw a plan that ideally balanced all these competing considerations, population shifts will make your masterpiece obsolete within 10 years. At which point, the whole expensive, protracted, divisive ordeal begins anew.

There must be a better way. The path to that better way may go through Ranked Choice Voting. The next chapter introduces Ranked Choice Voting in detail through its most simple variety: Instant Runoff Voting.

---

[33] FiveThirtyEight, *The Gerrymandering Project*, available at http://fivethirty eight.com/tag/the-gerrymandering-project/.

[34] Jowei Chen & Jonathan Rodden, *Unintentional Gerrymandering: Political Geography and Electoral Bias in Legislatures*, 8 QUARTERLY JOURNAL OF POLITICAL SCIENCE 239, 240 (2013).

[35] *See* Harry Enten, *Ending Gerrymandering Won't Fix What Ails America*, FIVETHIRTYEIGHT (Jan. 26, 2018), available at https://fivethirtyeight.com/features/ending-gerrymandering-wont-fix-what-ails-america/.

7.   Instant Runoff Voting

A.   THE FLAWS OF PLURALITY VOTING AND REGULAR RUNOFF ELECTIONS

1.   Plurality Voting

When we hold elections at-large or in single-member districts (SMDs), we have a choice between requiring a candidate to earn majority support (more than half of the overall vote), or allowing someone with less than a majority to win. If there are 3 or more candidates, it is possible for no one candidate to win a majority.[1] In the U.S., the oldest and most common system used is the plurality, or "first past the post" system, in which the candidate with the most votes wins, even if they do not achieve a majority of the vote.[2] This is the oldest electoral method, and the simplest.[3] We inherited it from England.[4]

However, it is problematic, because it allows for the "spoiler" or "vote-splitting" problem: if too many candidates sharing the views of the majority run, the majority's vote is split, allowing a candidate who may be the *least* preferred by the majority to squeak by with, say, 38% of the vote. Indeed, political scientists routinely rank plurality low among electoral systems when scored as accurately reflecting the popular will.[5]

---

[1]   Actually, this can happen in a race with only 2 candidates if there are a significant number of write-in votes, but this is rare.

[2]   *See generally Electoral Systems*, ACE PROJECT, available at http://aceproject. org/main/english/es/esd01.htm.

[3]   *Boundary Delimitation*, ACE PROJECT, available at http://aceproject.org/ main/english/bd/bda01a.htm.

[4]   While plurality has ancient roots internationally, it was far from the uniform practice in early America. Requiring a majority was the norm, even though a "top two" runoff election was impossible due to the lack of a government-printed ballot. As a result, state legislative and congressional elections would be declared failed if there was no majority winner, and the entire election would be held again weeks later, with all original candidates. The very first congressional elections in 1789 saw Massachusetts hold 5 separate rounds of election before a majority winner finally emerged in May 1789.

[5]   Charles King, ELECTORAL SYSTEMS (2000) available at http://faculty.geor getown.edu/kingch/Electoral_Systems.htm.

This is how Donald Trump came to be the Republican presidential nominee in 2016, by winning the early, crucial GOP primaries. The first 25 primaries, the ones which allowed Trump to move from novelty candidate to front-runner and then presumptive nominee, were almost all plurality winner-take-all elections, and in none of them did Trump win a majority.[6] Contemporaneous polling showed that GOP primary voters overall ranked Trump pretty low. Under either an instant runoff system or head-to-head matches, Trump would have lost to either Senator Ted Cruz or Senator Marco Rubio but because voters could only vote for one candidate and neither Cruz nor Rubio would drop out of the race, primary election after primary election saw their joint support split between them, allowing Trump to win the lion's share of delegates with low pluralities.[7]

This same dynamic occurs when third-party candidates play the role of "spoiler." For example, Ralph Nader played this role in Florida in 2000. The center-left Florida vote, a majority of the state, was split between Nader and Gore. Enough voters chose Nader to give Bush the edge (at least under the official, disputed certified vote count).[8] Jill Stein played the same Ralph Nader "spoiler" role in 2016, garnering enough votes to throw the key states of Pennsylvania, Michigan, and Wisconsin to Trump.[9]

2. Regular Runoff Elections

The other common form of winner-take-all system would require a majority of the vote to win. If no candidate achieves a majority, the top 2 vote-getters advance to a second round of elections some time later.[10] This

---

[6]   *CNN Delegate Estimate*, CNN POLITICS, available at https://www.cnn.com/election/2016/primaries/parties/republican.

[7]   Rob Richie, *Trump Moves into Majority Position in GOP Nomination Contest*, FAIRVOTE (Mar. 23, 2016), available at http://www.fairvote.org/trump_moves_into_majority_position_in_gop_nomination_contest.

[8]   2000 PRESIDENTIAL GENERAL ELECTION RESULTS–FLORIDA, available at https://uselectionatlas.org/RESULTS/state.php?year=2000&fips=12.

[9]   German Lopez, *Green Party Candidate Jill Stein Got More Votes than Trump's Victory Margin in 3 Key States*, VOX (Dec. 1, 2016), available at https://www.vox.com/policy-and-politics/2016/12/1/13811344/jill-stein-clinton-trump-nader-spoiler. Of course, we don't know for sure to what extent Nader and Stein voters would have also supported Gore and Clinton, respectively, but it is a fair inference. And there were right-of-center candidates who could have conceivably done the same to Bush and Trump had the election gone differently. At any rate, third party candidates are certainly perceived as playing the spoiler role, unnecessarily stigmatizing them.

[10]   *See generally, Electoral Systems*, ACE PROJECT, available at http://aceproject.org/ace-en/topics/es/ese/ese01/ese01b (providing examples of countries that use two-round election systems).

system is used widely in the U.S. and also internationally—for example, in the French presidential election.[11]

This can be an improvement over the plurality, winner-take-all system, but only barely; in some situations, it could arguably be considered worse. Like all winner-take-all systems, it can lead to disproportionate results from a votes-seats perspective. In France, it has resulted in the most disproportionate results of any Western democracy.[12] It is also more expensive and cumbersome for election administrators and voters because of the need to hold a separate, second election shortly after the first.

Further, it does not entirely fix the "vote-splitting" problem. To be sure, when a crowded field of candidates splits the vote, offering the voters a choice between the top 2 vote-getters in a final round would often allow voters to choose at least one candidate with broad majority support. If this system had been used in early 2016 GOP presidential primaries, for example, it is likely that there would have been runoffs between Trump and Rubio, or between Trump and Cruz; that Trump would have lost most of these runoffs; and that a majority of voters would have been satisfied with the final result, leading to the nomination of a less polarizing consensus candidate.

But two-round elections don't *always* fix this problem. For example, California has a "Top Two" system in which all candidates of all parties run together in a blanket "jungle" primary, with the top 2 vote-getters, regardless of party, advancing to the general election.[13] In 2018, many Democratic-majority districts had a plethora of Democratic jungle primary candidates, raising the specter that they would split the vote and allow 2 Republican candidates to advance to the general. This would force the majority of voters in the districts, who are Democrats, to have to choose between their 2 least-favorite candidates, electing a candidate strongly disliked by a significant majority of voters.

This fear was not speculative: in 2012, 4 Democratic candidates split the vote and allowed 2 Republicans to advance to the final round,

---

[11] Adam Taylor, *What You Need to Know about the French Presidential Election*, THE WASHINGTON POST (Apr. 23, 2017), available at https://www.washingtonpost.com/news/worldviews/wp/2017/04/20/a-guide-to-the-french-elections/?utm_term =.59680ebe16be.

[12] *Electoral Systems*, ACE PROJECT, available at https://aceproject.org/ace-en/topics/es/esd/esd01/esd01e/esd01e01.

[13] California's "Top Two" system isn't exactly a "runoff," because the top two still advance to the general election even if one of them acquired a majority. But California's two-round system still demonstrates the persistence of the vote-splitting problem.

electing a Republican in a district with a 15-percentage point advantage for Democrats in registered voters.[14] The next blanket primary election in 2014 came within a percentage point of repeating this result.[15] The prospect was serious enough in 2018 to cause the Democratic National Committee to take the unusual step of intervening in Democratic primary elections, trying to pressure Democratic candidates to withdraw and, when that didn't work, openly backing individual Democratic candidates against fellow Democratic candidates in the Democratic primaries.[16]

Aside from the trouble and expense of holding a second election, a runoff system also commonly sees significant declines in turnout from the first election to the runoff.[17] In Memphis, Tennessee, which has for years been delaying implementation of an instant runoff system decisively adopted via referendum in 2008,[18] this turnout drop-off is one of the most severe in the country. Approximately 28% of voters participate in the first round, yet only 5% participate in the runoff[19]—and that 5% is dispropor-

---

[14]   *See* Ballotpedia, *California's 31st Congressional District Elections, 2012*, available at https://ballotpedia.org/California%27s_31st_Congressional_District_electi ons,_2012.

[15]   Lily Mihalik, Anthony Pesce, & Ben Welsh, *California 2014 Primary Election Complete Results*, LOS ANGELES TIMES (June 3, 2014), available at http://graphics.latimes.com/calif-primary-election-results-2014/.

[16]   Alex Burns, *Fearing Chaos, National Democrats Plunge into Midterm Primary*, NEW YORK TIMES (Apr. 22, 2018), available at https://www.nytimes.com/2018/04/21/us/politics/democrats-house-midtermsalifornia.html?rref=collection%2Fsectionco llection%2Fus&action=click&contentCollection=us&region=stream&module=str eam_unit&version=latest&contentPlacement=8&pgtype=sectionfront.

[17]   Steven Wright, *Voter Turnout in Runoff Elections*, 51 JOURNAL OF POLITICS 385, 387–388 (1989) (finding that 77% of U.S. congressional and gubernatorial Democratic primaries between 1956 and 1984 showed turnout drop-offs in runoff elections; in "standalone" runoffs in SMDs unaccompanied by a high-profile statewide race, the turnout declined by over a third). In California-style two-round elections where the first round is a free-for-all primary, it is the first round that shows the low turnout. *See*, Jennifer Pae, *California's Top-Two Blues, and How to Break Out of Them*, FAIRVOTE CA (Sep. 8, 2017), available at http://www.fairvoteca.org/california_top_two_blues. Either way, forcing voters unnecessarily to go to the polls twice is going to depress overall turnout, leading to a decline in the number of voters participating both overall and at a key decision point.

[18]   Bill Dries, *Instant Runoff Voting Could Be in City's Future*, MEMPHIS DAILY NEWS (May 21, 2008), available at https://www.memphisdailynews.com/news/2008/may/21/instant-runoff-voting-could-be-in-citys-future/ (implementation of 2008 adoption delayed).

[19]   *See* SHELBY COUNTY ELECTION COMMISSION, STATEMENT OF VOTES CAST FOR PRECINCT, ALL COUNTER, ALL RACES (2015), available at https://www.shel byvote.com/sites/default/files/documents/elections/2015/Memphis%20City%20 Election/2015%20Memphis%20Municipal%20SOVC%20with%20Provisional_

tionately white and affluent. North Carolina's turnout has been as low as 1.8% in a statewide partisan primary runoff.[20] A turnout that low in the final round is subject to greater manipulation by well-financed candidates who can fund election-day get-out-the-vote efforts.

A more fundamental problem is the arbitrariness of limiting the final round to the top 2 candidates. While the selection of the top 2 has some intuitive appeal, and of course is necessary in order to guarantee that the final winner will receive a majority of the votes cast one election day,[21] it might not be the result most reflective of the popular will. Imagine a competitive four-way race among an extreme left, extreme right, and 2 moderate candidates. These candidates could receive, say, 27%, 26%, 25%, and 22% of the vote, respectively. But the more popular of the 2 moderates (with 25%) might be the second choice of *all* the other candidates' voters. Clearly the consensus candidate, she probably deserves to win. But under the regular runoff system, the voters are forced needlessly to choose between two very unpalatable options, extremes of the left and right whom distinct but overlapping majorities would point to as their least-favorite, "anybody but them" candidate.[22]

A different version of this vote-splitting scenario happens in California's Top Two system: the 2 candidates advancing to the general are sometimes both Democrats.[23] This was the case in California's Senate election. The millions of California voters statewide who preferred a Republican had no one reflecting their views in debates and no one to vote for on the ballot.[24]

And, just like with plurality elections, regular runoffs choke off the potential of third-party candidates (or, in nonpartisan elections, the less

---

RN746.pdf; Shelby County Election Commission, Statement of Votes Cast, Memphis Municipal Run-off Elections (2015), available at https://www.shel byvote.com/sites/default/files/documents/elections/2015/Memphis%20Run%20 Off%2011.19.15/SOVC%20Memphis%20Run-off%2011-3_RN767.pdf.

[20] North Carolina State Board of Elections, *Second Primary Election June 24, 2008*, available at http://results.enr.clarityelections.com/NC/4541/80793/en/summary.html.

[21] Of course, it is not really a guarantee, because of write-in votes, but it's pretty close.

[22] The plurality system would of course be even worse under this scenario, resulting in the automatic election of the extreme left candidate with only 27% of the vote.

[23] *See* Jonathan Nagler, *Voter Behavior in California's Top Two Primary*, 7 California Journal of Politics & Policy 2 (2015).

[24] John Myers, *Two Democrats Will Face Off for California's U.S. Senate Seat, Marking First Time a Republican Will Not Be in Contention*, Los Angeles Times (June 8, 2016), available at http://www.latimes.com/politics/la-pol-ca-senate-primary-election-20160607-snap-story.html.

establishment-oriented candidates). Scholars generally agree that winner-take-all elections of all stripes entrench the major parties' control and discourage the development of third parties.[25]

It is of course possible to spin hypothetical scenarios in any electoral system in which the outcome seems anomalous or undesirable. Indeed, the famed political scientist Kenneth Arrow proved mathematically that no election system (including plurality, regular runoffs, and Ranked Choice Voting) is perfect. His famous "Arrow's Impossibility Theorem" holds that given at least 3 candidates, you can always come up with a set of hypothetical voter preferences in any election system that theoretically could lead to anomalous results.[26] The theoretical possibility of anomalous results should not be enough to reject an electoral method, particularly one with a long history of U.S. use.

But the scenarios described above are not fanciful; they happen. More important, even if they were relatively rare, they are not *necessary*. That is, we do not need to put up with the possibility of these undemocratic

---

[25] *See, e.g.*, Michael S. Kang, *Sore Loser Laws and Democratic Contestation*, 99 GEORGETOWN LAW JOURNAL 1013, 1014 (2011).

[26] KENNETH ARROW, SOCIAL CHOICE AND INDIVIDUAL VALUES (2d ed. 1963). An "anomalous" result would include, for example, where increasing your support for a candidate can actually backfire and harm that candidate; or where increasing one's support for Candidate C affects whether you assist Candidate A or Candidate B, even though you clearly prefer A to B. Arrow's work earned him the Nobel Prize in Economics and spawned the modern discipline of "social choice theory."

Arrow excluded from his analysis systems like Range Voting, where voters gave a score (e.g., between 1 and 10) for candidates. Later scholars claim to have shown that Arrow's Theorem does not hold for such systems. Alan T. Sherman, Warren D. Smith, & Richard T. Carback III, *Scoring the Candidates*, MIT TECHNOLOGY REVIEW (Aug. 19, 2008), available at https://www.technologyreview.com/s/410622/scoring-the-candidates/; *see also* William Poundstone, GAMING THE VOTE: WHY ELECTIONS AREN'T FAIR (AND WHAT WE CAN DO ABOUT IT) 253–258 (2008). However, Range Voting, and other "cardinal" voting systems which let voters "grade" candidates on a scale, can suffer from their own anomalous results. For instance, there are plausible scenarios under which Range Voting will elect the "Condorcet loser" among a set of candidates—that is, the candidate that would lose to every single other candidate in the field head-to-head. *Cf.*, Michael Lewyn, *Two Cheers for Instant Runoff Voting*, 6 PHOENIX LAW REVIEW 117, 123–125 (2012) (showing how Condorcet winner can lose under Range Voting).

This book does not consider Range Voting, because (i) it has no track record of actual use anywhere in the modern world, and (ii) it is more vulnerable than RCV to manipulation by strategic voting. *See* Phil McKenna, *Vote of No Confidence*, 198 NEW SCIENTIST 30–33 (2008), available at https://www.sciencedirect.com/science/article/pii/S0262407908609148?via%3Dihub.

outcomes in order to get other benefits of the system, or to avoid other pitfalls of available alternatives. Limiting the voters' final choice to the top 2 candidates, even if a third-place challenger would have been the more popular consensus candidate, is *not*, in fact, a necessary evil because we have a viable alternative: Instant Runoff Voting (IRV), discussed briefly in Chapter 1.

B.   INSTANT RUNOFF VOTING[27]

As noted earlier, in IRV voters rank-order their candidate preferences.[28] Each vote initially counts for its first choice. If no one candidate receives a majority, the system eliminates the candidate with the fewest votes. If a voter's top choice is eliminated, their vote is added to the totals of their next candidate choice. If there is now a candidate with a majority, the system declares that candidate the winner. If not, the process of eliminating candidates round-by-round continues until a candidate wins with a majority.[29] Figure 7.1 illustrates a sample ballot for IRV. Figure 7.2 illustrates the vote-counting process.

Internationally, Australia has used IRV for almost a century to elect House members from SMDs at both the national and state level. Ireland and India both use it to elect their Presidents.[30] In the U.S., IRV has been

---

[27]   In the U.S., when RCV is used to select a single winner, it is "Instant Runoff Voting." Where it is used to fill multiple legislative seats in a single election, it is the "single transferable vote" (see Chapter 8). Both are forms of RCV. Abroad, IRV is sometimes referred to as the "alternative vote."

[28]   Usually, voters are allowed to (but not required to) provide as many rankings as there are candidates: If there are 12 candidates for a position, the voter could rank candidates from 1st through 12th preference; or rank, say, only the top 3 choices and leave all other spaces blank; or just indicate a preference for a single candidate. Some U.S. jurisdictions limit the number of choices—e.g., allowing voters to rank 1–3 only, even if there are 12 candidates. In Australia, many jurisdictions (including the national House) require that candidates rank all the way down for all listed candidates in order for the ballot to count. This is called "mandatory preference." Its only apparent advantage is that this minimizes "exhausted ballots" (*see* infra). This book advocates for maximum voter choice: in this case, that voters be free to rank as many or as few candidates as they wish.

[29]   If in the course of reassigning votes, a voter's 2nd choice is for a candidate who has already been eliminated in a previous round, then the voter's 3rd choice will be used. If the 3rd choice has also been previously eliminated, the 4th choice (if any) will be used, and so on. If all the choices on a ballot have been previously eliminated, the ballot is no longer counted; it is said to be an "exhausted" ballot.

[30]   There is a variation of IRV, sometimes called "the contingent vote,"

City Council						
Rank up to 6 candidates. Mark no more than 1 oval in each column.	First choice **1st**	Second choice **2nd**	Third choice **3rd**	Fourth choice **4th**	Fifth choice **5th**	Sixth choice **6th**
Valarie Altman Orange Party	◯	◯	◯	◯	◯	◯
George Hovis Yellow Party	◯	◯	◯	◯	◯	◯
Althea Sharp Purple Party	◯	◯	◯	◯	◯	◯
Mary Tawa Lime Party	◯	◯	◯	◯	◯	◯
Joe Lo Tan Party	◯	◯	◯	◯	◯	◯
Phil Wilkie Independent	◯	◯	◯	◯	◯	◯

Source: Whitney Quesenbery & Taaps Rarnchandani, Center For Civic Design. https://creativecommons.org/licenses/by/4.0/legalcode.

Figure 7.1   A sample Instant Runoff Voting ballot

used successfully for years in many cities, including Minneapolis (MN), Oakland (CA), Portland (ME), San Francisco (CA), and St. Paul (MN). As of this writing, IRV is in use in at least 11 cities or counties, with 4 more local jurisdictions scheduled to have their first use in the next few years, and proposals to adopt it are being considered in many more. Five states (Alabama, Arkansas, Louisiana, Mississippi, and South Carolina)

---

in which after the first round, all but the top 2 candidates are eliminated. The ballots for the eliminated candidates are redistributed among the remaining top 2 candidates only. This variation more closely simulates mathematically what actually happens in a regular runoff election. This method has been used in North Carolina. 2006 N.C. SESS. LAWS 192, available at https://www.ncga.state.nc.us/enactedlegislation/sessionlaws/html/2005-2006/sl2006-192.html. The contingent vote is an improvement over plurality because of the spoiler problem, and an improvement over regular runoffs because of the trouble, expense, and low turnout of regular runoffs. However, it is less preferable than the normal version of IRV, for the reasons described above about the problems in arbitrarily limiting the selection to the top 2 candidates.

Instant Runoff Voting

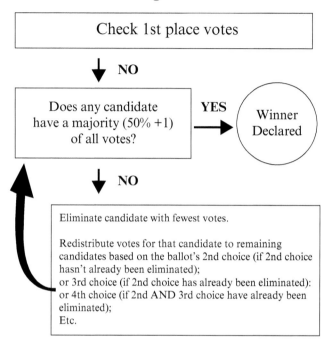

Figure 7.2   Flow chart for Instant Runoff Voting

use it for military and overseas voters, allowing them to participate in federal runoff elections without needing to mail a separate runoff ballot. The state Democratic Party of Texas and Iowa, as well as the Republican Party in Utah, use it for primary elections. In 2016, voters in a statewide referendum selected IRV to elect Maine's governor, state legislature, and members of Congress. It enjoyed its inaugural use in the 2018 elections.[31] Over 50 universities across the U.S. use it for student government elections. IRV is also the system used to select Oscar nominees and Heisman Trophy winners, and *Robert's Rules of Order* recommends it to select officeholders when voting must be conducted by mail.[32]

---

[31]   For an up-to-date list, see Ranked Choice Voting Resource Center, *Where Ranked Choice Voting Is Used*, available at https://www.rankedchoicevoting.org/where_used.

[32]   *Oscar's Instant Runoff*, USA TODAY (Mar. 5, 2010), available at https://usatoday30.usatoday.com/news/opinion/editorials/2010-03-05-editorial05_

IRV is ideal for single-office elections like mayor or district attorney. To fill *legislative* seats, multi-seat elections with proportional representation (PR) are generally preferable to SMD elections. But where a jurisdiction continues to use SMDs, either because of state law concerns, a well-considered preference for having some form of geography-based representation, easy constituent-incumbent interaction, or just plain inertia, then IRV is the best system. It avoids the "vote-splitting" problem of plurality elections and ensures that the winner enjoys majority support. It avoids the trouble, expense, and low turnout associated with regular runoffs, as well as the arbitrary limit in the final round between the top 2 candidates in the first round.

IRV also has other advantages. As discussed in Chapter 1, IRV gives third-party candidates in partisan elections a fighting chance: voters can risk voting for their favorite underdog or newcomer without worrying that they are "throwing away their vote";[33] if that candidate falls short and is eliminated, their votes will be transferred to their second choice. Similarly, even in nonpartisan elections, IRV lowers barriers to entry for first-time, lesser-known, and/or lesser-funded candidates. This makes elections more competitive, which boosts voter engagement and turnout. Indeed, cities using IRV have recently seen dramatic increases in turnout in municipal elections.[34]

ST2_N.htm; George Scoville, *Don't Let Politics Doom Instant Runoffs*, Commercial Appeal (Mar. 7, 2018), available at https://www.commercialappeal.com/story/opinion/contributors/2018/03/07/opinion-dont-let-politicians-kill-instant-run offs/395802002/; Robert's Rules of Order Newly Revised, Chapter XIII Sec 45.

[33] This regrettable dynamic of our current winner-take-all system was memorably illustrated in a 1996 Halloween episode of *The Simpsons* aired during the Bill Clinton–Bob Dole campaign. Evil aliens Kang and Kodos impersonate Clinton and Dole. On election eve, Homer unmasks them before a crowd of voters (including '90s third-party candidate Ross Perot). Kang tells them it's too late—he and Kodos have already been nominated. "What are you going to do," he scoffs, "throw away your vote on a third party?" The resigned crowd murmurs reluctant agreement with this fatalistic assessment, while a visibly frustrated Ross Perot angrily punches his fist through his straw hat. Later, when the newly elected President Kang has enslaved the human population, Homer says, "Don't blame me—I voted for Kodos."

[34] *See* City of Santa Fe, *Regular Municipal Election Results* (Mar. 6, 2018), available at https://www.santafenm.gov/media/files/Final Election Results.pdf (showing total turnout for mayor's race at 38% in 2018); Tripp Stelnicki, *Santa Fe Turns Out in City's First Choice Election*, The New Mexican (Mar. 5, 2018), available at http://www.santafenewmexican.com/news/local_news/santa-fe-turns-out-in-city-s-first-ranked-choice/article_b306198d-0542-50d2-9c77-157ff79e2780. html (noting last mayor's race had 29% turnout); City of Minneapolis, *Voter Turnout Information*, available at http://vote.minneapolismn.gov/rcv/index.htm

IRV also leads to better campaigning by discouraging attack-ad mud-slinging. Candidates want to be the first choice of their base, and the second choice of their rivals' bases. It's thus counterproductive to excoriate an opponent. Better to say to a rival candidate's supporters, "I respect that you may give Ms. Jones your first choice vote, but I'd sure appreciate your second choice vote." IRV thus leads to a more coalition-building campaign approach over a scorched-earth strategy, which is a healthier situation once the candidates take office and have to govern.[35] This has in fact been the campaign experience where IRV has been adopted.[36] Rutgers University polls in 2013 and 2014 of voters in 7 cities using IRV had voters reporting more positive campaigning, compared to voters in 14 cities using non-IRV methods.[37]

IRV should be the election system of choice whenever voters are choosing a single person to fill an office. States should use it to choose presidential

---

(showing turnout to be 78% in 2017 after adoption of IRV). *See e.g.*, James Walsh & Mary Smith, *Voter Turnout Surprises Twin Cities Poll Watchers*, STAR TRIBUNE (Nov. 7, 2017), available at http://www.startribune.com/voter-turnout-surprises-poll-watchers/455973653/ (stating turnout for pre-IRV Minneapolis municipal elections was 43%).

[35] Some opponents of IRV have criticized this very opportunity for cooperation among candidates, saying that candidates can engage in "collusion" and backroom deals to target incumbents. However, under RCV, this kind of cross-endorsement cannot work in secret: The voters must cooperate by ranking according to the cross-endorsement. Thus, these arrangements must be open and transparent, the opposite of "collusion" and backroom deals. Since voters are informed of the cross-endorsement arrangement, and are free to choose to follow or disregard the resulting suggestions for ranked choice ordering, this would be a salutary development rather than a sinister one. Contrast the situation with Australian STV Senate elections prior to 2016, where cross-party preference agreements were worked out among party leaders behind the scenes, and voters often voted just for the party and not for candidates. In this system, voters often did not fully appreciate the second- or third-round consequences of their votes, which could sometimes be counterintuitive (e.g., a progressive voter supporting the Labor Party would be surprised to find that Labor had struck a deal with a right-wing minor party). After the 2016 reforms, which required voters to affirmatively rank an alternate party as their second, third, etc. choice before their vote could be transferred, the system became more transparent, more intuitive, and far less subject to manipulation by party insiders.

[36] *Why Jurisdictions Adopt Ranked Choice Voting*, RANKED CHOICE VOTING RESOURCE CENTER, available at https://www.rankedchoicevoting.org/adopt.

[37] *Ranked Choice Voting and Civil Campaigning*, FAIRVOTE, available at http://www.fairvote.org/research_rcvcampaigncivility. This dynamic is not universal, however. It apparently did not much temper campaigning in Australia's 2007 election. *See* Michael Lewyn, *Two Cheers for Instant Runoff Voting*, 6 PHOENIX LAW REVIEW 117, 128–129 (2012).

candidates (see Chapter 2), U.S. Senators, governors, attorneys general, etc., and cities should use it to choose mayors. At the federal, state, and local level, where legislative seats are elected from SMDs, IRV would also be useful.

C.   OBJECTIONS TO INSTANT RUNOFF VOTING

One universal challenge of election reform is the reflexive resistance to change by officeholders to any proposed reform. Officials elected under the existing system have a natural wariness for changing the very system that elected them. They know how to play the current game: absent an obvious advantage for one's home team, why risk changing the rules? At times, the resistance can be sincere: there's a natural unconscious bias toward thinking that a system that elected you must be a very wise system indeed, and, to be fair, a natural resistance to the transition costs and potential confusion occasioned by any structural change, along with a healthy concern for unintended consequences.

IRV in the U.S. is a great example of this. Santa Fe, New Mexico adopted IRV via voter referendum back in 2008. The charter amendment passed with 65% voting in favor. However, to address the concerns of election administrators, it included a proviso, stating that it would only go into effect as soon as "equipment and software for tabulation of votes . . . is available at a reasonable price."[38] Although the equipment and software used in Santa Fe could have been used for RCV using a straightforward workaround, that language was interpreted to mean that the voting system must perform the entire tabulation from start to finish. For a decade, Santa Fe made no effort to acquire a voting system that would meet the requirements of its charter.

When the State of New Mexico decided to adopt a uniform voting system statewide that included readiness to run RCV elections, providing it to the city for free, the Santa Fe City Council brazenly voted that they would not implement RCV anyway, despite the dictates of the city charter. This led to a lawsuit brought by Santa Fe voters who wanted RCV implemented, which the city fought all the way to the State Supreme Court. Ultimately, Santa Fe was required to implement RCV for its March 2018 elections. Once implementation became inevitable, the city did a commendable job of implementing on a short timeline, and Santa Fe's first RCV election was a resounding success.[39]

---

[38]   Santa Fe, N.M. Mun. Charter, Art. IV § 4.06.
[39]   *See* Order Granting Peremptory Writ of Mandamus and Denying Motion to

In Maine, the state legislature legislatively blocked implementation of the 2016 referendum adopting IRV statewide, and state officials challenged its legality for use in state offices.[40] Voters had to produce over 80,000 petition signatures to force a second referendum in 2018 to repeal the legislature's repeal; that second referendum vote reaffirmed IRV by an even wider margin than the first. Maine finally began implementing IRV starting in 2018, and uses it for primary and general elections for the federal House and Senate.[41]

Memphis, Tennessee perhaps gets the award for the widest confederacy of the powers working to block IRV implementation. After voters approved IRV for City Council elections 71% in a 2008 referendum, the county election commission delayed implementation for 8 years, making the claim (later admitted to be inaccurate) that it could not implement IRV because of equipment issues. When a new election administrator announced in 2017 that implementation had been feasible all along[42] and that she planned to implement in the next City Council election in 2019, the City Council voted to place 2 different (and contradictory) IRV repeal referenda on the November 2018 ballot, one reinstating the former regular runoff system, the other providing for plurality elections. Not content with that, the City Council also quietly hired a lobbyist to persuade the state legislature to outlaw IRV statewide,[43] prompting a public outcry. That lobbying effort ultimately proved unsuccessful for that legislative session. In the meantime, the state election administrator, long an IRV opponent,

---

Dismiss and Motion for Relief from Judgment, State of New Mexico *ex rel* Maria Perez et al v. City Council of Santa Fe, Case No. D-101-CV-2017-02778, *petition for stay denied*, Santa Fe v. Thomson, No S-1-SC-36791 (N.M. Jan. 9, 2018); Tripp Stelnicki, *Court Clears Way for Ranked-Choice Voting in City Election*, THE NEW MEXICAN (Jan. 9, 2018), available at http://www.santafenewmexican. com/news/local_news/court-clears-way-for-ranked-choice-voting-in-city-election/ article_b12b039c-f590-11e7-b711-9f456ef43212.html.

[40]   Maine Senate v. Secretary of State, __ A.3d __, 2018 WL 1832874, *1–3, 7 (Maine Apr. 17, 2018).

[41]   Christopher Cousins, *Maine Again Backs Ranked-Choice Voting*, BANGOR DAILY NEWS (June 13, 2018), available at https://bangordailynews.com/2018/06/13/ politics/early-returns-show-evenly-split-electorate-on-ranked-choice-voting/.

[42]   Ryan Poe, *Memphis Will Scrap City Council Runoff Elections in 2019*, COMMERCIAL APPEAL (July 20, 2017), available at https://www.commercialappeal. com/story/news/politics/elections/2017/07/20/memphis-scrap-city-council-runoff -elections-2019/492299001/.

[43]   Ryan Poe, *Memphis City Council Quietly Works on Anti-Instant Runoffs Bill*, COMMERCIAL APPEAL (Feb. 19, 2018), available at https://www.commercialappeal. com/story/news/government/city/2018/02/19/memphis-council-quietly-works-an ti-instant-runoffs-bill/351732002/.

issued an opinion letter claiming (using strained interpretations of state election statutes) that state law forbade IRV.[44] That matter is currently being litigated.

Nonetheless, whether IRV's official opponents have in mind incumbency protection, inertia, or more sincere motivations, substantive objections to IRV exist.

Voter Confusion. The chief objection, common with all forms of RCV, is that voters will not understand how to rank their ballots. Australian experts scratch their heads at this argument: they've seen IRV successfully used for over a century, in a country where even the lowest-information voters are forced by law to vote.

The U.S. results are not much different: voter confusion is not a serious issue.[45] In the over 20 IRV elections held in 2014, for example, over 99% of voters cast a valid ballot. Polling firms find voters characterizing IRV as "simple" at 80 or 90% levels, with substantial majorities consistently reporting that they like IRV.[46] This holds even for the inaugural use of IRV, when voter confusion is presumably at its peak. Exit polling after Santa Fe's first use of IRV in 2018, for example, showed over 84% of voters finding IRV "not at all confusing" or "not too confusing."[47]

Election Administration Issues. Some opponents suggest that the multiple rounds of vote counting required under IRV will tax election administrators' ability, cause uncertainty, or unduly delay the reporting of results. Early on in IRV's adoption in the U.S., a few cities encountered such difficulties. But over the last 10 years, 15 cities and one state (North Carolina) have collectively conducted over 200 IRV elections without any significant election administration problems.[48]

---

[44] Ryan Poe, *State Official Questions Legality of Memphis Instant Runoffs*, COMMERCIAL APPEAL (Nov. 14, 2017), available at https://www.commercialappeal.com/story/news/politics/elections/2017/11/14/state-official-questions-legality-memphis-instant-runoffs/860092001/. The author is currently involved in local efforts advocating for IRV.

[45] *See* Michael Lewyn, *Two Cheers for Instant Runoff Voting*, 6 PHOENIX LAW REVIEW 117, 132–133 (2012) (collecting data sources).

[46] *Ranked Choice Voting and Civil Campaigning*, FAIRVOTE, available at http://www.fairvote.org/research_rcvcampaigncivility.

[47] FairVote, *Voters Liked Ranked Choice Voting in Santa Fe*, available at http://www.fairvote.org/fairvote_newmexico#2018_election.

[48] From 2008 to 2018, RCV elections have occurred in the following places: Berkeley (CA), Oakland (CA), San Francisco (CA), San Leandro (CA), Aspen (CO), Telluride (CO), Portland (ME), Takoma Park (MD), Minneapolis (MN), St. Paul (MN), Santa Fe (NM), Hendersonville (NC), Burlington (VT), and Pierce County (WA). North Carolina held a statewide RCV contest for a court of appeals vacancy in 2010.

Today, most voting machine systems now have optional RCV features as part of their systems. Some jurisdictions use off-the-shelf software to conduct the multiple rounds of calculations. Others use digital scanning technology of some kind to capture ballot images, and export the results into a spreadsheet like Excel to do the fairly simple (for a computer) RCV calculations. Either way, reliable results are reported on election night.

A few jurisdictions conduct manual counts of ballots, with final results reported either on election night or within a few days. Indeed, Australia has been conducting manual counts of IRV elections on a national level for many decades, reliably reporting results on election night. Compared to plurality systems, even a few days' wait does not seem too much to ask to ensure that the winner enjoys majority support, and is not the least preferred of the majority. And a few days' wait is still a quicker result than regular runoff elections, which postpone the final decision for many weeks so a second election can be held.

Cost of Voter Education. A related argument is that to avoid voter confusion, officials will have to do extensive voter education campaigns, driving up election administration costs. It is true that a robust voter education campaign would be a good idea, at least the first time that IRV is used in a jurisdiction. But such a campaign will still cost less than having to run a whole other, second election throughout that jurisdiction.

"Exhausted" Ballots. Critics also point to the risk that ballots will be "exhausted." This refers to the fact that if a voter ranks fewer candidates than the total that are on the ballot, leaving some lines on the ballot blank, and all candidates for which she expressed a preference end up being eliminated during early rounds, then there might be no preferences left to transfer over in the final rounds. At this point, the ballot is said to be "exhausted." In the U.S., this only happens to around 10–15% of ballots in RCV elections.[49]

Exhausted ballots are not ideal outcomes but they are largely under the voters' control, and at any rate are a minor phenomenon compared to the more common frustration of voter input present in competing systems. Where voters are allowed to rank "all the way down," any exhausted ballots are clearly the voters' choice. Even where the system allows voters to only rank a set number of preferences, exhausted ballots are still the exception rather than the rule, and preferable to the alternatives.

---

[49] Theodore Landsman, *RCV Elections and Runoffs: Exhausted Votes vs Exhausted Voters in the Bay Area*, FAIRVOTE (Oct. 19, 2016), available at http://www.fairvote.org/rcv_elections_and_runoffs_exhausted_votes_vs_exhausted_voters_in_the_bay_area (finding 12% rate of ballot exhaustion for set of RCV elections held in 4 California cities between 1995 and 2015).

Under plurality, voters are only allowed to express one preference. If they do not pick the winning candidate, the election ends, and their vote counts no more. We do not speak of this technically as an "exhausted" ballot, but the truncation of input from the voter ends up effectively the same.

Under regular runoffs, voters are only allowed to express 2 preferences, 1 in the first-round election, and 1 in the runoff. Again, after the second preference, the voter's input to the system ends. But under IRV, voters are allowed to express at least 3 preferences, and possibly more than that. If a ballot is ultimately exhausted, that is only because the voter chose losing candidates; just as with voters choosing losing candidates under plurality and regular runoff systems, their input ends—but after having more opportunities to affect the outcome.

The advantage of IRV becomes even clearer when one considers that many voters participating in the first-round election are not able to participate in the runoff round. As noted above, turnout from first round to runoff round drops significantly—varying from a 33% drop in cities like Santa Fe to the whopping 80% drop-off in Memphis, but in all cases far greater than the rate of exhausted ballots. There are many reasons for this drop-off but it seems like it is less of a conscious voter choice than the decision to rank, say, only 7 of 12 candidate spaces on a ballot. Since the turnout drop-off is most pronounced among lower socioeconomic levels,[50] surely major reasons include the difficulty of working people, persons juggling multiple jobs, persons with child care issues, etc., to make it back to the polls only a few weeks later on a workday.[51] Because of the dizzying array of primary and general elections held at the local, state, and federal level, voters are asked to return to the polls many times in an election cycle. Instead of exhausted ballots, we have exhausted voters. IRV eliminates this hurdle with "one-stop shopping," a voter-empowerment advantage far more significant as a practical matter than exhausted ballots.[52]

---

[50] *See, e.g.*, Pew Research Center, *Who Votes, Who Doesn't, and Why* (Oct. 18, 2006), available at http://www.people-press.org/2006/10/18/who-votes-who-doesnt-and-why/ (survey data showing "intermittent" voters are disproportionately minority and low-income, among other factors).

[51] *See* George Scoville, *Don't Let Politics Doom Instant Runoffs*, COMMERCIAL APPEAL (Mar. 7, 2018), available at https://www.commercialappeal.com/story/opinion/contributors/2018/03/07/opinion-dont-let-politicians-kill-instant-runoffs/395802002/ (making this argument).

[52] One can also object that IRV is not truly a majority-guarantee system, because if there is a significant number of exhausted ballots, then the candidate could win in the final round with a number of votes less than the total number of votes cast back in the first round. While this can happen, the number of votes for

Repeal by Some Jurisdictions. IRV critics also point to the 5 local jurisdictions which have repealed IRV as evidence that the above problems must be salient. However, the number of U.S. local jurisdictions which have retained IRV far exceeds the small number which repealed it. More important, the repeals often occurred for reasons unrelated to a principled, merits-based objection to IRV.[53] For example, voters in Ann Arbor, Michigan adopted and quickly repealed IRV in the 1970s after it resulted in the election of the city's first African-American mayor.[54] In Burlington, Vermont and Pierce County, Washington, IRV's ability to elect third-party candidates played a role in motivating a successful joint effort of both major parties to repeal it.[55] In Pierce County, a quirk of local law and election administration required the use of a separate ballot for IRV, which irritated voters.[56]

D. CONCLUSION

Where IRV has been used in the U.S. so far, it has been used at the local level. Starting in 2018, Maine has used it for federal elections to the U.S. House and Senate. While moving to IRV would be a salutary reform, even IRV retains the essential winner-take-all aspect of our election system. To really provide for fair representation, we need PR, and to get PR, we need to move to some form of multimember district system.[57] The next chapter discusses such systems.

---

the IRV winning candidate is still more likely to be a majority of total first-round votes than would be the case for the winner under a two-round system, given the substantial drop-off in turnout between the first round and the runoff. *See* Lewyn, *Two Cheers for Instant Runoff Voting, supra*, 131–132. And the IRV winner is certainly more likely to have a majority of first-round votes than under a straight plurality system.

[53] *See id.* at 135–136.

[54] *The History of IRV*, FAIRVOTE, available at http://archive.fairvote.org/irv/vt_lite/history.htm.

[55] *See, Lessons from Burlington*, FAIRVOTE (Mar. 4, 2010), available at http://www.fairvote.org/lessons-from-burlington; Kristin Eberhard, *What Really Happened with Instant Runoff Voting in Washington*, SIGHTLINE INSTITUTE (Sep. 19, 2017).

[56] *See*, Eberhard, *What Really Happened, supra*.

[57] Low-population states like Wyoming with only one House member should still use IRV for House elections, as PR would not be possible for them.

8. Proportional representation and the single transferable vote

Most people who have thought about this issue acknowledge that some type of "accidental gerrymander" is inherent in drawing district lines. Yet the inquiry often stops there because of an implicit or explicit assumption that we are stuck with districting.[1] But we have viable non-district election methods with proven track records in the U.S. which provide fairer representation without the many evils of gerrymandering. This chapter will briefly discuss election methods used around the world and in the U.S., and then examine more fully the most promising one, the single transferable vote (STV).

A.   SYSTEMS USED OUTSIDE THE U.S.

Some countries, like England, Canada, and India, use a "first past the post" system to elect at least one house of their national legislatures.[2] A few, like France and Iran, use the traditional runoff system, with a second round of voting used when no first-round candidate gets a majority. These two systems, discussed in Chapter 7, are familiar to Americans. They all suffer from the problems of winner-take-all systems.

But far more countries use other systems, including many with systems providing for proportional representation (PR). Every democracy in the developed world uses either PR or Ranked Choice Voting (RCV), or both, to elect either a national leader or at least one chamber of its national legislature. The U.S., along with Canada, are the odd ones out here.

---

[1]   *See, e.g.*, Nicholas Stephanopoulos, *Our Electoral Exceptionalism*, 80 UNIVERSITY OF CHICAGO LAW REVIEW 769, 776 & n. 16 (2013) (advocating for non-district remedies like preference voting, but focusing primarily on redistricting reform because of an assumption that most alternatives to SMDs are not politically viable in the U.S.).

[2]   Actually, most countries have only one house in their national legislature. *See* ACE Project, *Comparative Data*, ELECTORAL KNOWLEDGE NETWORK, available at http://aceproject.org/epic-en.

Many countries, including most of Europe and South America, use a "party list" system of PR. Under this system, political parties compile lists of candidates who are available to fill seats.[3] Each party is given a number of seats in the parliament according to its overall proportional share of the vote. Once a party is assigned X number of seats, the seats are filled from the party's list. The party may have 20 candidates on its list, for example, but only 10 of those candidates may be seated. The first 10 on the party's list (determined ahead of time by the party organization itself through internal deliberations) are then seated. To get at least one seat, a party has to meet a minimum threshold of the vote, usually determined by the number of seats up for election—for example, if there are 20 seats up, then a party would need 5% of the vote (one-twentieth). This is the most common form of electing a national legislature, with traditional plurality the second most common.[4]

The party list has two main subcategories, relating to how one selects the order in which candidates from the list are chosen to fill seats. Under the "closed list" system, the voter just votes for parties. Candidates from the list are given seats in the order that the party organization lists them. Albania, Argentina, Turkey, and Israel, among others, use this system. Under the "open list" system, voters vote for individual candidates associated on the ballot with parties. Votes for candidates go towards the party's total percentage share of the vote, used to determine the number of seats the party gets. They also usually (though not always) help to determine which candidates for that party get priority. Finland, the Netherlands, and Brazil, among other countries, use this system. (Until 2016, Australia used a hybrid form in which voters could choose either to rank individual candidates within a party's list, or simply vote for a party itself.)

---

[3] Thus, they do not conduct primary elections to determine the party nominees, as in the U.S. Indeed, U.S.-style partisan primaries are the exception rather than the rule around the world. *See* Int'l Foundation for Electoral Systems, PROPORTIONAL REPRESENTATION OPEN LIST ELECTORAL SYSTEMS IN EUROPE 2 (2009). This is not necessarily a good thing for the rest of the world. *See, e.g.*, Jed Ober, *Here's Why Primaries Are Good for Democracy*, FOREIGN POLICY (July 13, 2015), available at http://foreignpolicy.com/2015/07/13/heres-why-primaries-are-good-for-democracy/.

[4] *See* ACE Project, *Comparative Data*, ELECTORAL KNOWLEDGE NETWORK, available at http://aceproject.org/epic-en (party list used in 36% of countries compared to 26% for plurality). *See Party List Proportional Representation*, ELECTORAL REFORM SOCIETY, available at https://www.electoral-reform.org.uk/voting-systems/types-of-voting-system/party-list-pr/. There are many variations and subcategories within party list, and indeed among many of the other international election systems discussed herein. This section is intended to discuss the most commonly used only rather than be an exhaustive compilation.

Both main types of systems have the advantage of providing for PR, but have challenges which eliminate them as persuasive models for the U.S. The closed list variety arguably leaves too much power in the hands of party insiders, who can decide in backroom deals which members of the party get priority over other members as to who gets seated, who doesn't, and in what order. These decisions are usually made without significant voter input. Such a system would be anathema to many Americans, who proudly maintain (whether it is true or not) that they "vote for the candidate, not the party,"[5] and who in any event would insist on having a direct say as to which candidates from a party get priority over others in terms of seating.

The open list system addresses those concerns but it, like its cousin the closed list system, presents other issues. Fundamentally, by not providing that the voter rank-order her choices, much of value is lost. In a party list system, all votes below the minimum threshold to seat a party's candidate are wasted votes. Rank-ordering minimizes wasted votes by transferring votes to other candidates. And even where a smaller party does not have a plausible chance of actually taking seats, it can use its ability to cross-endorse ("Vote for us first, vote for Labor second") as leverage in getting policy concessions from larger parties, thus allowing for at least some influence on policymaking.

To add to the variety of choices worldwide, some countries use various hybrid forms of systems which combine a party list system with a plurality system. While variations abound, there are two main forms of this kind of hybrid. In the more common Mixed Member Majoritarian system (MMM), also known as the "Parallel" system, some seats in the legislature are filled from single-member districts (SMDs) using first past the post voting, with the remainder using a party list system. Russia, Mexico, Pakistan, and a number of African countries use this system. It is not a true PR system because a party's share of the vote translates into proportional seats only for those seats reserved for the party lists; the remaining

---

[5]   While many American voters make this claim, it is not clear how true it has been in practice, especially in recent decades. *See* Abigail Geiger, *For Many Voters, It's Not Which Presidential Candidate They're For But Which They're Against*, Pew Research Center (Sept. 2, 2016), available at http://www.pewresearch.org/fact-tank/2016/09/02/for-many-voters-its-not-which-presidential-candidate-theyre-for-but-which-theyre-against/. Polling data shows that Americans have become increasingly polarized along party lines, with crossover voting (self-identified Democrats voting for Republicans, and vice versa) ever rarer. Matthew Gentzkow, Polarization in 2016 9 (2016), available at https://web.stanford.edu/~gentzkow/research/PolarizationIn2016.pdf.

seats are elected using a non-proportional winner-take-all method, from SMDs. In the Mixed Member Proportional (MMP) system, the legislative seats are also divided into party list seats plus SMDs with plurality voting. The difference is that MMP uses true proportional allocation rules. If a party wins either at least 5% of the party list vote, or else at least 1 SMD, that party gets a number of seats proportional to its national share of the party list vote. If a party is entitled to, say, 7 seats, and has won 3 SMDs, those 3 SMD winners are seated first, and the remaining 4 are seated based on the rank order of the party's previously submitted list.

These kinds of hybrids offer some guidance for the U.S. The choice between winner-take-all systems and proportional systems is not all or nothing. Some decision-makers in the U.S. would cling to some form of SMDs because of arguments about local concerns, constituent–incumbent interaction, simplicity, and the like. A compromise could combine SMDs with PR in like manner, especially at the state or local legislative level.

Finally, some countries use Instant Runoff Voting (IRV), or another ranked choice system, the Single Transferable Vote (discussed below in Section B), at the national legislative level. Australia uses IRV in SMDs to elect its House, while using Single Transferable Vote to elect its Senate. Papua New Guinea also uses IRV, and Ireland and Malta also use Single Transferable Vote (for multi-seat legislative races) and IRV (for single-office races like President). As discussed in Chapter 7, if one must use a winner-take-all system, IRV is better than alternatives like plurality or regular runoffs. But because IRV is not a PR system, it is not as good as Single Transferable Vote.

B.   SYSTEMS USED IN THE U.S.

At the national level, the U.S. uses SMDs for House elections and at-large elections in each state for the Senate. This is provided for by federal law.[6] But at the state and local level, there is more variety, including the use of multimember districts – which could plausibly use PR methods of election.

At the state legislative level, most states use SMDs for both the state House and the state Senate. But 9 states use *multimember* districts, where voters elect 2 or more representatives per district to elect members to at least one house, and 4 states (Arizona, New Jersey, South Dakota,

---

[6]   *See* 2 U.S.C. § 2c (2012) (mandating SMDs for U.S. House); U.S. CONST. amend. XVII (providing that each state shall have two senators chosen by the people of that state).

and Washington) use multimember districts to elect all state legislators. Indeed, over 1,000 state legislative seats, about 15% of the country's total, are elected from multimember districts,[7] although state legislative use of multimember districts is in decline today from their heyday decades ago.[8]

These state legislative multimember districts use a winner-take-all approach (although Illinois used "cumulative voting" (see below) from 1890 to 1980). But there is even more variety at the local level, for city councils, county commissions, school boards, and the like. True, most local jurisdictions use either traditional winner-take-all at-large systems, SMD systems, or some combination of the two.[9] But many use multimember districts.

And at the local level, these districts do not simply use a winner-take-all approach. Several of them use innovative voting methods which help to

---

[7] *See* National Conference of State Legislatures (NCSL), *Changes in Legislatures Using Multimember Districts after Redistricting*, THE THICKET (Sept. 11, 2012), available at http://ncsl.typepad.com/the_thicket/2012/09/a-slight-decline-in-legislatures-using-multimember-districts-after-redistricting.html. For an excellent summary of the various methods of election used, see the blog of Loyola Law School Los Angeles Prof. Justin Levitt, *All about Redistricting*, available at http://redistricting.lls.edu/where-state.php. Some of these multimember district elections are the functional equivalent of SMD elections. For example, some states have 2 legislators elected from one district, but their terms are staggered, so that in any one election, voters are only electing a single representative. Lilliard Richardson and Christopher Cooper, *The Mismeasure of MMD: Reassessing the Impact of Multi Member Districts on Descriptive Representation in U.S. State Legislatures*, WEST NORTH CAROLINA LIBRARY NETWORK, available at https://www.researchgate.net/publication/228433036_The_Mismeasure_of_M MD_Reassessing_the_Impact_of_Multi_Member_Districts_on_Descriptive_ Representation_in_US_State_Legislatures. Others have candidates run for a designated numbered post within a multimember district, so each separate pool of candidates competes for one seat—again, the functional equivalent of SMDs. For this reason, one could use preference voting to effectuate PR in such systems, but only after eliminating staggered terms or numbered posts. I put these aside for purposes of this discussion. But most multimember districts still in use are "readily convertible" to PR, and there are a sizable number of such districts.

[8] NCSL, *Declining Use in Multimember Districts*, THE THICKET (Jul. 13, 2011), available at http://ncsl.typepad.com/the_thicket/2012/09/a-slight-decline-in-legislatures-using-multimember-districts-after-redistricting.html.

[9] *See* Steven J. Mulroy, *The Way Out: A Legal Standard for Imposing Alternative Electoral Systems as Voting Rights Remedies*, 33 HARVARD CIVIL RIGHTS-CIVIL LIBERTIES LAW REVIEW 333, 334 (1998); Heywood T. Sanders, *The Government of American Cities: Continuity and Change in Structure*, 1982 MUNICIPAL YEAR BOOK 178, 179–80 (1982); Edward Still, *Alternatives to Single Member Districts*, in Chandler Davidson ed., MINORITY VOTE DILUTION 249 (1989).

achieve PR.[10] All involve multiple seats being filled in the same election, either in a multimember district or just in an at-large election covering the entire jurisdiction. Three such methods are in use in the U.S.

1.   Limited Voting

In limited voting, a voter casts one vote per candidate, but the total number of votes she may cast is less than the total number of seats to be filled. For example, if 5 city council seats are up for election, with, say, 15 candidates running, the traditional winner-take-all method would be to allow a voter to cast 1 vote each for up to 5 candidates, with the top 5 vote-getters taking a seat. This system allows the majority to elect candidates of choice to all 5 seats, shutting out a significant politically cohesive minority. Under limited voting, by contrast, the voter might be limited to cast only 4 votes, or perhaps only 1, 2, or 3. This limit keeps the majority voting bloc from sweeping the election, and allows a cohesive minority to have at least some representation on the city council (though of course not a majority).

Limited voting is used in Philadelphia, Pennsylvania; Hartford, Connecticut; in about two dozen city councils in Alabama; about a dozen school boards and county commissions in North Carolina; and in scores of local jurisdictions elsewhere in Connecticut and Pennsylvania. Where it has been used, it has helped previously shut-out racial and ethnic minority groups to achieve greater representation by electing candidates of choice.

2.   Cumulative Voting

In cumulative voting, a voter has a set number of votes to cast among the candidates, and may allocate those votes among candidates however she wants. The number of votes usually is equal to the number of seats to be filled. In our example of the 5-member city council, a voter could "plump" all 5 votes for one especially preferred candidate, or give 5 candidates one vote each in traditional style, or split up her votes between 2 candidates 3–2, etc.[11]

---

[10]   The description of voting systems below is taken from Steven J. Mulroy, *Coloring Outside the Lines: Erasing "One-Person, One-Vote" & Voting Rights Act Line-Drawing Dilemmas by Erasing District Lines*, 85 MISSISSIPPI LAW JOURNAL 1271, 1292–1295 (2017).

[11]   The variation of cumulative voting used in Peoria, Illinois is the "equal and even" method, in which the total number of votes each voter has is equally divided among all the candidates for which the voter has indicated a preference. In Peoria, a voter is given 3 votes. If she indicates a preference for only 1 candidate, all 3 go to that candidate; if she checks 2 candidates, each gets 1.5 votes, and so on.

Cumulative voting is used in Peoria, Illinois; Chilton County, Alabama; by a number of city councils in Alabama; and by about 40 school boards in Alabama, South Dakota, and Texas. Historically, Illinois used cumulative voting statewide to elect members of the state House for about a century leading up to 1980. In 1870, a bill in Congress to elect the U.S. House entirely by cumulative voting came within 2 votes of passage. Like limited voting, cumulative voting has enabled previously frustrated racial and ethnic minorities to elect candidates of choice.

3.   Single Transferable Vote

In Single Transferable Vote (STV), a form of RCV also called preference voting,[12] the voter ranks available candidates in order of preference, from most preferred to least preferred. The voter is free to rank all the candidates, some of the candidates, or just vote for 1 candidate.[13] In the same 5-member city council example, a voter faced with a list of 15 candidates vying for 5 seats could, say, rank her preferences from 1 to 7, leaving other candidate spaces blank. Once she indicates a rank order, her job is done.

The counting of these ballots is a little more involved. Where voters are electing only one person from the jurisdiction (like a mayor), or only one person from an SMD, the election would be resolved using IRV, described in Chapter 7.[14] But that system would not allow for PR.

---

[12]   Both IRV and STV are RCV systems, with the former used in single-office races and the latter in multiple-seat races. When I use RCV in this book, I refer to both systems.

[13]   This is true inside the U.S. In other countries, voters are sometimes required to "rank all the way down." Australia has such a requirement for its House of Representatives elections, and had a similar one for its Senate elections up until 2016. *See* Kelly Buchanan, *Australia: Changes to Senate Electoral Law Passed Following Overnight Debate*, LIBRARY OF CONGRESS (Mar. 28, 2016), available at http://www.loc.gov/law/foreign-news/article/australia-changes-to-senate-electoral-law-passed-following-overnight-debate. While proponents of this requirement argue that this reduces or eliminates "exhausted ballots" (see Chapter 7), this rigid requirement of ranking all candidates seems ill-advised. In Australia, for example, it leads to much higher rates of ballots which are not counted due to voters failing to follow the directions. Damon Muller, *The New Senate Voting System and the 2016 Election*, Parliamentary Library Research Paper Series (25 Jan. 2018), available at http://parlinfo.aph.gov.au/parlInfo/download/library/prspub/5753272/upload_binary/5753272.pdf. Even where voters rank all the way down, in many cases they will be doing so in an uninformed way.

[14]   There actually is a form of IRV, called Block Voting, which can be used to fill multiple seats from within one jurisdiction. Where there were insufficient majority vote winners, the system would eliminate the weakest candidate and

Under STV, election officials calculate a minimum number of votes needed to fill a seat, the "Droop quota." This is the {total number of votes} divided by {the total number of seats plus 1}. In our example, if there were a total of 1,000 votes cast, the Droop quota would be {1,000 votes/5 seats + 1} = 1,000/6 = 167. Any candidate receiving more than 167 votes is seated. Any "surplus" votes (i.e., votes won by a candidate over the Droop quota) are then reassigned to other candidates based on those voters' second-rank selections.[15] In the second round, after this reassignment, any candidates with votes above the Droop quota are seated, and surplus votes reassigned as above. If in any round no candidate has votes above the quota, then the weakest candidate is eliminated and votes redistributed as under IRV. This process of seating candidates, eliminating candidates, and reassigning both the "surplus" votes of winners and all votes for eliminated losers, continues until all the seats are filled. Figure 8.1 illustrates this process.

While the above may sound confusing, it actually tracks nicely with our discussion of gerrymandering in Chapter 4. Recall that the hallmarks of gerrymandered plans are large numbers of "wasted" votes, wasted either by votes for losing candidates in "cracked" districts, or wasted by having too many votes for winning candidates in "packed" districts. Minimizing wasted votes maximizes the number of voters who vote for winning candidates, as well as the number of voters who are fairly represented. STV addresses both types of wasted votes. A vote for a losing candidate is transferred to remaining candidates, as in IRV. "Extra" votes for winning candidates (like in a packed district) over and above the Droop quota are transferred to remaining candidates using the STV method.

---

transfer those votes based on voter rankings, just as in IRV. This process would continue until all seats are filled. This book does not discuss it in detail, for two reasons. First, it does not provide for PR; it is just another species of winner-take-all. Second, it is not in current use. Australia used it to elect its national Senate members from 1918 to 1948, but then replaced it with STV.

[15]   There are two main ways of accomplishing this. Election officials could randomly draw a "surplus" number of ballots from the ballots listing this winning candidate first, and redistribute those particular ballots. This is called the "Cincinnati method." Or they can redistribute all of said ballots, but reassign a proportional fraction of each ballot, so that each such transferred ballot counts for some fraction less than one full vote (using the fractional method). Cambridge, Massachusetts uses the Cincinnati method. Minneapolis uses the fractional method for its STV elections. For example, if a candidate needed 100 votes to be elected, but received 120 votes, then that candidate would be elected and all 120 ballots would count for their next choice, but only at 20/120, or 1/6 of a vote each. That way, 20 total votes count for their next choice, but it perfectly reflects the proportion of voters who favored each remaining candidate as a back-up choice.

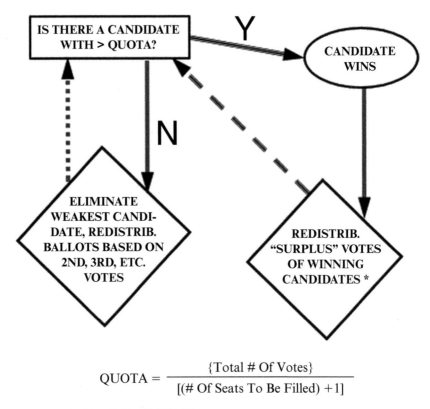

$$\text{QUOTA} = \frac{\{\text{Total \# Of Votes}\}}{[(\# \text{ Of Seats To Be Filled)} +1]}$$

REPEAT UNTIL ALL SEATS FILLED

Note: **Surplus votes* = votes for a winning candidate over and above the Quota. E.g., Quota = 100, Winning Candidate gets 120 votes: there are 20 Surplus votes.
Redistribution Methods (using example of 120 votes for candidate with 100 vote quota):
A. *Cincinnati Method*: Randomly draw 20 ballots from the 120; reassign 20 votes to remaining candidates based on 2nd, 3rd, etc. choices.
B. *Fractional Method*: redistribute all 120 ballots to remaining candidates based on 2nd, 3rd, etc. choices, but give each such vote a 20/120 or one-sixth of a vote value.

Figure 8.1   Flow chart for single transferable vote

STV is used in Cambridge, Massachusetts, and Minneapolis, Minnesota. Historically, New York City used it in local community school board elections throughout the 1990s, and city councils in about two dozen American cities (including New York) used it throughout the early to mid-20th century. Like limited and cumulative voting, where they have been used, these STV elections have enabled cohesive minority groups to elect candidates of choice roughly in proportion to their share of the electorate. For example, after the first STV election for New York City community school boards in 1970, the percentage of black and Hispanic community school board members jumped to levels close to the corresponding black and Hispanic percentages of the citywide population. These percentages increased with the rising populations of blacks and Hispanics throughout the succeeding decades. STV resulted in more proportional results than in the single-member district city council elections held during the same period, despite the presence of a number of minority-oriented SMDs in the city council districting plan.[16]

4. "Threshold of Exclusion"

For each of these systems used in the U.S.—limited voting, cumulative voting, and preference voting—political scientists have derived a formula which can be used to reliably calculate the minimum percentage of the electorate a politically cohesive group needs to be in order to be assured to elect at least one candidate of choice. This formula, the *threshold of exclusion*, conservatively assumes that all voters who are not members of the minority group cast all available votes; cast no votes for the minority-preferred candidates; concentrate their votes entirely on a number of candidates equal to the number of seats to be filled; and divide their votes equally among those candidates. In other words, it assumes that the majority votes with perfect strategic efficiency against the preferences of the minority.

For limited voting, the threshold of exclusion is

$$\frac{\{\text{the number of votes each voter has}\}}{\{\text{the number of votes each voter has}\} + \{\text{the number of seats to be filled}\}}$$

In our example, if each voter is given 4 votes to fill 5 seats, the threshold of exclusion is $4/\{4+5\} = 4/9$ = roughly 44% of the vote. The threshold drops the fewer votes each voter is allowed to cast. If each voter casts only 1 vote, for example, the threshold drops to $1/\{4+5\} = 1/9$ = roughly 11%.

For both cumulative voting and RCV choice voting, the threshold formula is

$$\frac{1}{\{\text{number of seats to be filled} +1\}}$$

In our example, the threshold is $1/\{5+1\} = 1/6$ = roughly 17%.

---

[16]   Douglas Amy, Real Choices, New Voices 138 (1993).

This formula also scales: if the politically cohesive group has twice or thrice the threshold of exclusion, they can reasonably be expected to elect 2 or 3 candidates of choice. In our ranked choice example here, a minority group with 34% of the vote could be expected to elect 2 candidates of choice.[17]

Political scientists consider RCV to be a true "proportional representation" system, in that a voting bloc's percentage of the votes correlates relatively closely with its share of the seats. Limited voting and cumulative voting are considered only a "semi-proportional" system. It less reliably achieves PR.[18] Further, under limited voting, for the threshold of exclusion to get low enough to give most politically cohesive groups a good chance of electing a candidate of choice, one must significantly reduce the number of votes each voter has (as we reduced said available votes from 4 to 1 in the prior example). This is problematic, in that it reduces choice for all voters across the board. For these reasons, most election reform advocates interested in PR do not focus on limited voting. Indeed, when New York City tried to replace STV with limited voting for community school board elections, the Justice Department denied Section 5 preclearance, finding that a switch to limited voting would dilute minority voting strength.

Cumulative is a better option than limited voting, but still has issues. One of them is that it requires voters to understand how to vote strategically, which usually means to "plump" all their votes for one favored candidate. As a practical matter, this is not an insurmountable obstacle. Where cumulative voting has been used to address issues of racial or

---

[17]   The formula is an estimate only. It assumes that minority voters are voting efficiently and strategically. For cumulative voting, that may mean "plumping" all votes for a single agreed-upon candidate (where the threshold suggests a potential to elect 1 candidate of choice) or 2 agreed-upon candidates (where the threshold suggests a potential to elect 2). This does not always happen. Also, the formula relates to the percentage of voters in the minority group who actually participate in the election on election day, as opposed to the percentage of registered voters, or of the voting age population. Thus, in our ranked choice example above, politically cohesive Hispanic voters might constitute 20% of the total population but only 18% of the voting age population, 16% of the citizen voting age population, 14% of the registered voters, and only 12% of those turning out on election day. Since 12% is lower than the threshold of exclusion of 17%, even if they vote perfectly strategically, Hispanic voters would need to rely on at least some non-Hispanic crossover to elect a candidate of choice.

[18]   Steven J. Mulroy, *The Way Out: A Legal Standard for Imposing Alternative Electoral Systems as Voting Rights Remedies*, 33 HARVARD CIVIL RIGHTS-CIVIL LIBERTIES LAW REVIEW 333, 339–340 (1998).

ethnic vote dilution, minority voters have demonstrated that they understand how to vote, and to vote strategically by "plumping" their votes.[19]

But the possibility of "strategic voter error" nonetheless exists, and can
prevent minority candidates of choice from winning election in a few close
cases.[20] The risk of strategic failure increases somewhat when the goal is to
elect more than one candidate of choice, for voters have the slightly more
complex task of coordinating how to divide their multiple votes among 2
or more candidates—in our example, say, agreeing to plump 2 votes for
one favored candidate and 3 votes for the other. In preference voting, by
contrast, there are no such strategic decisions to be made. The voter's best
strategic outcome is to sincerely rank-order their candidates in order of
preference.

A more significant problem with cumulative voting is "intra-group
competition." This is another variation of the "spoiler" or "vote-splitting"
problem discussed above regarding plurality voting. To take our Hispanic
empowerment example above, suppose that the threshold of exclusion
suggests that Hispanic voters could elect 1 candidate of choice. If 2 or
more Hispanic candidates run,[21] and the Hispanic vote is split among
them, it is possible that no one candidate receives enough votes under the
threshold of exclusion to win a seat.

Again, this is not an issue with RCV. In our example, if the Hispanic
minority was truly politically cohesive, then a sincere ranking of candidates under RCV could not harm Hispanic voters' interests, no matter
how many Hispanic candidates ran. Presumably, Hispanic voters would
all rank the Hispanic candidates at the top of their lists in various orders,

[19] *See* Richard L. Engstrom, *Cumulative and Limited Voting: Minority
Electoral Opportunities and More*, 30 ST. LOUIS UNIVERSITY PUBLIC LAW REVIEW
97, 105 (2010) (citing numerous election results, exit polls, and surveys, by both the
author himself and others).
[20] *See* Richard H. Pildes & Kristen A. Donoghue, *Cumulative Voting in the
United States*, UNIVERSITY OF CHICAGO LEGAL FORUM 241, 243–251 (1995).
[21] For simplicity's sake, I assume here that the candidates of choice of the
Hispanic voters happen to also be Hispanic. It is commonly the case in Voting
Rights Act litigation that minority-preferred candidates are personally of the same
minority. However, this is by no means universal, or required. The Voting Rights
Act speaks of the ability of minority voters to elect "candidates of choice," who
may personally be of any race or ethnicity. For example, in the majority-black U.S.
House District 9 in Tennessee, the candidate of choice of African-American voters
has for years been long-time progressive Democratic incumbent Steve Cohen,
who happens to be white. He has soundly defeated single black challengers in
the Democratic primary in head-to-head matchups. (However, he was originally
nominated in 2006 in a crowded Democratic primary with many black candidates,
where "vote-splitting" in a plurality election may have played some role.)

but rank all of them before ranking any non-Hispanic candidates. As long as that were true, intra-group competition could not interfere with Hispanic voter empowerment. Votes for a Hispanic candidate who did not garner enough votes to win a seat or advance to the next round would simply be transferred to another Hispanic candidate based on the voters' ranked preferences, continuing in this manner until a preferred candidate met the Droop quota and was seated. For this reason, there is never a "spoiler" problem with RCV.

Substitute for Hispanics the word "Republican," "libertarian," "environmentalist," or "LGBTQ-friendly," and the analysis is the same. If a politically cohesive group which is a minority of the multimember district strives for fair representation—i.e., representation which comes close to their proportional share of the electorate—their best option is RCV. RCV beats all winner-take-all systems, as well as limited voting and cumulative voting. Political scientists generally rank PR systems, including RCV systems like STV and IRV, higher than SMD plurality or SMD with two-round runoff systems.[22] The rest of this book focuses on STV.

C.   FAIR REPRESENTATION ACT

STV has natural appeal in local multimember elections using an at-large or multimember district system, and could also be profitably adapted for use at the state legislative level. How would RCV work at the national level? Chapter 3 explained why STV could not practically be used in the Senate, so the best approach is to use it in the House. A bill in Congress provides for exactly that.

The Fair Representation Act, sponsored by Virginia Democrat Don Beyer, would require the use of RCV in both primary and general elections for the U.S. House. In states with just one House member, the states

---

[22]   Shaun Bowler, David M. Farrell, & Robin T. Pettitt, *Expert Opinion on Electoral Systems: So Which Electoral System Is "Best"?*, 15 JOURNAL OF ELECTIONS, PUBLIC OPINION & PARTIES 3, 7–8 (2005) (survey of 170 political scientist/electoral experts worldwide ranked plurality 6th out of 9 major systems), available at https:// www.tandfonline.com/doi/abs/10.1080/13689880500064544#aHR0cHM6Ly93d 3cudGFuZGZvbmxpbmUuY29tL2RvaS9wZGYvMTAuMTA4MC8xMzY4OT g4MDUwMDA2NDU0ND9uZWVkQWNjZXNzPXRydWVAQEAw; *see also* FairVote, COMPARATIVE STRUCTURAL REFORM, Aug. 28, 2015, available at http:// www.fairvote.org/comparative-structural-reform (survey of 14 American election law scholars concluded that some version of RCV was among the top 3 structural electoral reforms in terms of impact, ranked higher than conventional redistricting reform).

would use IRV. In states with 2–5 House members, the state would elect its House members at-large using STV. In states with more than 5 House members, a nonpartisan redistricting commission would draw multi-member districts for between 3 and 5 House members[23] using identified redistricting criteria. The state would use STV to elect the members within each multimember district.[24]

Adopting RCV in this way does not require a constitutional amendment. The Constitution already gives Congress the authority to "make or alter" any state regulations regarding the "Times, Places and Manner of holding Elections for Senators and Representatives."[25] Congress has already used this authority to require that all House elections occur on a uniform date in November, and that they occur within SMDs.[26] The Fair Representation Act would repeal this second requirement.

The RCV process begins with the partisan primary elections. Each party will hold a primary as before, but now using RCV. And not just 1 but multiple top winners from each party will advance to the general election, usually a number equal to the number of seats to be filled. This will ensure competition both among parties and within parties in each general election.

Where multimember districts must be drawn, the Act describes the non-partisan redistricting commission process. The commission would have equal numbers of Democratic, Republican, and Independent members. While a simple majority suffices to approve a multimember districting plan after notice and comment, the majority must contain at least 1 vote from each of the 3 groups, and must draw the multimember districts according to statutorily specified criteria.[27] If the commission deadlocks, a panel of federal judges would use the statutory criteria to draw a plan.

---

[23] This comports with the range of seats available in the form of STV used in Ireland's national legislative elections.

[24] *See* Fair Representation Act, H.R. 3057, 115th Congress § 332(a) (2018), available at https://www.congress.gov/bill/115th-congress/house-bill/3057/text#t oc-H5E6F74FC8800422AB4982E416FD318C3. The STV method would use the "reweighted Gregory" system of fractional redistribution of "surplus" votes.

[25] U.S. Const. Art. I, § 4, cl. 1.

[26] *See* 2 U.S.C. § 7 (2012) (mandating uniform date for federal elections); 2 U.S.C. § 2c (2012) (requiring SMDs).

[27] In order of importance: contiguity; Voting Rights Act compliance; avoiding districts "safe" for either party, so that each major party has a chance to elect at least one member in each district; avoiding 4-member districts (to prevent 2–2 splits); maximizing the number of 5-member districts (to lower the threshold of exclusion); respect for existing political boundaries and communities of interest; compactness; and respect for visible geographic features. The Act forbids

Experts at the RCV advocacy group FairVote have drawn simulated multimember district maps for each state using the statutorily designated criteria. Using available data on partisanship and race, they made predictions about its likely effects. The number of districts with an unpredictable electoral outcome (party-wise) rose from 15% of districts to 43% of districts. Partisan bias drops from 5 percentage points in favor of the GOP to only 1 percentage point. States become less lopsided party-wise regarding their congressional delegations. For example, Massachusetts (60% Democratic) goes from 9 Democrats and 0 Republicans to an expected 6 Democrats and 3 Republicans. Texas (40% Democratic) goes from 12 Democrats and 24 Republicans to roughly 16 Democrats and 20 Republicans.

Minority representation would improve as well. The South, for example, would go from having 19% of its SMDs with black majorities to 27% of multimember districts where black voters, based on the threshold of exclusion, would be able to elect at least 1 candidate of choice. As a result, the South would go from a region in which 60% of black voters lived in majority-white, Republican districts to a region where 98% of black voters would live in a district where they could elect at least one candidate of choice.[28]

Of course, there is no guarantee that the resulting maps would be the same as those projected here. States would have the discretion to draw their own lines. But if the size of the districts were limited to 3–5, and the lines drawn only by a truly nonpartisan redistricting commission, then it is reasonable to expect that competition would increase, partisan fairness would get better, and racial/ethnic fairness would either improve or at least get no worse.

An alternative rule would be to allow for conversion to STV only where the result would be no worse for racial and ethnic minorities currently protected by the Voting Rights Act. This is analogous to the "retrogression" principle under the "preclearance" provision of the Voting Rights Act, Section 5, which was in place prior to the Supreme Court's 2013 decision suspending the preclearance process indefinitely.[29] Covered jurisdictions seeking advance preclearance had to prove, at a minimum, that a proposed voting change would be no worse for minorities' ability to elect candidates of choice.[30] Courts and Justice Department officials applied

---

consideration of residences of officeholders or candidates. *See* https://beyer.house. gov/uploadedfiles/fair_representation_act.pdf.

[28] *The Fair Representation Act in Your State*, FAIRVOTE, available at http:// www.fairvote.org/the_fair_representation_act_in_your_state.

[29] 52 U.S.C. § 10304 (Supp. II 2014).

[30] *See* Beer v. U.S., 425 U.S. 130, 140 (1976) (interpreting Section 5 of the Act to incorporate a retrogression principle).

the retrogression standard for decades, and there are well-understood, well-accepted metrics for it. The redistricting commissions could be required to apply that standard as well, subject to correction by federal courts.

There are other ways in which the current proposal could be improved. Perhaps the redistricting commission could be required to adopt a plan with a supermajority, to further ensure bipartisan consensus. If states' rights were a concern, the adoption of STV could be made optional on a state-by-state basis. The main point is, while STV and PR have been used in the U.S. only at the local level, there are good reasons to consider it at the federal and state level as well.

D. ADVANTAGES OF PROPORTIONAL, NON-DISTRICT SYSTEMS

There are numerous reasons why we should prefer a non-district voting system using some form of PR[31] over a traditional district-based system.

1. Avoiding the Evils of Redistricting

As mentioned earlier, non-district voting systems have the obvious advantage of obviating redistricting. Gerrymandered districts will be with us as long as we have districts. As long as we carve the jurisdiction up into geographic subunits, the carving will create winners and losers. Without districts, those problems go away.

Depending on the number of seats available in the jurisdiction, it might be necessary to draw a *few* multimember districts to keep the number of seats up for election at any one time to a manageable number. But the opportunities for gerrymandering mischief, or "accidental" gerrymandering, are much, much fewer when one is only drawing 3 to 5 multimember districts than when one is drawing, say, 12 to 25 SMDs. So, a switch to alternative, non-district, non-winner-take-all methods would reduce both intentional and unintentional gerrymandering of both the partisan and racial/ethnic varieties.

Eliminating (or substantially reducing) redistricting also ameliorates the

---

[31] Non-SMD systems using traditional winner-take-all voting rules would *not* be better than SMD systems. At-large or multimember district systems using winner-take-all rules have long been acknowledged to tend to dilute minority voting strength. *See* Rogers v. Lodge, 458 U.S. 613, 616 (1982); Chapman v. Meier, 420 U.S. 1, 16 n.10 (1975); Whitcomb v. Chavis, 403 U.S. 124, 158–159 (1971).

practical problems involved in the 10-year reliance on decennial Census data. One of the polite fictions of redistricting is that the Census-based plans have any accuracy past the early part of the decade. As migrant as modern Americans are, population shifts quickly render Census-based redistricting plans obsolete, as residents move from one district to another within the jurisdiction, or residents move into and out of the jurisdiction entirely. Non-district PR systems adjust automatically to these population shifts.

A proportional electoral method can also eliminate or reduce redistricting litigation. As Prof. Pam Karlan has written,[32] redistricting litigation in the U.S. is now extremely common, with various sides using legal theories to advance their narrow partisan ends. Republicans without a long track record of aggressive advocacy for minority electoral empowerment are suddenly interested in aggressive use of the Voting Rights Act. Democrats who had earlier decried the intellectual vapidity of the *Shaw/Miller* cause of action now use it to prevent perceived packing of minority districts. Observers both domestic[33] and foreign[34] have noted that America is at the extreme end of litigiousness when it comes to redistricting.

This has many costs, not only in wasted money, time, and effort, but also in political uncertainty. Voters and candidates are not sure what the final redistricting map will look like. This often translates into legislative inaction on broader issues. Courts often end up deciding the cases on narrow, technical grounds that are beside the point when it comes to fundamental issues of fair representation. As judges themselves will tell you, they should be a last resort when it comes to redistricting.[35] The uncertainty and technical opacity contribute to increased public cynicism about both the political process and the judiciary, as the entire enterprise looks to outside observers (with much justification) as gamesmanship, an amoral jostling for power—*Game of Thrones* without the dragons, sex, and witty dwarves.

In the U.S., the main sources of federal litigation over redistricting are issues of race and ethnicity. Abroad, countries either fail to address these issues, or have formal representational "set-asides" for minority groups,

---

[32] Pamela Karlan, *Federal Court Involvement in Redistricting Litigation*, 114 HARVARD LAW REVIEW 878, 879–880 (2001).

[33] Nicholas Stephanopoulos, *Our Electoral Exceptionalism*, 80 UNIVERSITY OF CHICAGO LAW REVIEW 769 (2013).

[34] Ron Levy & Graeme Orr, THE LAW OF DELIBERATIVE DEMOCRACY 179 (2016).

[35] *See* Upham v. Seamon, 456 U.S. 37, 40–41 (1982); Whitcomb v. Chavis, 403 U.S. 124, 160–61 (1971).

or use PR systems in multimember districts.[36] The former would be a political nonstarter for the left, the second a nonstarter for the right. Both seem generally problematic. But the latter has much to commend it.

One particularly vexatious litigation trap in modern American redistricting, one unique for those interested in racial and ethnic fairness, is the tension discussed in Chapter 5 between the Voting Rights Act and the *Shaw/Miller* "reverse racial gerrymandering" cause of action. Non-district remedies allow jurisdictions to achieve roughly proportional representation for minorities without any risk of running afoul of *Shaw/Miller*.

2. Ending the Reliance on Residential Segregation

Eliminating or reducing districting also ameliorates the other inherent problems in redistricting. Politically cohesive groups which happen to be geographically scattered in a jurisdiction have no chance for representation in the SMD framework. This again has particular salience for racial and ethnic minorities like Hispanics and Asians, who tend to be less residentially segregated than African-Americans in the U.S.[37] Hispanics make up 17% of the U.S. population, yet only 7% of House districts have Hispanic majorities, and only 8.5% of Representatives are Hispanic. Asians are roughly 5% of the population, yet only 3.2% of House members are Asian, and there is only one Asian-majority House district—or 0.002%.[38]

As noted earlier in Chapter 4, the more racial and ethnic minorities successfully fight housing discrimination to achieve housing integration, the less voting power they have to fight other forms of discrimination. Because of this, even African-Americans, a less geographically dispersed minority group, suffer electorally because of integration. They make up 12% of the population, yet less than 10% of House members, and only 5% of House districts have a black majority.[39]

---

[36] Stephanopoulos, *Our Electoral Exceptionalism, supra*, 772.

[37] *See* Mulroy, *Coloring Outside the Lines, supra*, 1295–1297.

[38] *Demographics*, U.S. HOUSE OF REPRESENTATIVES PRESS GALLERY, available at https://pressgallery.house.gov/member-data/demographics/asian-americans. Not even Hawaii has a fully Asian-majority House district.

[39] The fact that there are so many black Representatives in non-black-majority districts might be seen as an indication that voting is no longer racially polarized, such that we no longer need to be concerned about racial representation. However, that is not the case. Of the 22 African-Americans elected to non-black-majority districts, 8 were elected from "crossover" districts over 40% in black population where some white (largely Democratic) crossover voting enabled them to win, even though substantial majorities of white voters voted for other candidates. Others were elected from "coalition" districts with a significant percentage of another

A close variation of this situation is when a minority group is geographically concentrated to allow for the creation of *one* compact majority district, but their overall share of the jurisdiction population would suggest that, from a seats/votes or threshold of exclusion perspective, they deserve more than one seat.[40] A related situation occurs when concentrations of two minority groups, like blacks and Hispanics, occur close to each other, such that it is possible to create a compact majority district for one group or the other, but not both.[41] Only single-member districting creates all these tensions, and non-district PR systems resolve (or moot) them.

Nor are all these tensions (except the one between the Voting Rights Act and *Shaw/Miller*) limited to racial and ethnic minorities. Any politically cohesive group, be it racial, partisan, LGBTQ, or ideological, suffers under the existing system if they happen to enjoy residential integration. All minorities escape the ghetto at their peril.

3. Transcending the Tyranny of Geography

A common theme in all these arguments for the preferability of preference/proportional systems over SMDs is the idea that geography, as a basis for representation, is overrated. Below are some illustrations of this concept.

Transcending "Virtual" Representation. Even more fundamental advantages of non-district systems stem from the fact that no matter how careful and well-intentioned, districting always creates winners and losers, even within individual districts. Democrats in Republican districts,

---

minority which voted cohesively with black voters. At any rate, polling data shows that racially polarized voting is sadly still alive and well in the U.S.; though it varies from state to state in its intensity, there are still many states where it is a relevant electoral phenomenon. *See* Harr Enten, *It's Much Harder to Protect Southern Black Voters' Influence than It Was 10 Years Ago*, FIVETHIRTYEIGHT, Dec. 5, 2016, available at https://fivethirtyeight.com/features/its-much-harder-to-protect-southern-black-voters-influence-than-it-was-10-years-ago/.

[40] The author litigated precisely such a case, resulting in the first federal court-ordered use of cumulative voting as Voting Rights Act remedy. *See* United States v. Vill. of Port Chester, 704 F. Supp. 2d 411 (S.D.N.Y. 2010).

[41] *See* Steven J. Mulroy, *Alternative Ways Out: A Remedial Road Map for the Use of Alternative Electoral Systems as Voting Rights Remedies*, 77 NORTH CAROLINA LAW REVIEW 1867, 1883 (1999) (making this observation in arguing for non-district remedies in minority vote dilution cases under the Voting Rights Act, and citing exemplifying cases). The author's first redistricting case involved exactly such a black-versus-Hispanic dilemma. *See* De Grandy v. Wetherell, 815 F. Supp. 1550, 1576 (N.D. Fla. 1992) (three-judge court) (noting that the creation of a Hispanic state senate district in the Miami area would sacrifice creation of a third black senate district), *aff'd in part, rev'd in part sub nom.* Johnson v. De Grandy, 512 U.S. 997 (1994).

conservatives in liberal districts, blacks in white districts, Anglos in Hispanic districts, etc.—someone will always be left out. Some commentators have referred to these persons as "filler people"—as in, we want to draw a Democratic district, but, lest we pack it with Democrats, we will put in some Republicans as "filler."[42]

The standard defense of this state of affairs (aside from just shrugging it off as inevitable, given an implicit assumption that we are stuck with districting) is the concept of "virtual" representation. That is, Democrats stuck in Republican districts may not like their representative, but they console themselves with the knowledge that there is a Democratic representative two districts over, and he will "virtually" represent their interests.

This is an imperfect rationalization at best. The Democratic incumbent two districts over may not in fact adequately represent those voters' interests. For one thing, there may be issues that are local in nature (the main rationale for having SMDs to begin with), which the Democrat two districts over has little knowledge of or interest in. For another, the "filler" Democrats may be liberal Democrats, and the Democratic incumbent two districts over may be a moderate Democrat. And all that's true even with a districting plan that gets the votes–seats curve right—which, as we've seen, is rarely the case, either because of intentional gerrymandering or the natural result of demographic clustering. At day's end, "virtual representation" is cold comfort if you know you're one of the filler people.

PR systems do not need to rely on virtual representation. They provide representation for all voters in the district of the cohesive political minority, not just those lucky enough to be placed in a district with the right kind of majority. (Of course, they also provide PR for the majority voting bloc as well.) There are no filler people.

Representing All Voters Equally Throughout the Jurisdiction. Even where a cohesive group is blessed with a majority in a particular district, their cohorts in other districts are still left out. For example, in the Voting Rights Act case the author litigated in the Village of Port Chester, New York, the court found that a winner-take-all, at-large system illegally diluted the Hispanic population. The plaintiffs' proposed remedial plan featured an SMD map with one Hispanic-majority district in one part of the village. That plan would have left 82% of the village's Latino citizen voting-age population to reside *outside* the Latino-majority district. The cumulative voting plan adopted by the court, by contrast, allowed all Latinos in the village to participate in electing a Latino candidate of

---

[42] *See* Paul Finkelman, *Who Counted, Who Voted, and Who Could They Vote for*, 48 St. Louis University Law Journal 1071, 1072 (2014).

choice. This candidate was beholden to, needed the votes of, and thus represented, all Latino voters in the village, not just the subset in a particular district. Similarly, in another Voting Rights Act case decided around the same time, the court-adopted limited voting scheme provided representation for all the city's black population, not just the 44% of the city's black voting-age population who happened to reside within the originally proposed black-majority SMD.[43]

"Descriptive" Representation versus Substantive Representation. Another advantage, at least in the context of balancing partisan fairness with civil rights concerns, involves the conflict between "descriptive" representation and "substantive" representation.

"Descriptive" representation occurs when the candidate elected is actually a member of the voters' group—of the same race, or class, or geographic sublocation. For example, in a state with no recent history of electing a black congressman, there is value, symbolic and otherwise, to having a system which affords black voters the chance to elect one.[44] Such a representative may have life experiences (like personal experience with discrimination, for example) which would enhance their ability to appreciate black voters' concerns, or be seen as more accessible and approachable, both about policy input and requests for constituent service.

Substantive representation occurs when the candidate elected actually votes in a way aligned with the voters' preferences. For example, black voters in a district may be concerned about mass incarceration and felon disenfranchisement; a representative who votes to oppose those two perceived evils would be substantively representative.

Descriptive and substantive representation often go hand in hand: increase the number of blacks elected to a legislature, and you will likely improve the substantive representation for black voters. But in a single-member districting system, this is not always the case. Aggressive attempts to draw minority districts can sometimes "bleach" the surrounding districts, making them both white and more conservative. These whiter, "righter" districts can elect representatives more hostile to the black voters' policy preferences, with the sum total result that the legislative

---

[43] Mulroy, *Coloring Outside the Lines*, *supra*, 1295–1296 (discussing Voting Rights Act cases in Port Chester, NY and Euclid, OH).

[44] Again, as a legal matter, and even as a philosophical matter, the Voting Rights Act does not speak in terms of electing candidates of a particular skin color, but rather the opportunity for racial and ethnic minority voters to elect "candidates of choice"—of any color. But some advocates support the value of "descriptive" representation in the sense above, separate and apart from whether it is called for by the letter or spirit of the Voting Rights Act.

delegation as a whole is more hostile. Gains in descriptive representation paradoxically can come at the expense of substantive representation.

Take, for example, Georgia's congressional redistricting in the 1990s. Georgia went from having 9 center-left Democratic representatives (8 white, 1 black) and 1 Republican representative (white) to only 3 Democratic representatives (all black) and 8 conservative Republican representatives (all white).[45] The typical black voter with typical policy preferences had little to cheer about this state of affairs, which has been replicated in subsequent decades.[46]

The apotheosis of this tension was seen in the last round of redistricting, where some Republican line-drawers in the South deliberately eliminated white-majority, Democratic-leaning state legislative and House Democratic districts while preserving or enhancing black-majority Democratic districts, with the result that white Democratic officeholders became rare. Voters saw Democratic officeholders who were almost all black, and Republican officeholders who were all white. This optic was seen as helpful to Republicans in states with white majorities and racially polarized voting.[47]

Of course, there are other causes of the decline of Democratic representation in the South. Gerrymandering is by no means the only, or even primary, explanation.[48] And the tradeoff between descriptive and substantive representation could be ameliorated with more artful line-drawing.[49] But

---

[45]   *See* Jeffrey Rosen, *Southern Comfort*, NEW REPUBLIC (Jan. 7, 1996), 8–15, at 4.

[46]   *See, e.g.*, Damion Waymer, *How Gerrymandering Black Districts Backfired in the South*, NEWSWEEK (Sept. 17, 2016), available at http://www.newsweek.com/how-gerrymandering-black-district-backfired-south-498036 (making this argument regarding the post-2010 round of redistricting).

[47]   *See, e.g.*, Eric Black, *Why Congress Has So Few White Democrats from the South*, MINNEAPOLIS POST (Apr. 8, 2016), available at https://www.minnpost.com/eric-black-ink/2016/04/why-congress-has-so-few-white-democrats-south (describing this argument made by author and former Texas congressman Martin Frost).

[48]   *See* DAVID LUBLIN, THE PARADOX OF REPRESENTATION: RACIAL GERRYMANDERING AND MINORITY INTERESTS IN CONGRESS 123 (1997) (noting that new minority districts cost Democrats only 9 seats in 1992 and 1994, compared to 54 total seats lost in 1994 when the Democrats lost control of the House); David A. Bositis, *The Future of Majority-Minority Districts and Black and Hispanic Legislative Representation*, in David A. Bositis ed., REDISTRICTING AND MINORITY REPRESENTATION 9, 19 (1998); Allan J. Lichtman, *Quotas Aren't The Issue*, N.Y. TIMES (Dec. 10, 1994), at A23 (finding that equally significant Democratic losses in non-district, at-large races and an overall decline in Democratic support were more important reasons for the Democrat's 1994 loss of control of the House of Representatives).

[49]   *See* Lublin, PARADOX OF REPRESENTATION, *supra*, 89–102 (describing how

the tension between descriptive representation and substantive representation is real. It can occur whether the descriptive representation at issue is race, ethnicity, gender, LGBTQ status, or class. And it applies only to winner-take-all districted systems.

PR systems do not have this tension. There is no "bleaching" of surrounding districts, because there are no districts (or at least very few). A voter is entirely free to vote on the basis of descriptive representation, substantive representation, or some combination. A hypothetical black, female, lesbian, pro-life Democrat can vote on the basis of race, gender, LGBTQ status, position on abortion, party affiliation, or any mixture of those. The choice is hers. Her choices will not be made for her, or at least limited, by a line-drawer who puts her in a district with a majority of black/Democratic/etc. voters. In this sense, PR allows each voter to "self-district."[50]

Equality of Representation Versus Minority Voter Empowerment. Yet another tension inherent in districting is that between equality of representation and the prevention of vote dilution. Under our "one person, one vote" jurisprudence, districts are required to be relatively equal in population.[51] Traditionally, courts have measured that based on *total* population, which includes both eligible voters and ineligible voters—those under 18, noncitizens, felons, and the mentally incompetent. However, in recent years some states and advocates have argued that a different measure, one closer to actual voters, should be used, like citizen voting age population (CVAP) or registered voters. Since the goal of "one person, one vote" is to make everyone's vote mathematically equal, the argument goes, redistricting should strive for equality in the number of *voters*, or at least the number of people who could legally vote if they so chose. The counterargument is that districting is also about *representation*, and even those who cannot vote still deserved to be represented. They deserve an equal chance at constituent

---

districts with slightly over 40% black population could achieve the same goals for black voter empowerment without creating significant costs in substantive representation).

[50]   Mulroy, *Alternative Ways Out, supra*, 1896.

[51]   Reynolds v. Sims, 377 U.S. 533, 577 (1964). For state and local districts in the U.S., courts will typically allow districts to deviate +/− 10% from the "ideal" district population. *Id.* at 562. This 10% "allowance" is fairly typical in Western democracies around the world. Australia, for example, uses this benchmark. *See Redistribution Overview*, AUSTRALIAN ELECTORAL COMMISSION (Sept. 28, 2011), available at https://www.aec.gov.au/Electorates/Redistributions/Overview.htm. For U.S. House districts, the Court is much stricter, requiring districts be as "equal as practicable." Wesberry v. Sanders, 376 U.S. 1, 7 (1964). As a practical matter, a deviation of more than +/− 1% will be presumptively unconstitutional.

service, an equal chance to urge policies upon representatives, and an equal chance simply to be counted for purposes of representation.

The Supreme Court recently ruled that states may continue to use total population for redistricting and are not *required* to switch to voter proxy measures. But it has not ruled out the idea that states could choose voluntarily to so switch.[52] So the debate continues. A switch to voter proxy measures like CVAP or voter registration would reduce representation for Latinos, who have lower citizenship rates than other Americans (and a higher-than-average number of persons under 18).[53] Opponents could also assail such a switch for being anti-immigrant, or a policy that, coupled with mass incarceration of minorities and strict felon disenfranchisement laws, has the purpose or effect of disproportionately burdening persons of color.

This is a significant issue, one which may become even more significant in the next few years. It underscores a fundamental philosophical tension with districting—one eliminated, or at least substantially alleviated, respectively, with non-district or multimember district systems using PR.

Relative Salience of Geography versus Other Factors. Given all these inherent tensions caused uniquely by drawing districts, why do we do it? What is the fundamental advantage of carving a jurisdiction up into representational subunits?

One answer might be that districts help with representational focus on local issues, that people living near each other do indeed have local concerns in common. There is certainly much traditional thinking along these lines (so to speak). Legendary former Speaker of the House Tip O'Neill is credited with the well-worn political aphorism, "All politics is local." It implies that local issues and constituent service matter in a congressional race much more than national issues.

If that was ever true in O'Neill's time in politics (the 1950s through 1980s), it is certainly not true today. Polling data shows that congressional politics has become increasingly nationalized in recent decades.[54] Recent election experiences seem to bear this out. Ever since Newt Gingrich's

---

[52] Evenwel v. Abbot, 136 S. Ct. 1120 (2016).

[53] Mulroy, *Coloring Outside the Lines*, *supra*, 1274–1275.

[54] *See, e.g.*, Andrew Gelman, *All Politics Is Local? The Debate and the Graphs*, NEW YORK TIMES (Jan. 3, 2011), available at FIVETHIRYEIGHT: NATE SILVER'S POLITICAL CALCULUS, https://fivethirtyeight.blogs.nytimes.com/2011/01/03/all-politics-is-local-the-debate-and-the-graphs/; *see also* Morris P. Fiorina, THE (RE) NATIONALIZATION OF CONGRESSIONAL ELECTIONS, available at https://www.hoover.org/sites/default/files/research/docs/fiorina_renationalizationofcongressionalelections_7.pdf.

"Contract with America" in 1994, which was a deliberate (and success-ful) effort to nationalize House elections, we have seen increasingly nationalized congressional elections. A moment's reflection will show no shortage of congressional elections since, which seemed obviously domi-nated by one or two nationwide issues: impeachment (1998); terrorism and the build-up to Iraq (2002); second thoughts on Iraq (2006); the Obama "hope and change" phenomenon and the reaction thereto (2008); the Tea Party uprising (2010); and immigration, "MAGA," and the reaction thereto (2016). The other elections in that time period may not have an obvious one or two overarching themes, but there were national issues in the mix then, too.[55]

The decreasing salience of local issues in recent decades makes sense from a technological and cultural perspective. Thanks to smartphones, laptops, and the Internet, the world gets smaller, telecommuting gets easier, and the primacy of place wanes.

And to whatever extent local issues remain salient, it is not clear that they are salient on a district-by-district level, or in a way that coherently correlates to district lines. For example, many local issues are issues about the needs and shortcomings of local governments, but congressional districts today rarely follow local government boundaries. It makes sense that Chicagoans may have common concerns with fellow Chicagoans, be it about crime, how much federal funding Chicago gets, or whether Chicago is doing enough to mitigate Lake Michigan water pollution. But there are 7 different congressional districts which include some part of Chicago, with none of them entirely contained within Chicago.[56]

Search your own preferences as a quick check on this premise that "All politics is local." Think to yourself of the top 3 issues affecting your vote for Congress. Expand that to the top 5. Where are local issues on this list, if they appear at all?

Even to the extent there persist salient local issues that are in some coherent way included within, or otherwise tied to, a particular House district or cluster of House districts, is it clear that they are *more* salient than co-occurring regional, state, national, or international issues? If not, why give them more prominence? Because that is what we are doing when we force electoral choices into district-sized boxes. A voter in a regional, 5-member district using preference voting and PR can choose to vote

---

[55] *See* Daniel J. Hopkins, THE INCREASINGLY UNITED STATES: HOW AND WHY AMERICAN POLITICAL BEHAVIOR NATIONALIZED 2–7 and *passim* (2018) (making this argument).

[56] By population, Chicago would normally be expected to have 4 House members.

for candidates who live near her and presumably understand her local concerns. Or, she can vote for candidates living further away because they share her passion for the environment; or are from the LGBTQ community and presumably can be trusted on LGBTQ issues; or have committed to tax cuts; or some combination of these. A voter in an SMD has no such choice; all candidate choices are filtered through the narrow restriction that they must live relatively close by[57] within a 700,000-person bubble. The candidate who lives closest to her and is best on local issues may actually be on the other side of the district line—as must often be the case for the 2 million Chicagoans who share 7 House Representatives among them.

Another variation on this "local issues" defense of districts is that districts ensure that representatives will come from all over a state (or subregion of a state), rather than all reside in one tiny, well-populated or otherwise influential area. In Southern California, for example, we wouldn't want all the congressional representatives to come from Hollywood, or Bel Air. Again, this concern, while legitimate, must be balanced against the other, non-geographic concerns that voters may find equally worthy. Using PR allows voters to decide the relative weight of those concerns for themselves, rather than having the decision made for them by politicians or redistricting commission members.

And it's by no means certain that such geographic clustering of representatives would result. In Cambridge, for example, STV-elected council members tend to be pretty dispersed throughout the city, and often choose to campaign as "neighborhood" candidates. The difference is that the neighborhoods are organic and voter-chosen, not fixed by arbitrary lines.

Of course, the objection that at-large, multimember systems elect representatives too distant from constituents certainly doesn't apply where the jurisdiction is very small, as with a diminutive city or town. Indeed, in such locations, non-district systems may also help where districts are simply impractical—for example, it would be wasteful to draw voting precinct lines, and set up and staff multiple polling places, etc.[58]

---

[57] And not even necessarily close by. New Mexico's 2nd Congressional District takes up half the area of the state of New Mexico, over 300 miles long and over 200 miles wide.

[58] This was the situation in the Port Chester case the author litigated, *see* Defendant's Pre-Hearing Remedy Brief at 14–15, United States v. Village of Port Chester, 704 F. Supp. 2d 411 (S.D.N.Y. 2010) (No. 06-CV-15173) (making the same argument for use of cumulative voting), as well as another Voting Rights Act case. *See* Cottier v. City of Martin, 475 F. Supp. 2d 932, 940–941 (D.S.D. 2007) (imposing cumulative voting in part on these grounds where the city was less than a square mile in area), *rev'd on other grounds*, 04 F.3d 553, 562 (8th Cir. 2010)

4. Other Advantages

Aside from avoiding the obvious pitfalls of redistricting, PR systems offer other, less immediately apparent advantages.

Accurate Reflection of Popular Will. First and most fundamentally, they do a better job of matching seats with votes, and do so along more dimensions. We have already seen how districting can lead to racial gerrymanders or partisan gerrymanders, either intentionally or accidentally. But even where districting plans are ideal, at-large PR systems still inherently do better at measuring voter sentiment. And, multimember-district PR generally does a better job than SMDs.

For example, after the first STV election for New York City community school boards in 1970, the percentage of black and Hispanic community school board members jumped to levels close to the corresponding black and Hispanic percentages of the population.[59] These percentages increased with the rising population of blacks and Hispanics throughout the following decades. The use of preference voting resulted in much more proportional results than in the SMD city council elections held during this period, despite the presence of a number of minority-oriented SMDs in the city council districting plan.

A useful analogy here is to calculus. Before the invention of calculus, scientists and mathematicians trying to measure things very accurately would divide the thing to be measured—the area under a curve, the acceleration (change in rate of speed) of a body at a given point in time—into small subsets, measure those in the aggregate, and approximate. For example, mathematicians could approximate the area under a curve by dividing the area into a number of rectangles, measuring the area of those rectangles using a crude, simple, well-understood formula (height × width), and adding up the rectangles' areas. To get a more accurate measurement, mathematicians would break the area up into ever-smaller, ever-more-numerous rectangles. Calculus allowed them to simulate the use of an infinite number of infinitely small rectangles.

(finding that the plaintiffs did not satisfy the third *Gingles* precondition regarding white bloc voting).

[59] Again, we assume for simplicity's sake that same-race identifying of the candidates is a useful proxy for the candidate being the candidate of choice of that minority community. This is a pretty safe assumption wherever voting has been shown to be racially polarized. In the examples cited herein, regarding the use of alternative electoral systems in response to actual or threatened Voting Rights Act litigation, such racial bloc voting exists.

So it is with PR. The goal of an electoral system is to measure, as accurately as possible, the popular will. If one uses a winner-take-all at-large system, there is much room for error. If you divide the jurisdiction into a few large districts, there is less room for error (assuming no intentional gerrymander), but it is still crude and approximate. The more, and smaller, the districts, the more accurate the measurement of popular will jurisdiction-wide. If we had 100 districts, each very small, the sum total of their mini-elections would on average be even more accurate (again, assuming no intentional gerrymanders). Even more so for 1000 districts. The ultimate measuring tool would be a number of tiny districts equal to the number of voters—one for each voter. In effect, that is what PR is: allowing each individual voter to express an individual preference that is measured equally against all other voters jurisdiction-wide, without the skewing effect of assigning arbitrary bunches of them into winner-take-all districts for counting purposes. The inherent potential of line-drawing to skew results is eliminated. Each voter controls their own district. As mentioned before, each voter can "self-district."

Representation and Diversity Over More Dimensions. Even when districting plans are drawn with scrupulous efforts to match seats with votes, they usually achieve either racial fairness, or partisan fairness, but not both. Rare is the plan which is a close votes/seats match re: both partisanship and minority representation, in jurisdictions with significant racial/ethnic minority populations.[60] Non-district systems can achieve both—or, where a choice between the two is inevitable, allow the *voters* to make the choice rather than line-drawers.

Indeed, where they are used, these systems tend to promote ideological and gender diversity as well as partisan, racial, and ethnic diversity. When Illinois used cumulative voting for state legislative elections, there was far more partisan diversity per multimember district. There were Republicans in mostly-Democratic Chicago-area districts, and Democrats in the mostly-Republican "downstate" districts. This led to more bipartisan cooperation on projects that had local or regional salience. Regarding gender, the experience has been that non-district, PR systems provide better opportunities for female candidates, at least as compared to SMD systems.[61] This result probably occurs in part because when parties nominate slates rather than a single

---

[60]   *See generally* Liz Kennedy et al., *Redistricting and Representation: Drawing Fair Election Districts Instead of Manipulated Maps*, CENTER FOR AMERICAN PROGRESS (Dec. 5, 2016), available at https://www.americanprogress.org/issues/democracy/reports/2016/12/05/294272/redistricting-and-representation/.

[61]   *See*; R. Darcy et al., WOMEN, ELECTIONS, & REPRESENTATION 159–168 (2d ed. 1994); Mulroy, *Alternative Ways Out, supra*, 1894.

individual, they try to diversify—including by gender—to appeal to as many voters as possible. A similar dynamic may also be at work among voters, who when given the chance to express preferences for several candidates rather than one, may be more inclined to include at least one woman in their preferences. In Germany, which has a mixture of PR, plurality, and SMD elections, female candidates consistently perform better in the PR races.[62]

More Coalition-Building. This increased diversity increases the number of voters who feel represented by *somebody* in the legislature, and thus can ameliorate the alienation currently felt by the many people in SMDs who are in the voting minority. The increased diversity also dovetails with other features to encourage coalition-building across racial, partisan, and other divides. In some circumstances, two distinct groups (racial, ethnic, ideological, etc.), each of which is too small to control a district, may often vote similarly. If they are too geographically distant to be included within one SMD, they have no opportunity for cooperation and are doomed to political irrelevance. A non-district (or multimember district) PR system provides these voters with an opportunity for coalition that they would not otherwise have.

Competition and Turnout. This flexibility in candidate selection dovetails with other features of PR to increase competition and turnout. In most districts, the outcome of the election is pretty much decided before the campaigning begins.[63] The district usually comes with a significant majority of Republicans, Democrats, African-Americans, Latinos, etc. There may be some competition in the primary election, but by the final, decisive round of the general election, the outcome is foreordained. As seen earlier, this is not just true where intentional gerrymandering has occurred, but is a natural consequence of demographic clustering.

These general election contests are not competitive. Campaigning is not as robust. Voters have less of an opportunity to see a real debate with engaged advocates, to be informed, to deliberate among themselves, and to reconsider their views. Voters from the "losing" side see participation as futile so they don't turn out. Voters from the "winning" side see their votes as not needed, and don't turn out. The result is turnout levels even lower than the abysmal rates which the U.S. has seen in recent decades.[64]

---

[62] *See* Tracy-Ann Johnson-Myers, THE MIXED MEMBER PROPORTIONAL SYSTEM: PROVIDING GREATER REPRESENTATION FOR WOMEN? 9 (2017).

[63] *See* Georgetown University, *The House's Competitiveness Problem. . . or Lack Thereof*, THE GOVERNMENT AFFAIRS INSTITUTE, available at https://gai.georgetown.edu/the-houses-competitiveness-problem-or-lack-thereof/; DAVID HILL, AMERICAN VOTER TURNOUT: AN INSTITUTIONAL PROSPECTIVE 12–14 (2006).

[64] Drew Desilver, *U.S. Trails Most Developed Countries in Voter Turnout*,

By reducing the threshold of exclusion from 51% to a lower figure, PR systems lower barriers to entry for candidates, thus easing the path for less well-known, less well-funded candidates.[65] By allowing "underdog" candidates a chance, they increase electoral competition, which in turn increases turnout. In 2017, for example, turnout increased dramatically in all 4 U.S. cities which used RCV.[66] Comparative studies among Western industrialized democracies have found that on average, countries with PR systems tend to have turnout rates about 10 percentage points higher than countries using traditional, winner-take-all systems.[67]

These results make intuitive sense. Citizens trying to engage fellow voters in SMDs have an uphill battle. In most districts, if you organize an increase in turnout of like-minded voters, you will merely convert a preordained narrow victory into a landslide, or convert a preordained lopsided loss into a more respectable loss. Only in the rare particularly close swing district would such an effort have a reasonable chance of making a difference. But in a PR system, even a relatively small increase in turnout will cause a proportional increase in representation for your side. You will have a better shot at making a difference, so you will be more likely to organize your side. Further, you know that the other side is aware of this dynamic, and may be doing likewise. Thus, competition.

The results of the election can also spur turnout due to voter psychology. Voters generally prefer to vote for a candidate and see her win than vote for a candidate and see her lose. In districts, many voters have the dispiriting experience of voting for losing candidates time and time again. In PR with a relatively low threshold of exclusion, almost all voters will be able to point to at least one winning candidate and say, "Yes, I voted for her." In preference voting, the percentage of ballots cast for at least some winning candidates rises with the number of seats to be filled (as the threshold of exclusion drops): at least five-sixths of voters for an election

---

PEW RESEARCH CENTER (May 15, 2017), available at http://www.pewresearch.org/fact-tank/2017/05/15/u-s-voter-turnout-trails-most-developed-countries/.

[65]   Douglas Amy, REAL CHOICES, NEW VOICES 76–98 (1993) (citing multiple sources).

[66]   Drew Penrose, *Voter Turnout Surges in All Four Cities with Ranked Choice Voting*, FAIRVOTE (Nov. 8, 2017), available at http://www.fairvote.org/voter_turnout_surges_in_all_four_cities_with_ranked_choice_voting.

[67]   *See* Arend Lijphart, *Unequal Participation: Democracy's Unresolved Dilemma*, 91 AMERICAN POLITICAL SCIENCE REVIEW 1, 7 (1997) (citing four different studies); Gary Cox et al., *The Contraction Effect: How Proportional Representation Affects Mobilization and Turnout*, 78 JOURNAL OF LAW AND POLITICS 1249, 1250 (2016).

to fill 5 seats, for example.[68] In practice, the percentage can be higher: one study of preference voting in Cambridge, Massachusetts showed that 96% of the electorate ranked at least one winning candidate in their top 3 choices, with 80% seeing their first or second choice elected.[69] When this becomes the norm, the voters' sense of futility decreases and participation rises.

E. THE SENATE

This chapter discusses the adoption of STV for House races. It would also be possible to use it for Senate races as well, though it would not help as much. Since each state has 2 Senators, the threshold of exclusion would be $1/(2 +1) = 33\%$. Thus, in a red state, if Democrats were at least one-third of voters, they would get some representation. Likewise, in blue states, if Republicans were at least one-third of voters, they would get at least one Senator. This would help the minority "trapped" in overwhelmingly blue or red states from feeling that their votes didn't count and their participation was futile. Also, to have more states with mixed-party Senate delegations might be a healthy thing; it might lead to more across-the-aisle cooperation, especially on issues of regional concern (as occurred during Illinois Legislature's century-long use of cumulative voting). But one could also argue that it overrepresents a minority. When you only have 2 seats up for election, PR is a crude thing. Rounding up or down can result in significant votes–seats deviations. It might seem unfair to give a 35% minority 50% of the Senate seats. Of course, that is closer to proportionality than the current system, where they would get 0% of the Senate seats.

Accomplishing this (admittedly radical) reform would not take a constitutional amendment, but it would take congressional action. Congress could change the process which determines how Senate terms are staggered. Currently, Congress ensures that each of a state's 2 Senator positions gets elected on a different schedule than the other: one in 2014 and one in 2016, for example, rather than both in 2016.[70] If Congress acted to put both Senate slots from a given state up for election at the same time, this rather crude form of STV could be implemented. Ultimately, it seems a long walk for a short beer.

---

[68]   *See* Edward Still & Robert Richie, *Alternative Electoral Systems as Voting Rights Remedies*, 1997 FED. ELECTIONS COMM'N J. ELECTIONS ADMIN. 18, 22.

[69]   Amy, REAL CHOICES, NEW VOICES, *supra*, 26.

[70]   *See* United States Senate, *Frequently Asked Questions*, available at https://www.senate.gov/general/common/generic/NewCongress_faq.htm#class_assignments.

F. CRITICISMS OF PROPORTIONAL SYSTEMS AND PREFERENCE VOTING

1. Parliamentary System Problems

Many of the most common criticisms against PR systems are actually criticisms against the parliamentary systems in which they are commonly found. Under many party list PR systems, the internal party leadership decides (a) who will stand for election under that party's slate, and (b) in what order of preference on the party list. The decision in (a) takes the place of U.S. primary elections, and that in (b) occurs during general elections. This system arguably gives the party leadership too much of a say, and voters too little, in who will serve in the legislature. Similarly, in a parliamentary system the chief executive is chosen by the newly elected legislative majority, and not directly elected by the people as in the U.S. Again, this arguably gives politicians too much of a say, and voters too little, in which person will run the government.

Worse, the parliamentary nature can create real instability. Whenever a majority of the parliament votes "no confidence" in the prime minster, he must step down, triggering a new election. In some parliamentary countries, the governing party itself can simply decide to switch leaders as part of intramural infighting. In Australia, this has happened 4 times in the last 8 years, with both the No. 2 of the left-leaning Labor Party and the right-leaning Liberal Party ousting their own No. 1. in intra-party maneuvering. Between such maneuvering and regular elections, no prime minister in this century has been in office more than 3 years. In the latter half of the 20th century, Italy averaged one new government every year, with some governments lasting less than a month.

These criticisms have some merit, but are irrelevant to the debate concerning PR within the U.S. None of the above problems can occur in an STV system with RCV. In partisan races, voters could still participate in primaries. Either way, voters would vote for candidates, not parties, and voters would have the say over party leaders. "No confidence" votes could not occur. We would still directly elect a President, governor, and mayor for set terms, with the resulting predictability and stability we are accustomed to.

2. Criticisms of Ranked Choice Voting

Many of the criticisms of the STV version of PR are essentially criticisms of RCV itself. Such criticisms, like voter confusion, election administration, and exhausted ballots, were previously addressed in Chapter 7 regarding IRV. That discussion applies for the most part to STV as well.

Admittedly, STV is more complex than IRV. Like IRV, STV involves eliminating the weakest candidate, and transferring those votes to remaining candidates based on 2nd, 3rd, etc. choices. But STV also adds the element of transferring "surplus" votes of wining candidates—votes over and above the quota necessary to win—to remaining candidates as well. This crucial extra feature is what allows STV to lead to proportional results. But it also makes the vote-counting rules more complicated to explain and to implement. This could make administration and voter confusion more of a concern.

Fortunately, we have a track record of use to draw from. STV has been used at the national level for almost a century in Ireland and Malta, and for almost 70 years in Australia. Cambridge, Massachusetts has used STV to elect its city council for over 75 years, and the Minneapolis Park & Recreation Board for 9 years. Further, over two dozen two major U.S. cities used it for decades and decades. In this use of STV we have not seen voter confusion or election administration problems.

More important, the extra complexity of STV over IRV is a matter only for those who count the votes. From the perspective of the voter, there is no difference. Once one enters the voting booth, all one needs to understand is that one ranks their first choice 1st, their second choice 2nd, and their third choice 3rd. So there is no reason to be more concerned about voter confusion than there is with IRV. By analogy, most U.S. voters would be incapable of explaining fully and in detail exactly how the Electoral College works. But they do not find voting for President too confusing, because all they need to know once they enter the booth is to vote for their favored candidate.

3. History of Repeal of STV

As noted earlier, about two dozen U.S. cities used STV for their city council elections in the first half of the 20th century. These cities adopted STV at various points from 1915 through 1950 and continued using it for periods varying from several years to several decades. A fair question is why those cities discontinued their use of STV. Repeal often came as a result of public hostility to the election of blacks (as in Cincinnati) or Communists (as in New York), mostly in the years after World War II.[71]

---

[71] *See* Amy, Real Choices, New Voices, *supra*, 173 (noting the role of fear of Communism in the New York repeal); Robert A. Burnham, *Reform, Politics, and Race in Cincinnati: Proportional Representation and the City Charter Committee, 1924–1959*, 23 JOURNAL OF URBAN HISTORY 131, 153 (1996) (discussing the role of race in repeal in Cincinnati). A 1988 effort to bring back STV to Cincinnati was also

A similar history occurred in Canada, with STV used at the local level in a few cities including Calgary and Edmonton, and also at the provincial level in Alberta, from 1926 through 1955. Cambridge, by contrast, soldiered on with STV despite 5 different attempts at repeal from the 1940s through early 1960s.

While hostility to the election of "outsiders" is not the only reason for the discontinued use in the 20th century, it certainly did play a role. As did some of the concerns about complexity discussed above. It has also been suggested that STV's empowerment of individual candidates weakened party discipline, encouraging opposition by both major parties, which eventually led to repeal.[72]

More recently, a 2018 referendum to adopt STV for city council elections in Santa Clara, California failed by 471 votes (4.7%). It is not clear what role RCV or PR played in the rejection. The proposal would have remedied a court finding of Asian-American minority vote dilution under the Voting Rights Act by moving from an at-large, winner-take-all system to a system of 2 multimember districts using STV. Some opposition might have been to the move away from at-large elections. In addition, the Asian-American Voting Rights Act plaintiffs argued for the traditional SMD remedy, in part due to a preference for neighborhood-based representation.[73]

Certainly, STV will not meet with universal acclaim among voters. Its track record of retention by jurisdictions having adopted it is more mixed than that of the simpler IRV system. But Cambridge's successful experience demonstrates both its electoral viability and its merit.

4.   Other Criticisms

There are other, more fundamental criticisms of the idea of PR which deserve consideration.[74] The most basic is the objection that PR systems,

---

marked by racial overtones; the effort was narrowly defeated mostly because white opposition overcame black support. *See* Richard L. Engstrom, *Cincinnati's 1988 Proportional Representation Initiative*, 9 ELECTORAL STUDIES 217, 221–222 (1990).

[72]   Jack Santucci, *Bad for Party Discipline: Why Unions Attacked the Single Transferable Vote in Cincinnati* (June 28, 2017), available at http://jacksantucci. com/docs/papers/cincinnatiJune2017.pdf.

[73]   Tatiana Sanchez, *Santa Clara Voters Reject Measure A, Switch To District Elections*, THE MERCURY NEWS (June 5, 2018), available at https://www.mercurynews. com/2018/06/05/santa-clara-voters-approve-measure-a-switch-to-district-elections/.

[74]   One such argument, that the law does not entitle anyone to PR, that PR is not a part of the American system and should thus be viewed with suspicion, has already been addressed. The fact that PR is not an entitlement does not mean

including STV, do away with or fatally undermine the geographic basis of representation. This argument assumes that (i) geography is a useful proxy for representational communities of interest, and (ii) that it is a better proxy than the self-selected preferences of voters themselves, be they inflected by race, gender, party, ideology, LGBTQ status, issue-specific positions, etc. These assumptions are addressed above in Section D.2.

A related objection is that the decoupling from geography would encourage lax constituent service, and/or make constituents feel less comfortable making constituent service demands, where constituents and representatives became more physically distant.

There certainly is some merit to the objection that increased distance could make constituent–incumbent interaction more difficult. The author has served on an elected body with both single-member and multimember districts. In the latter, responsibility for constituent services can be diffused. Presumably, though, consistent failure to respond to constituent service requests would eventually harm any representative's reputation and electoral chances, discouraging the worst derelictions of duty. And in the age of email, social media, and cell phones, contacting one's representative, regardless of geographic location, has never been easier. The author's own (admittedly anecdotal) experience as an elected official suggests skepticism that members of the public would ever, under any circumstances, become shy about making demands on their representatives.

Another common criticism of PR systems, including STV, is that they allow the election of radical or "fringe" candidates. A common example is the prominence of religious extremist parties in Israel.[75] However, the party list form of PR used in Israel's Knesset has an extraordinarily low threshold of exclusion. Until the 1990s, it was only 1%; now, by law, a party must meet a threshold of 3.25% to get representation in the Knesset. Contrast Germany, which since World War II has seen a relatively stable and moderate series of governments in a system imposing an across-the-board requirement of 5% of the vote for all national elections.

Under the Fair Representation Act, House members would be elected in districts (or states) with 3–5 seats up at a time. The threshold of exclusion would then be somewhere between 17% $[1/(5 +1) = 1/6]$ and

---

it is forbidden, or suspect; indeed, courts evaluating racial gerrymandering cases routinely take it into account. *See* Chapter 5.

[75]   Even when extremist candidates make it into the Knesset, they do not have a significant influence on actual legislation. Raphael Ahren, *The Extremist Who Could Bring Kahanism Back to the Knesset*, THE TIMES OF ISRAEL (Feb. 18, 2015), available at https://www.timesofisrael.com/the-extremist-who-could-bring-kahanis m-back-to-the-knesset/.

25% [1/(3+1) = 1/4] of the vote. If a group has this percentage of the vote, they are almost by definition not a "fringe" group. They deserve a seat at the table. Under STV, that is exactly what they would get.

Indeed, one could argue that winner-take-all systems are more likely to cause problems of extremism, precisely because they freeze out significant minority groups with grievances. Realizing that they have no realistic chance for representation, such groups are more likely to turn to extralegal methods of conveying their grievances. The single-member plurality system formerly used in Northern Ireland has been blamed for inflaming religious tensions by shutting out the Catholic minority. Protestants crowded out Catholics "until all too many Catholics replaced their meaningless ballots with bullets."[76] It was no accident, then, that the Good Friday Accords peace agreement in Northern Ireland made STV a key component.[77]

The use of STV at the state or local level would trigger varying thresholds of exclusion depending on the number of seats in the legislative body, the decision to elect at-large or in multimember districts, the use of staggered terms, etc., all determining the number of seats up for election at any one time. For practical reasons of avoiding an overly long and complicated ballot, it seems unlikely that such jurisdictions would ever have more than 8 or 9 seats up at one time, meaning that the threshold of exclusion would never drop below 11%. At any rate, if this were viewed as too low, the jurisdiction in question could always titrate these structural features to craft a consensus threshold of exclusion, one low enough to ensure that legitimate cohesive political minorities were not shut out, but not so low as to invite fringe groups.

Although critics of PR and STV may overstate the extent to which extremist candidates would be elected and pay too little heed to the ability of winner-take-all systems to fuel extremism among excluded minorities in highly polarized societies, they are correct about the inherent moderating effect of a winner-take-all system. Such systems tend to elect politically moderate candidates and force parties to hover around the political center.[78] This is either a feature or a bug, depending on your point of view.

---

[76] Rein Taagapera & Matthew S. Shugart, SEATS AND VOTES: THE EFFECTS AND DETERMINANTS OF ELECTORAL SYSTEMS 63 (1989).

[77] *See* Deaglan de Breadun, *News Features*, IRISH TIMES (May 30, 1998), at 10 (discussing the proportionality electoral features of the new governing body in Ireland and its role in ensuring cooperation in the "divided society" of Northern Ireland).

[78] This moderating, centrist effect is not in serious dispute among political scientists. *See, e.g.,* Anthony Downs, AN ECONOMIC THEORY OF DEMOCRACY 114–141 (1957); Theodore Lowi & Benjamin Ginsberg, AMERICAN GOVERNMENT: FREEDOM AND POWER 498 (1980).

If stability is one's chief concern, winner-take-all systems have a natural attraction. Another view is that we should favor stability only to the extent that it accurately reflects the popular will.

F. HOW PLAUSIBLE IS THIS?

A final objection to discussing these systems is that they will never fly politically in the U.S. Respected electoral scholars have taken this position.[79] It is true that RCV and PR are seen as exotic in the U.S., despite their prevalence throughout the world.

But even in the U.S., familiarity with RCV is on the rise. Currently, there are over 2 million Americans living in cities with RCV. Once Maine implements, there will be members of the U.S. House and Senate familiar with the system. At the same time, dissatisfaction with the current electoral system is widespread and deeply felt.[80] While no one expects the passage of Fair Representation Act-style reforms overnight, structural reforms of our electoral system have occurred throughout our history. Direct election of Senators is one example. Others might include the widespread conversion of winner-take-all, at-large election systems into district systems to address concerns of minority vote dilution, along with the dramatic increase in minority registration, voting, and election to office occurring during the civil rights era, changes which have been called a "quiet revolution."[81] Another example might be the ongoing move toward nonpartisan redistricting commissions discussed in Chapter 6, which is gaining momentum throughout the U.S.

Of course, adoption of STV might be more plausible at first at the local level, which is where it currently is used in the U.S. Local adoptions could lead to statewide adoptions, as happened in Maine; use of RCV in the form of IRV started in Portland, and gained sufficient popularity to be adopted by referendum at the statewide level. For this reason, it is useful to look at the adoption of these reforms at the local and state level.

---

[79] *See, e.g.*, Nicholas Stephanopoulos, *Our Electoral Exceptionalism*, *supra*, 769 n.16 (taking districting systems "as a given" because "the American commitment to territorial districting is so strong that prescriptions that call it into question are highly implausible").

[80] *See* Hannah Fingerhut, *Already-low Voter Satisfaction with Choice of Candidates Falls Even Further*, PEW RESEARCH CENTER (Sept. 12, 2016), available at http://www.pewresearch.org/fact-tank/2016/09/12/already-low-voter-satis faction-with-choice-of-candidates-falls-even-further/ (providing polling data on voter satisfaction with election candidates).

[81] *See* Chandler Davidson & Bernard Grofman, eds., QUIET REVOLUTION IN THE SOUTH: THE IMPACT OF THE VOTING RIGHTS ACT 1965–1990 (1994).

9. State and local applications

Chapter 8 focused on the use of proportional representation (PR) and single transferable vote (STV) in federal elections for the House. But perhaps a more politically plausible route would be the continued adoption of these systems at the local and state level to prove their merit.

A. LOCAL GOVERNING BODIES

General. STV has a long history of use at the local level in the U.S. As noted previously, over two dozen cities from 1915 through the early 1960s, including Cleveland, Cincinnati, New York, Sacramento, and Kalamazoo, adopted STV and continued using it for periods ranging from several years to several decades.[1] It has been in continued use in Cambridge, Massachusetts since 1941 for both its city council and its school board, having voted down 5 separate repeal efforts. Minneapolis adopted it in 2009 for its Park and Recreation Board and its Board of Estimate & Taxation, and has been using it ever since.

There are several reasons why adopting STV makes particular sense at the local level. First, many local jurisdictions currently use a pure, winner-take-all, at-large system. Switching to STV would not involve a debate over abandoning districts, but simply adjusting the voting rules of an already at-large system to allow for rank choice voting and proportional representation.

Second, many local jurisdictions already use multimember districts. Adopting STV in such multimember districts would in many cases be a simple matter of retaining existing district boundaries and changing the voting rules from winner-take-all to STV.

Third, moving away from single-member districts (SMDs), and thus loosening the geographic basis of representation, may be less of a concern at the local level. If the issue is having a representative who knows local

---

[1] *See* Leon Weaver, *The Rise, Decline, and Resurrection of Proportional Representation in the United States*, in Bernard Grofman & Arend Lijphart eds., ELECTORAL LAWS AND THEIR POLITICAL CONSEQUENCES 139–141 (1986).

issues, lives nearby, and understands your concerns, that is surely less of a concern when the person lives in the same town.

If the issue is constituent access to representatives, this is also likely less of a concern: if phone or email won't suffice, the citizen just needs to travel from one part of town to another for an in-person meeting. While that may still be an inconvenience in cities with very large land footprints, those cities tend to have larger city council sizes, and could divide their area into multimember districts. Even the largest population cities (over 50,000) average only about 50 square miles in size.[2] The vast majority, over 90%, are smaller.[3] On average, it should be manageable for most, and certainly less of a concern than multimember districts at the federal or state level reaching beyond the boundaries of a city.

As a legal matter, authority to enact these reforms varies widely from state to state. In some states, state legislatures would need to amend state law to permit these electoral forms. In others, local governments may be free to do it through enactment of the local legislature itself. In many, it would require an amendment to the city or county charter, which would in turn require a local referendum. To get such a referendum on the ballot, depending on the jurisdiction, one could either petition the local government body to place it on the ballot, or citizens could place it on the ballot through a petition-signature-driven citizen initiative.[4]

Where available, the latter mechanism is the most fruitful. It bypasses incumbents who are naturally disposed toward supporting the status quo and resisting change to the electoral methods that brought them into power.

Cities. The number of members on city councils would by and large be amenable to the use of STV. U.S. city councils have an average of about 6 members, and at least 3 members.[5] For many such cities, STV could be employed at-large with acceptable thresholds of exclusion ranging from 14% to 25%.

---

[2] Demographia, *2000 Census: US Municipalities Over 50,000: Ranked By 2000 Population*, http://demographia.com/db-uscity98.htm (detailing land area for 601 cities over 50,000 in population as of 2000).

[3] *See* National League of Cities, *Number of Municipal Governments & Population Distribution*, available at https://www.nlc.org/number-of-municipal-governments-population-distribution (2007) (listing over 19,000 municipal entities in the U.S. as of 2007).

[4] *Initiative, Referendum and Recall*, NCSL.ORG, available at http://www.ncsl.org/research/elections-and-campaigns/initiative-referendum-and-recall-overview.aspx.

[5] Steven Mulroy, *The Way Out: Toward a Legal Standard for Imposing Alternative Electoral Systems as Voting Rights Remedies*, 33 HARVARD CIVIL RIGHTS-CIVIL LIBERTIES LAW REVIEW 333, 354 n.110 (citing sources).

Larger-population cities naturally tend to have much larger city councils. As of the beginning of the decade, of the 50 largest cities in population, city council size ranged from 5 seats in Miami to 51 in New York, with an average of 14 seats.[6] Most of these cities would require multimember districts rather than at-large voting to use STV, for several reasons.

As the number of seats to be filled increases over, say, 9, the number of candidates rises into the 20s, 30s, or more. This starts to make the ballot impractically long. The threshold of exclusion also starts to dip into the single digits, raising the specter of a "fringe" candidate winning a seat. Both these concerns could be alternatively addressed by staggering the legislators' terms, to reduce the number of seats up in any one election. However, some of those larger-population cities might tend to need multimember districts for the separate reason that larger-population cities tend to have larger land area footprints.

Counties. The analysis is similar for counties. County legislative bodies tend to have more members than cities, but only slightly more. County commissions range from 3 to 51 members, with most at 6 or fewer.[7] County commissions from the 50 largest counties in population average 8 members.[8] Consolidated county-city metropolitan governing legislatures can be larger. For example, after the City of Jacksonville, Florida and Duval County merged several decades ago, the size of the combined local legislature rose to 19 members.[9] Counties also tend to take up more land area. Thus, for most counties, using STV would probably require the use of multimember districts rather than an at-large framework.

Mixing PR with winner-take-all. With local elections, there is room to experiment with a mixture of geographic-based and proportional election systems. Many cities and counties have a mixture of SMDs and at-large elections, or SMDs and multimember districts.[10]

Memphis, for example, had until 2011 a county commission with a mixture of 3-member districts with numbered posts covering one part of the county, and one SMD covering the remainder of the county. The rationale

---

[6] Josh Whitehead, *A Look at City Council Size Around the Country*, Smart City Memphis (May 3, 2010), available at http://www.smartcitymemphis. com/2010/05/a-look-at-city-councils-around-the-country/.

[7] Nat'l Assoc. of Counties, *NACo County Explorer*, available at http:// explorer.naco.org/#.

[8] Whitehead, *A Look at County Commission Size Around the Country*, *supra*.

[9] Jacksonville City Council, COJ.NET, available at http://www.coj.net/city-council.aspx.

[10] *See, e.g.*, *Cities 101 – At-Large and District Elections*, NLC.ORG, available at https://www.nlc.org/resource/cities-101-at-large-and-district-elections (confirming this situation with respect to cities).

was to have a rough partisan balance between the multimember districts, with a "swing" SMD serving as the partisan tiebreaker.[11] In contrast, the city council has had 7 SMDs since the 1990s, with two overlapping 3-member "Superdistricts" superimposed over the SMDs. This was in part a compromise between civil rights advocates who favored single districts for minority empowerment, and traditionalists who favored something closer to the preexisting at-large framework. A modern rationale for this overlapping mixed system is that it combines localized, neighborhood-based representation (SMDs) with representatives who are encouraged to think beyond parochial neighborhood concerns and consider the interests of the city as a whole (or, at least their half of the city).

Such hybrid systems allow a combination of election methods, with multimember districts providing the advantages of PR, and SMDs providing the advantages of neighborhood-based representation. Where they use SMDs, however, jurisdictions should at least adopt Instant Runoff Voting (IRV) for the reasons discussed in Chapter 7. Santa Clara, California considered a 2018 referendum which would have used STV in multimember districts for city council races, and IRV for citywide single-office elections like mayor.

B.   STATE LEGISLATURES

As mentioned previously, unlike the federal House and Senate, some state legislatures use multimember districts to elect their members. As with the federal House, they were common in the early days of the Republic. Unlike the House, which switched to SMDs as early as 1842,[12] multimember districts continued in the state legislatures until the mid-20th century. The civil rights era highlighted the ability of multimember districts using winner-take-all methods to dilute the voting strength of racial and ethnic minorities, as well as partisan minorities. Through a combination of voluntary adoption and litigation, states moved toward SMDs. Multimember districts went from being about half of state legislative seats at the start of

---

[11]   The county switched to 13 SMDs during the 2010 round of redistricting, largely due to the author's legislative advocacy while serving as an elected member of the County Commission.

[12]   *See* Act of June 25, 1842, ch. 47, 5 Stat. 491 (1842) (requiring House elections to be held from SMDs). Electoral practice varied by state somewhat over the ensuing century, but single districts were the norm and became universal in 1967 after another congressional enactment. Rob Richie & Andrew Spencer, *The Right Choice for Elections,* 47 UNIVERSITY OF RICHMOND LAW REVIEW 959, 963–964 (2013).

the 1960s to roughly a quarter of the House members and a twelfth of state senators by the 1980s.[13] They represent less than 15% of state legislative seats today.

Currently, 9 states use multimember districts for at least some of their state legislative seats, with the multimember districts ranging in size from a minimum of 2 members in many of those states to a maximum of 11 members in some parts of New Hampshire.[14]

The districts with only 2 members pose the same issue as discussed in Chapter 3 regarding U.S. Senate seats: STV is feasible, but perhaps undesirable. The threshold of exclusion would be one-third. Since there are many districts less lopsided than 67% for one party, there would be districts where it is plausible that the minority party (representing 33% or more) would be able to elect at least one candidate of choice. Even where the districts are more lopsided than 67% for one party, a minority party that approached the threshold of exclusion but didn't quite meet it might still be able to *influence* the outcome of the election. Or such an electoral structure might afford heightened opportunities for racial and ethnic minorities to form coalitions with other groups, at least as compared to a winner-take-all multimember election.

As with the U.S. Senate, though, it might be deemed undesirable to have 1 out of 2 state senators be from the minority party if the multimember district has a decided majority in favor of one party. If a district is, say, 65% Republican, a majority of voters may be troubled by having to share representation 50–50 with a Democrat. So, a push toward STV in such 2-member districts may not be worth it.

In the states currently using 3 or more members per district, however (Maryland, New Hampshire, Vermont, and West Virginia), STV could be used quite profitably under the existing system. These states, with multimember districts electing anywhere from as many as 11 to as few as 3 members, would have thresholds of exclusion varying from 8% [$1/(11+1)$ $= 1/12 = 8\%$] up to 25% [$1/(3+1) = 1/4 = 25\%$]. These are acceptable thresholds of exclusion: not so low as to invite "fringe" candidates, yet not so high as to shut out significant minority voting blocs which deserve a seat at the table.

As the number of seats rose up toward 11, it might be advisable to consider staggering terms, so that the number of candidates did not become

---

[13] *See State Legislative Chambers that Use Multi-Member Districts*, BALLOTPEDIA, available at https://ballotpedia.org/State_legislative_chambers_that_use_multi-member_districts.

[14] Michael Barone et al., STATE LEGISLATIVE ELECTIONS: VOTING PATTERNS AND DEMOGRAPHICS, *passim* (1998).

too great to be practical based on ballot length and other considerations of election administration. And, of course, there is nothing preventing state legislatures which do not use multimember districts from legislatively changing their electoral systems to convert to multimember districts in whole or in part.

As with local governments, there is room to experiment with a mixture of geography-based methods and proportional methods. State legislatures could use IRV for their House elections, for example, and STV in multi-member districts for their Senate elections. Australia does precisely this at the national level. Or, within a legislative chamber, multimember districts could abut neighboring SMDs, as Memphis' county commission districts used to do, except that the multimember districts would use STV, and the single districts IRV. Still another alternative would be for a single chamber to have SMDs and overlapping multimember districts occupying the same territory, as occurs in Memphis City Council elections, with a similar mixture of STV and IRV. There are many combinations, each of them better for democracy than the current status quo.

10. Conclusion

One common response to any argument for a national popular presidential vote is "we live in a republic, not a democracy."[1] Indeed, that response comes up in just about any discussion of any significant election reform, including Senate representation, the filibuster, and proportional representation (PR).[2] It is, of course, a shibboleth more than an argument. The U.S. is both a *democracy* (governed by the people) and more specifically a *republic* (governed by the people through elected representatives). It is not a direct democracy, in the style of a New England town hall meeting where the people vote directly, item by item, on every decision; rather, it is a representative democracy. But both terms are consistent with the Founders' original understanding, and any purported distinction between the two sheds no real light on the merit or lack thereof of any of the above reform proposals.[3]

But while this semantic sloganeering may have no actual weight to it in and of itself, it is suggestive of a more general mindset that constitutes the greatest resistance to any attempt to reform the American electoral system. That mindset is a traditionalist one, a feeling that proper reverence for the wisdom of the founding generation, and respect for our long experience with the current system, are reason enough to oppose restructuring.

Traditionalists say that the Constitution is a work of genius, written by men who, for all the flaws of their time, were true visionaries. They're

---

[1]   *See, e.g.*, Chris Stirewalt, *A Republic, Not a Democracy,* Fox News Politics (Nov. 23, 2016), available at http://www.foxnews.com/politics/2016/11/23/republic-not-democracy.html.

[2]   *See, e.g.*, Walter Williams, *Why We Are a Republic, Not a Democracy*, The Daily Signal (Jan. 17, 2018), available at https://www.dailysignal.com/2018/01/17/republic-not-democracy/.

[3]   *See* Eugene Volokh, *Is The United States of America a Republic or a Democracy?*, The Washington Post (May 13, 2015), available at https://www.washingtonpost.com/news/volokh-conspiracy/wp/2015/05/13/is-the-united-states-of-america-a-republic-or-a-democracy/?noredirect=on&utm_term=.3c58c8fd1461 (making this same observation); Lawrence Lessig, *The United States Is Not a "Democracy," It Is a "Republic"*, Medium (Nov. 25, 2016), available at https://medium.com/@lessig/the-united-states-is-not-a-democracy-it-is-a-republic-54e8036c781c (same).

correct. But the Founders weren't perfect, and they were the products of their time. The Founders themselves recognized this. Thomas Jefferson famously cautioned against ascribing to the Founders "a wisdom more than human," and against looking at the Constitution with a "sanctimonious reverence" like "the ark of the covenant, too sacred to be touched." Of the Founders, he wrote that "were they to arise from the dead," they would say "institutions must go hand in hand with the progress of the human mind." They must "advance also, and keep pace with the times."[4]

The U.S. can always be proud that it was the first modern democracy, the first colony to break off from the parent stem. We *invented* constitutional democracy, checks and balances, and an organized system of elections suitable for a large, modern polity. That is a world-historical distinction that can never be taken away.

But other democracies sprouted up in our wake, inspired by our example. With the advantage of our experience, they were able to learn from our mistakes and improve on our invention. They learned from us; now it's time for us to learn from them.

In like fashion, natural skepticism about unintended consequences should make us "conservative" in the original sense of being cautious about change. There is a legitimate case to be made for a little healthy structural inertia in our electoral system. We need to know what the rules are, and it's harder to do that if we're constantly tinkering with them. As Jefferson put it in the Declaration of Independence, "Prudence, indeed will dictate that Governments long established should not be changed for light and transient causes." The burden should definitely be on reformers to show that it's broke before we go fixin' it.

But that burden seems more than met. A candidate who yields fewer nationwide votes becomes President over the candidate who receives more nationwide votes, 1 in 12 times in our history, 2 in 5 times in the last 2 decades. A Senate in which 41% of the Senators routinely blocks what a majority of both the House and Senate have voted on, and where that 41% of Senators routinely represents less than 33% of the population. A House so gerrymandered, either intentionally or unintentionally, that there is a nationwide *average* of a 6% difference between the votes a party receives and the seats it fills, and where that differential is triple or quadruple in some states. A majority of Americans wanting to see third parties in our politics, and a U.S. Congress without a single third-party representative.

---

[4] Letter from Thomas Jefferson to Samuel Kercheval (July 12, 1816), *reprinted in* Paul L. Ford ed., 12 THE WORKS OF THOMAS JEFFERSON 11–12 (1905).

Even when these institutions avoid the most egregious of deviations between votes and representation, the system fundamentally encourages bad behavior. The Electoral College encourages candidates to focus on 10 key states and ignore the other 40, a dynamic that continues through to governance. The Senate encourages individual Senators to use anonymous holds to hijack major legislation to extract petty concessions, and minority parties to engage in long-term tactics of obstruction, biding their time until they regain power. Single-member districts (SMDs) in the House, even under the best of circumstances, give most incumbents safe seats, insulating them from public outcry; this incentivizes them to pander to the extremes of left and right to avoid primary challenges, and to abjure cross-partisan compromise. The zero-sum nature of the campaign encourages attack ads and mudslinging and discourages cooperative debate. Winner-take-all voting turns third parties into spoilers—thwarting them getting a chance to be heard and thwarting fair outcomes for the majority.

And the bad behavioral incentives apply just as much to the rest of us. The winner-take-all nature and preordained conclusions of so many of the above electoral frameworks encourage rational voters to recognize the futility of voting, to stay home and drop out. Those who continue to go to the polls are discouraged from ever giving a chance to third parties, to lesser-known candidates, or to lesser-funded candidates, lest they "throw away their votes" or end up electing the candidate they fear the most.

Even if one is convinced of the need for structural reform, one may not be convinced it's feasible. Like any election reform, the elected officials with the ability to reform the system have every incentive not to. After all, they won under the existing rules; why risk losing by changing the rules? Even officials who are not so brazenly cynical tend to be sincerely convinced that a system that resulted in their own election must be working pretty well.

But that same skepticism could be applied to any of the many fundamental structural reforms we have already accomplished in our electoral system. At the beginning of our republic, many states did not even hold elections for President; those that did used a "long ballot" which required voters to vote for individual Electors rather than presidential candidates. Voting was generally not anonymous, and in most states was limited to white males who owned property. And state legislatures chose U.S. Senators without regular elections. Each of these things changed over time, state by state. Even the federal constitutional amendment ensuring popular election of Senators was finalized through a state-by-state ratification campaign.

Nor did structural change stop in the modern era. As a result of the civil rights movement, millions of racial and ethnic minorities gained the practical ability to register and cast a ballot, and the percentage of elected officials of color skyrocketed. Around the country, especially in the South, winner-take-all, at-large elections changed to SMD elections wherever significant concentrations of minority populations pushed back against discrimination. Women started achieving high elected office, 18-year-olds won the right to vote, and D.C. residents won the right to vote for President.

Some of these reforms took years, and some took decades. Some even took generations to complete. But every one of them was viewed as infeasible at the inception.

More recently, we have seen early voting periods transform the pace and schedule of elections and campaigns in dozens of states. Some states have adopted automatic and same-day registration. Nonpartisan redistricting commissions are sprouting up in many states. States as recently as 2018 signed on to the National Popular Vote compact, raising the score to 172 out of the needed 270 Electoral votes. The number of cities that have adopted some form of RCV is 15 and growing fast, including 3 that use or will soon use single transferable vote. The entire state of Maine now uses Instant Runoff Voting for statewide elections. We have a congressman and a U.S. Senator elected through IRV.

The Fair Representation Act would be a milestone achievement, fundamentally reshaping our democracy for the better in one fell swoop. Aside from that, though, these reforms would best be pursued as they have always been: at the local level, and state legislature by state legislature. These reforms take root early on in those states which are already predisposed toward being open to change. With a track record of success in these cities and states, they gradually spread until they are commonplace.

Additionally, as a tactical matter, hope lies in at least two ways around the natural resistance of the establishment to any change to the status quo.

One is the tendency of a party in power, fearing an upcoming electoral loss, to be more open to structural reforms. That happened in Australia when the majority Liberal Party saw its right-leaning vote being split by the rise of another right-of-center party, the Country Party (now the National Party). It then was open to calls for IRV.

The other is the initiative process. Many states allow citizens to place referenda measures on the ballot directly by obtaining a number of petition signatures. This allows the citizens to bypass the elected incumbents. Many of the adoptions of RCV and PR were achieved this way, including the recent statewide adoption in Maine.

The plausibility of citizen initiative-driven electoral reform ties directly to the level of citizen hunger for change. Citizen dissatisfaction with the electoral process has risen in recent years, as has activist energy.

Since the election of Donald Trump, more Americans are questioning whether the U.S. is, or will remain, a functioning democracy. But the breakdown of our system goes far beyond Trump, who is as much a symptom of that breakdown as a cause. Politically, the time may be ripe for a fundamental reexamination of our election system. On the merits, it's not only ripe, but overdue.

Afterword

The U.S. 2018 midterm elections provided further illustration of the skew, as well as further progress for Ranked Choice Voting and redistricting reform.

The Senate showed a pronounced skew, and another instance of the party receiving the most votes nationwide failing to capture a majority of the body's seats. Nationwide, Democratic candidates received over 12 million more votes than their Republican counterparts. However, Republicans still maintained the Senate majority, and appear to have a net gain of seats. [1] As of this writing, the outcome in 3 states was still uncertain, as two states went into a recount and one went into a runoff election. But despite gaining over 57% of the nationwide vote, Democrats will have anywhere between 46 and 49% of the seats.[2]

The votes-seats gap in the House was slighter: with 11 close races still up for grabs (out of 435 total) as of this writing, Democrats gained control of the House and anywhere from 52% to 54% of the seats, while winning about 51.5% of the vote.[3] Democrats' biggest gains came in Pennsylvania following a state court decision striking down a Republican-drawn gerrymander.[4] The contrast between the Senate and House results illustrates the strong skew caused by equal state suffrage in the Senate.[5]

---

[1] Only 35 out of 100 total seats were up for election in 2018 due to the Senate's staggered terms.

[2] *Senate Election Results: Republicans Keep Majority*, NEW YORK TIMES (Nov. 10, 2018), available at https://www.nyti-mes.com/interactive/2018/11/06/us/elections/results-senate-elections.html. Two Independents from Maine and Vermont who caucus with the Democrats were counted in the Democrats' total.

[3] *House Election Results: Democrats Take Control*, NEW YORK TIMES (Nov. 10, 2018), available at https://www.nytimes.com/interactive/2018/11/06/us/elections/results-house-elections.html.

[4] Demetrios Pogkas, Jackie Gu, David Ingold, & Mira Rojanasakul, *How Democrats Broke The House Map Republicans Drew,* BLOOMBERG NEWS (Nov. 10, 2018), available at https://www.bloomberg.com/graphics/2018-house-seats-vs-votes/.

[5] *See* Paul Krugman, *Real America Versus Senate America*, NEW YORK TIMES (Nov. 8, 2018), available at https://www.nytimes.com/2018/11/08/opinion/midterms-senate-rural-urban.html?fbclid=IwAR3q4zXOo-VJJvML1GEaCNI-

Ranked Choice Voting was also on the ballot in a significant way. Maine used RCV for its U.S. House and Senate races. In most cases, a candidate won with a majority in the first round. However, one House race triggered an RCV count, because of the presence of two left-leaning Independents on the ballot who together garnered 8% of the vote and deprived both major party candidates of a majority. The "instant runoff" is expected to result in the election of the Democratic candidate, thus illustrating how RCV can address the "spoiler" problem.[6]

And in the author's home town of Memphis, Tennessee, one of the 25 largest U.S. cities, voters decisively rejected two different attempts by incumbent local elected officials to repeal RCV (called "Instant Runoff Voting" in Memphis) for city elections. Referendum voters had originally adopted Instant Runoffs by referendum in 2008, but official opposition had delayed implementation.[7] City Council incumbents placed on the November 2018 referendum ballot two different repeal proposals. One would return to a separate second, runoff election for certain races, while the other would adopt plurality across the board. Voters rejected both.[8] While questions remain about implementation in time for the regularly scheduled October 2019 municipal elections, it was, in the words of Aaron Fowles, the head of the local IRV advocacy group, "a clear victory for Ranked Choice Voting."

At least three states, Colorado, Missouri, and Michigan, overwhelmingly adopted nonpartisan redistricting commissions via referendum. A fourth, Utah, where vote-counting continues as of this writing, also appears to have adopted this reform.[9] Colorado, Michigan, and Utah followed the standard approach of an independent commission. Missouri

---

HZznBsN8BXSwnVrwujzMnaYKyZrqog5AtH2E&login=email&auth=login-em ail (making this point).

[6]   Michael Shepherd, *What Happens Next As Maine's 2nd District Race Heads To A New Round Of Ranked-Choice Voting*, BANGOR DAILY NEWS (Nov. 8, 2018), available at https://bangordailynews.com/2018/11/08/politics/daily-brief/what-ha ppens-next-as-maines-2nd-district-race-heads-to-the-next-round-of-ranked-cho ice-voting/.

[7]   *See* Chapter 7.

[8]   Jamie Munks, *Memphis Voters Shoot Down Longer City Council Terms, Instant Runoff Voting Repeal*, MEMPHIS COMMERCIAL APPEAL (Nov. 6, 2018), available at   https://www.commercialappeal.com/story/news/2018/11/06/early-votes-show-memphis-voters-overwhelming-against-three-ballot-questions/1857987002/.

[9]   David Daley, *As Polarized As Americans Are, They Agree On This: Gerrymandering Is Wrong*, LOS ANGELES TIMES (Nov. 8, 2018), available at http:// www.latimes.com/opinion/op-ed/la-oe-daley-gerrymandering-reform-20181109-story.html.

mandates the appointment of a state demographer to play a principal role in drawing lines.[10]

Overall, the results both illustrated the need for fundamental electoral reform and highlighted a path forward.

---

[10]   Katie Zezima and Emily Wax-Thibodeaux, *Voters Are Stripping Partisan Redistricting Power From Politicians In Anti-gerrymandering Efforts*, WASHINGTON POST (Nov. 7, 2018), available at https://www.washingtonpost.com/national/ voters-are-stripping-partisan-redistricting-power-from-politicians-in-anti-gerrym andering-efforts/2018/11/07/2a239a5e-e1d9-11e8-b759-3d88a5ce9e19_story.html? utm_term=.7dddcc25399c.

Index